October 18–21, 2014
Portland, OR, USA

Association for Computing Machinery

Advancing Computing as a Science & Profession

HILT 2014

Proceedings of the ACM Conference on
High Integrity Language Technology

Sponsored by:
ACM SIGAda

In cooperation with:
**ACM SIGAPP, ACM SIGBED, ACM SIGCAS,
ACM SIGCSE, ACM SIGPLAN, ACM SIGSOFT,** *and Ada-Europe*

**Association for
Computing Machinery**

Advancing Computing as a Science & Profession

The Association for Computing Machinery
2 Penn Plaza, Suite 701
New York, New York 10121-0701

Notice to Past Authors of ACM-Published Articles
ACM intends to create a complete electronic archive of all articles and/or other material previously published by ACM. If you have written a work that has been previously published by ACM in any journal or conference proceedings prior to 1978, or any SIG Newsletter at any time, and you do NOT want this work to appear in the ACM Digital Library, please inform permissions@acm.org, stating the title of the work, the author(s), and where and when published.

ISBN: 978-1-4503-3217-0

Additional copies may be ordered prepaid from:

ACM Order Department
PO Box 30777
New York, NY 10087-0777, USA

Phone: 1-800-342-6626 (USA and Canada)
+1-212-626-0500 (Global)
Fax: +1-212-944-1318
E-mail: acmhelp@acm.org
Hours of Operation: 8:30 am – 4:30 pm ET

Printed in the USA

Welcome to ACM SIGAda's Annual International Conference High Integrity Language Technology – HILT 2014

Welcome to Portland and to HILT 2014, this year's annual international conference of the ACM Special Interest Group on the Ada Programming Language (SIGAda). This year we are pleased to be co-located with the SPLASH 2014 conference, enabling even more chances for interactions with colleagues in industry, academia, and government.

HILT 2014 features a top-quality technical program focused on the issues associated with **high integrity software** – where a failure could cause loss of human life or have other unacceptable consequences – and on the solutions provided by **language technology**. "Language technology" here encompasses not only programming languages but also languages for expressing specifications, program properties, domain models, and other attributes of the software or the overall system.

HILT 2014 consists of two days of tutorials, and two days of conference sessions. The **tutorials** cover a wide range of topics: Ada 2012, SPARK 2014, High-Integrity OOP, AADLv2, and the Rust language. The conference program includes **keynote and invited presentations** from internationally recognized experts:

- **Christine Anderson** (Spaceport America) on From Ada9X to Spaceport America: Going Where No One Has Gone Before;
- **Peter Feiler** (Software Engineering Institute /Carnegie Mellon University), on AADL and Model-Based Engineering; and
- **Tom Ball** (Microsoft Research), on Correctness via Compilation to Logic.

HILT 2014 **conference sessions** deal with a range of topics associated with **safe, secure and reliable software**: enhancing and evolving embedded systems languages for safety; behavioral modeling and code generation; practical use of assertions and formal methods in industry; and safe programming languages for the multicore era. You will learn the latest developments in model and program verification technologies, and hear industrial presentations from practitioners. The accompanying **exhibits** will give you the opportunity to meet our corporate sponsors and find out about their latest offerings. Sponsors include AdaCore (Platinum Level); Microsoft Research (Gold Level); Ellidiss (Silver Level).

At HILT 2014 you will learn about both the challenges confronting high integrity software and the solutions available to address them. Perhaps just as important are the social interactions that you get at a live conference, this year co-located with the SPLASH 2014 conference: the chance to meet and talk with researchers and practitioners in industry, academia, and government, to ask them questions, and to explain your own work and interests. These renewed and new associations can be as valuable as the technical program at professional conferences, and their benefits will continue to reward you well after you return home.

HILT 2014 Conference Chair

Michael Feldman
Professor, George Washington University (retired)

HILT 2014 Program Chair

S. Tucker Taft
Director of Language Research, AdaCore

Table of Contents

Session: Applying Formal Methods
Session Chair: Tucker Taft *(AdaCore)*

Session: Safe Programming Languages for the Multicore Era (I)
Session Chair: Brad Moore *(General Dynamics Canada)*

Session: Safe Programming Languages for the Multicore Era (II)
Chair: Clyde Roby *(Institute for Defense Analyses)*

ACM SIGAda HILT 2014 Conference Organization

Conference Chair:	Michael Feldman *(George Washington University, retired)*
Program Chair:	Tucker Taft *(AdaCore)*
Exhibits and Sponsorships Chair:	Greg Gicca *(Verocel, Inc.)*
Proceedings Chair:	Tucker Taft *(AdaCore)*
Local Arrangements Chair:	Michael Feldman *(George Washington University, retired)*
Workshops Chair:	John W. McCormick *(University of Northern Iowa)*
Publicity Chair:	Alok Srivastava *(TASC, Inc.)*
Treasurer:	Jeff Boleng *(The Software Engineering Institute)*
Registration Chair:	Thomas Panfil *(Washington, D.C.)*
Tutorials Chair:	John W. McCormick *(University of Northern Iowa)*
Academic Community Liaison:	Michael Feldman *(George Washington University, retired)*
Webmaster:	Clyde Roby *(Institute for Defense Analyses)*
Logo Designer:	Weston Pan *(Raytheon Space and Airborne Systems)*
SIGAda Chair:	David Cook *(Stephen F. Austin State University)*
SIGAda Vice Chair for Meetings and Conferences:	Tucker Taft *(AdaCore)*
SIGAda International Representative:	Dirk Craeynest *(K. U. Leuven, Belgium)*
Program Committee:	Tucker Taft *(AdaCore)*
	Howard Ausden *(Lockheed Martin Corporation)*
	Anya Helene Bagge *(University of Bergen, Norway)*
	Lennart Beringer *(Princeton University)*
	Judith Bishop *(Microsoft Research)*
	Robert Bocchino *(NASA Jet Propulsion Laboratory))*
	Stephen Chong *(Harvard University)*
	David Cook *(Stephen F. Austin State University)*
	Julien Delange *(Carnegie Mellon University, SEI)*

Program Committee:
(continued):

Claire Dross *(AdaCore)*

Arjun Guha *(University of Massachusetts, Amherst)*

Matt Heaney *(Google, Inc.)*

James Hunt *(aicas, Germany)*

John Kassie *(Rockwell Collins, Inc.)*

Y. Annie Liu *(SUNY at Stony Brook)*

Brad Moore *(General Dynamics Canada)*

Michael Norrish *(NICTA, Australia)*

Weston Pan *(Raytheon Space and Airborne Systems)*

David Pearce *(Victoria University of Wellington, New Zealand)*

Luis Miguel Pinho *(CISTER Research Centre/ISEP, Portugal)*

Erhard Ploedereder *(University of Stuttgart, Germany)*

Norman Ramsey *(Tufts University)*

Jean-Pierre Rosen *(Adalog, France)*

Sukyoung Ryu *(KAIST -- Korean Advanced Institute of Science and Technology, Korea)*

Julien Signoles *(French Alternative Energies and Atomic Energy Commission, France)*

Mehmet Sindel *(Symbiontronic Technologies Corporation, Turkey)*

Jack Wileden *(University of Massachusetts, Apmherst)*

Lukasz Ziarek *(SUNY at Buffalo)*

ACM SIGAda HILT 2014 Sponsor & Supporters

Sponsor:

In cooperation with:

Supporters:

Microsoft Research

From Ada 9X to Spaceport America: Going Where No One Has Gone Before

Christine Anderson
Spaceport America

ABSTRACT

Ada 95, aka Ada9X at the time because we didn't know when we would be done, was a labor of love for most of us. A spectacular team was assembled from all over the world. I had the distinct pleasure and honor of being the Department of Defense Ada 9X Project Manager. The lessons I learned and the experience I gained allowed me to do many other things after Ada 95 was completed. I ran an Air Force space technology laboratory. I was responsible for building military satellites and launching them from the Cape. Currently, I am responsible for developing and operating the first purpose-built commercial spaceport. Looking back, the common thread through all of these endeavors is innovation, dedication, strong team work, and a passion for the job at hand. That *can do* spirit and boundless energy is a must for success and I have been fortunate to work on unprecedented projects with colleagues who possessed these qualities. Anecdotes from the Ada9X Project to today's emerging commercial space industry will be provided from my experiences and observations.

Categories and Subject Descriptors

D3.0 [**Programming Languages**]: General – *standards*

General Terms

Reliability, Human Factors, Standardization, Languages.

Keywords

Ada 95; Commercial Space Industry

BIO

Christine Anderson is the Executive Director of the New Mexico Spaceport Authority, a position she assumed in 2011. She is responsible for the development and operation of the first purpose-built commercial spaceport -- Spaceport America. Spaceport America, situated on 18,000 acres in southern New Mexico, has hosted 20 vertical launches and supports several tenants including Virgin Galactic and SpaceX as well several other launch customers. Anderson retired from the United States Air Force as a civilian with 30 years' service. In the Air Force she achieved the rank of Senior Executive Service, the civilian equivalent of the military rank of General Officer. Anderson was the DOD Project Manager for Ada 95, an international standard software programming language. Anderson was the founding Director of the Space Vehicles Directorate at the Air Force Research Laboratory, Kirtland Air Force Base, New Mexico. She also served as the Director of the Space Technology Directorate at the Air Force Phillips Laboratory at Kirtland, and as the Director of the Military Satellite Communications Joint Program Office at the Air Force Space and Missile Systems Center in Los Angeles where she directed the development, acquisition and execution of a $50 billion portfolio. She is a Fellow of the American Institute of Aeronautics and Astronautics. Anderson earned a B.S. in mathematics from the University of Maryland, and completed the National Security Leadership Program at Johns Hopkins University and the Senior Management in Government Program at Harvard University.

HILT 2014, October 18–21, 2014, Portland, Oregon, USA.
ACM 978-1-4503-3217-0/14/10.
http://dx.doi.org/10.1145/2663171.2663172

Ada83 to Ada 2012

Lessons Learned Over 30 Years of Language Design

John Barnes
John Barnes Informatics
11 Albert Road, Caversham
Reading RG4 7AN, UK
+44 118 947 4125
jgpb@jbinfo.demon.co.uk

S. Tucker Taft
AdaCore, Inc.
24 Muzzey St, 3rd Fl
Lexington, MA 02421 USA
+1 781 750 8068
taft@adacore.com

ABSTRACT

This presentation will comprise a discussion between two language designers, John Barnes and Tucker Taft, who have been intimately involved with the design of Ada over the past 30 years. During the discussion they will review the successful and less than completely successful features of the various versions of Ada, going from the original Ada 83, through the latest Ada 2012 version, and will attempt to identify some lessons to be learned about programming language design and evolution.

Categories and Subject Descriptors

D3.0 [**Programming Languages**]: General – *standards;* D.3.3 [**Programming Languages**]: Language Constructs and Features – *modules/packages, abstract data types, concurrent programming structures, polymorphism.*

General Terms

Reliability, Human Factors, Standardization, Languages

Keywords

Ada; Programming Language Evolution; Human Engineering

1. OVERVIEW

The Ada programming language was first standardized by ANSI in 1983 and by ISO in 1987. Since then there have been three additional revisions, Ada 95 (standardized by ISO in 1995), Ada 2005 (standardized by ISO in 2007), and Ada 2012 (standardized by ISO in 2012). From the beginning Ada was designed with the recognition that programming was a human activity, and the language was explicitly *human engineered* toward readability, reliability, and predictability. As the language has evolved, this focus on human engineering has always remained, as additional requirements have been identified, and new capabilities have been added to the language.

During this process of evolution, most of the elements of the language have been preserved or enhanced because they have been demonstrated to serve the needs of a programmer focused on building reliable systems. But some elements of the language have been recognized as less successful, and have been largely replaced by new approaches to reliability. This presentation will comprise a discussion between two language designers, John Barnes and Tucker Taft, who have been intimately involved with the design of Ada, John from the very beginning as a member of the *Green* team which produced the first design of Ada, and Tucker as an early user starting in 1980, and then as the lead language designer of Ada 95 starting in 1990. John and Tucker will review some of the key features of the various versions of Ada, and glean what lessons can be learned from the more or less successful history of these features as they were actually used in the field.

HILT 2014, Oct 18-21, 2014, Portland, Oregon, USA.
ACM 978-1-4503-3217-0/14/10.
http://dx.doi.org/10.1145/2663171.2663173

Can C++ Be Made as Safe as SPARK?

David Crocker
Escher Technologies Ltd.
Mallard House, Hillside Road
Ash Vale, Aldershot GU12 5BJ, UK
+44 20 8144 3265
dcrocker@eschertech.com

ABSTRACT

SPARK offers a way to develop formally-verified software in a language (Ada) that is designed with safety in mind and is further restricted by the SPARK language subset. However, much critical embedded software is developed in C or C++. We look at whether and how benefits similar to those offered by the SPARK language subset and associated tools can be brought to a C++ development environment.

Categories and Subject Descriptors

F.3.1 [**Logics and meanings of programs**]: Specifying and Verifying and Reasoning about Programs – *assertions, invariants, mechanical verification, pre- and post-conditions, specification techniques.*

General Terms

Reliability, Security, Languages, Verification

Keywords

Formal methods; software verification; design by contract; C++; high integrity software

1.   INTRODUCTION

The Ada language is generally considered to be well-designed from a safety perspective. The SPARK [1] subset, designed for use in developing high-integrity software, restricts the Ada language by removing constructs that are considered unsafe or difficult to reason about, and adds notation for information flow, function contracts, and other formal specifications. The SPARK tool set allows the annotated program to be analyzed, in particular it can generate verification conditions and attempt to prove them. The most recent versions of the SPARK tools use the function contract notation of Ada 2012 in preference to the older notation involving comments that start with a special character.

Despite the advantages of the Ada programming language and the SPARK subset, much critical embedded software is today written in C and there is an increasing use of C++ in this field. C and C++ are both supported on a wide range of embedded processors by a number of compilers and development

environments of good quality. However, in comparison with Ada, from a correctness and safety perspective C is a poorly designed language. To mitigate this, subsets of C are widely used in developing high-integrity software, of which the best known is MISRA-C, now in its third version [2]. Many commercial static checking tools for C are available, and most of these can be configured to enforce MISRA-C compliance to a greater or lesser extent.

Unfortunately, C also lacks important features, such as encapsulation at the object level, and generics. Lack of object encapsulation makes it difficult to protect data from unintended modification and enforce object invariants, except where there is only a single instance of the type. Lack of generics means that either the same code is written more than once to work on different types, or type safety has to be sacrificed by using void pointers for parameter passing, for example in the standard library functions *qsort* and *bsearch*. C++ provides object-level encapsulation by supporting classes, and generics by supporting template declarations. So when developing critical software, a subset of C++ could offer advantages over MISRA-C, given suitable support from static checking and verification tools.

There are already subsets of C++ designed for high-integrity software, notably MISRA-C++ 2008 [3] and JSF-C++ [4]. Both are based on sets of rules that prohibit the use of various features of C++. We have concerns over the use of these subsets in the most critical software, for example at Safety Integrity Level 4 which is where formal verification is most often performed. Our concerns are these:

- C++ is a large and complicated language. It is difficult to identify all the weaknesses in it that may contribute towards inadvertent errors.

- Because of its size, it is difficult to develop formal semantics and associated verification tool support for the language in its entirety.

In practice, critical embedded software developers do not need the full C++ language. Dynamic memory allocation is generally prohibited in critical embedded software, and this in turn limits the C++ features that can be used.

We therefore propose a different approach. Most well-written C programs are also valid C++ programs, and programs that are valid in both C and C++ have the same semantics in both languages, provided that a small number of potential issues are avoided. So our approach is:

- Start with the MISRA-C:2012 subset of C;

- Add selected features from C++ along with rules limiting how they may be used;

- Further constrain the MISRA-C:2012 rules by banning C constructs that are not needed because better C++ constructs can replace them, and by banning constructs that can have different semantics in C and C++;

- Add notation for adding SPARK-like function contracts and other specifications to C++ source code;

- Implement formal verification of all constructs permitted by the resulting C++ subset, using the Verified Design-by-Contract paradigm [20].

Our aim was to produce a C++ language subset that is sufficient for critical embedded software development, that addresses the main safety-related limitations of C, that is amenable to formal verification, and for which we can provide tool support in a reasonable time frame.

In keeping with the theme of this conference, this paper addresses the contribution to software safety that is made by the programming language and the analysis techniques that it supports. There are of course many other factors that contribute to software safety.

2. DESIGN OF THE C++ LANGUAGE SUBSET

2.1 C++ Safety Issues Inherited From C

The C++ language [5, 6] includes several features that do not fit well with safety. Fortunately for us, most of them are inherited from C, and the C language has been widely-studied in relation to safety. Some known vulnerabilities in a number of programming languages, including Ada, SPARK and C, are listed in [7]. Unfortunately, that publication does not list vulnerabilities in C++. Vulnerabilities in C are also listed in the MISRA-C:2012 guidelines [2], along with rules to avoid them. Examples of such vulnerabilities include: excessive automatic type conversion, identifier re-use, accidental use of '=' where '==' was intended, and operator precedence issues. When the MISRA-C guidelines are enforced, these vulnerabilities are for the most part avoided. Enforcing some of them requires the use of formal techniques in the general case. Almost all the MISRA-C 2012 guidelines can be mapped directly or with only minor modifications to our subset of C++.

Many vulnerabilities of C fall into the categories of undefined, unspecified and implementation-dependent behaviour. For the most part, we can avoid these behaviours by defining appropriate preconditions for the constructs concerned, and using formal verification to ensure that these preconditions are satisfied. This is akin to proving exception freedom in SPARK. Some implementation-defined behaviours cannot be avoided, and for those we provide tool configuration options to describe the behaviour of the compiler and platform. For example, we provide a means to specify the ranges of the built-in integral types, and whether integer division of a negative by a positive number rounds up or down.

There are some particular weaknesses in C that cannot be mitigated simply by subsetting the language. Three of them are concerned with pointers. Whereas SPARK bans the use of Ada access types, in C it is necessary to use pointers at least for passing array parameters between functions. However, the C language does not distinguish between a pointer to an object and a pointer to an array of objects. On receiving a pointer to an array, it is not possible to inquire of the pointer how many elements are in the array. Furthermore, C allows any pointer type to take the value NULL; but in most instances of using pointers to pass parameters, a null pointer is not an appropriate value.

We have already solved two of these problems in our earlier tool [8]. When a pointer is declared using standard C syntax, our tool requires that every initialization of or assignment to that pointer is not the value NULL. Furthermore, use of the array index and pointer arithmetic operators on such a pointer is forbidden. To specify a pointer to an array of objects, the user adds the keyword **array**. Such a pointer may only be initialized or assigned to point to an array, not to a single object. To specify that NULL is an allowed value, the user adds the keyword **null**. For example:

```
char * p1;              // pointer to a single
                        // character
char * array p2;        // pointer to an array
                        // of characters
char * null p3;         // pointer to a single
                        // character, or NULL
char * array null p4;   // pointer to an array
                        // of characters or
NULL
```

In order that the code may still be compiled by a standard C or C++ compiler, we define C preprocessor macros that cause **array** and **null** to be expanded to nothing, except when the source code is being analyzed by our tool. These macros are defined in a header file that is referenced at the start of each C source file by a **#include** directive. We also provide a **not_null**(...) macro for asserting that a nullable pointer is not null and converting its type to the corresponding non-nullable pointer.

Although C++ does not include bounds information in pointers to arrays, for verification purposes we pretend that it does. We do this by augmenting the array pointer type with 'ghost' fields. A ghost entity is one that can be used in a specification construct, but not in executable code. We provide a ghost field to yield the number of elements in the array, and another to yield the offset of the array pointer into the array (because a C++ array pointer can point part way into an array). These ghost fields can be referred to in function contracts and other formal specifications, allowing us (for example) to write preconditions to ensure that accesses to array elements are within the bounds of the array.

Where the bounds of an array that is passed as a function parameter need to be available not just in the specification but in the code as well, we adopt the notion of a generic Array class that was recommended by the JSF-C++ standard. Unfortunately, the *array.doc* file describing the JSF-C++ Array class has not been put in the public domain. We therefore defined our own *array_ref<T>* class template for passing array parameters. This class is small enough to be passed by value, and it contains both the pointer to the start of the array and the number of array elements. It can also be configured to perform run-time bounds checks when indexing into the array, if this is desired.

Another weakness of C is that there is a single type conversion syntax that is used not only for expressing relatively safe conversions (for example, converting between different integral types) but also for more dangerous conversions, such as converting between pointer types or casting away **const**. We avoid this issue by mandating use of the C++ type conversion operators for these more dangerous conversions, as described in the next section.

2.2   C++ Constructs Included in our Subset

Our C++ subset is focused on including those features of C++ that offer significant benefits over C to the writers of high-integrity embedded software, while leaving out features that are of doubtful utility or safety, or for which we feel that the safety implications are not well understood.

The first items in our list of C++ constructs to include are the C++ type conversion operators **static_cast**, **reinterpret_cast** and **const_cast**. The C++ conversion operators show what sort of conversion is intended, and are therefore safer to use than the single type casting notation of C. Therefore, we mandate the use of C++ type conversion notation for the more dangerous forms of conversion. We continue to allow the C type casting operator to be used where it has the same meaning as a **static_cast** to the same type.

Next on our list are classes, in order to provide the object-level encapsulation that is missing from C. A further benefit of using classes is that if a class has at least one declared constructor, then it is impossible to declare or create an instance of that class without a constructor being called. Our subset requires all classes to have at least one constructor, and all constructors to initialize all member variables of the class. In this way, use of uninitialized or partially-initialized objects is avoided.

Use of class inheritance and dynamic binding remains controversial in high-integrity software. However, there is increasing interest in using these techniques in some sectors, notably aviation. When doing formal verification of source code annotated with function contracts, it is relatively straightforward to ensure that local type consistency is satisfied as required by the DO-332 Object Oriented Supplement to DO-178C [9]. Furthermore, we consider that use of inheritance and dynamic binding is preferable to using function pointers, which is the usual solution adopted by C programmers faced with similar requirements. We therefore include single inheritance and virtual functions in our subset.

Support for function templates is needed in order to allow generic functions to be written without sacrificing strong typing, as discussed earlier. Class templates are needed, both to support the *array_ref<T>* class and to support other useful classes, such as a bounded vector class. It is less obvious that template specialization is needed and safe to use, so for the time being we have not included it in our subset.

Our C++ subset also permits side-effect free user-defined operator declarations (but not type conversion operators), and reference types. These are needed to support the *array_ref<T>* class as well as being useful features in their own right.

2.3   Mitigating Unsafe Features of C++

Although C++ inherits a lot of poorly-designed language features from C, most of the new constructs it adds to C are fairly well-designed, in our opinion. C++ strengthens the type system of C a little, despite the issues with migrating C code to C++ that this causes. However, C++ introduces a small number of unsafe new features that require mitigation for high-integrity software.

One such feature is the treatment of string literals. Although a string literal yields type **const char*** in most C++ contexts, in some contexts it can be implicitly converted to **char***. This was done to improve backwards-compatibility with C. We ban the use of this conversion in our subset.

Another concerns the overloading of functions, operators and constructors by argument number and type. We are forced to support overloading in our C++ subset, because it is needed to support class constructors and user-defined operators. Unfortunately, overloading interacts badly with implicit type conversion of actual parameters. A call to a function, operator or constructor may potentially match more than one of the overloaded declarations, depending on which implicit type conversions are applied to the actual parameters. The C++ rules for resolving such ambiguities are complex and occasionally give surprising results. Therefore, our subset requires that if a call potentially matches more than one overloaded declaration, then it must match one of them without the use of automatic type conversions.

When a class constructor is declared with a single parameter, that constructor introduces an implicit type conversion from the argument type to the class type, unless the constructor is flagged **explicit**. So in common with MISRA-C++ and JSF-C++, we require all single-argument constructors to be declared **explicit**.

When a derived class declares a function with the same name and parameter types as a virtual function in the parent class, it overrides the parent class function. Such overriding could be inadvertent. The 2011 revision of the C++ language standard [6] provides a way of indicating intentional overriding by adding the reserved identifier **override**. We elevate **override** to the status of a keyword and mandate its use. When using a C++ compiler that implements the older 2003 C++ standard, to preserve compatibility we define **override** as a macro expanding to nothing in the usual way.

Other safety-enhancing language additions in C++ 2011 include the **final** reserved identifier and the **nullptr** keyword. Again, we allow these in our subset and we define macros to make them acceptable to older C++ compilers.

When a C++ program declares statically-allocated variables that need to be constructed, the order in which these initializations are performed is defined for the declarations within a single translation unit, but not between different translation units. This raises the possibility that the initialization of a statically-allocated object in one translation unit could depend on the value of another statically-allocated object in another translation unit that has not yet been initialized. Our subset therefore prohibits the declaration of any statically-initialized object whose initialization is non-trivial and whose value depends on the value of an object with non-trivial initialization in another translation unit. In contrast, the Ada language requires the translator to determine a suitable elaboration order for all the packages that make up the program.

2.4   Expressing Contracts and Other Specifications

Unlike Ada 2012, C++ does not have built-in language constructs for expressing function contracts or other specifications, apart from a macro for declaring assertions. Fortunately, such constructs can be readily added to C++ by choosing suitable keywords such as **pre** and **post**, following the keyword by a bracketed list of expressions, and once again defining these in a header file as macros that expand to nothing. The C++ preprocessor discards the entire specification construct when the source file is processed by a standard C++ compiler. We prefer this approach over the alternative custom of expressing specifications as specially-formatted comments, because it gives specifications the visual impact associated with source code rather than comments, and text editors that understand C++ will perform their usual syntax highlighting on the expressions in the specifications. Many text editors for C++ can also be configured to treat **pre**, **post** etc. as additional keywords and highlight them appropriately.

A minor annoyance is that macros in C++ 2003 must have a fixed number of parameters, so comma cannot be used as a separator in specification expression lists. We use semicolon instead.

The main specification constructs we support are listed in Table 1. Where a construct supports a list of Boolean expressions, the individual expressions are conjoined implicitly by 'and', although separate verification conditions are generated for each expression.

Table 1. Primary specification constructs

pre(*expression-list*)	Declares preconditions
post(*expression-list*)	Declares postconditions
returns(*expression*)	Declares the value returned by a function. Equivalent to **post**(**result** == *expression*) except that recursion is permitted in *expression*
assert(*expression-list*)	Asserts conditions
invariant(*expression-list*)	Used in class declarations to declare class invariants, and in **typedef** declarations to declare constraints
keep(*expression-list*)	Declares loop invariants
decrease(*expression-list*)	Declares loop variant or recursion variant expressions
writes(*lvalue-expression-list*)	Declares what non-local variables the function modifies. If a function is declared without a writes-clause, then a default writes-clause is constructed based on the signature of the function.
assume(*expression-list*)	Declares predicates to be assumed without proof
ghost(*declaration-list*)	Declares ghost variables, functions, parameters etc.

2.5   Specification Expressions

Within specification macros such as **pre**(...) we allow side-effect-free C++ expressions. Of course this is not sufficient, and we add syntax for additional forms of expression. The main ones are listed in Table 2.

We add ghost members to a number of standard C++ types. For the array pointer types, the fundamental ones are *offset* (which returns the offset of the pointer from start of the array that it points into), *lim* (which returns the number of elements that can be addressed in a non-negative direction), and *all* (which yields the entire array addressed by the array pointer). For convenience

we also provide *lwb* (lower bound i.e. lowest valid index, equal to *-offset*) and *upb* (upper bound, equal to *lim-1*), *isndec* (is-non-decrementing according to the < operator for the type) and *isninc*.

Table 2. Additional specification expressions

exists *identifier* **in** *expression* :- *predicate*	Existential quantification over the elements of *expression*, which must be an array or an abstract collection type
exists *type identifier* :- *predicate*	Existential quantification over all values of *type*
forall *identifier* **in** *expression* :- *predicate*	Universal quantification over the elements of *expression*, which must be an array or an abstract collection type
forall *type identifier* :- *predicate*	Universal quantification over all values of *type*
for *identifier* **in** *expression1* **yield** *expression2*	Applies the mapping function *expression2* to each element of collection *expression1*, yielding a new collection
those *identifier* **in** *expression1* :- *predicate*	Selects those elements of collection *expression1* for which *predicate* is true
that *identifier* **in** *expression1* :- *predicate*	Selects the single element of the collection *expression1* for which *predicate* is true
expression1 **in** *expression2*	Shorthand for **exists** *id* **in** *expression2* :- *id* == *expression1*, where *id* is a new identifier
expression **holds** *member*	*expression* must have union type, and *member* must be a member of that type. Yields true if and only if the value of *expression* was defined by assignment or initialization through *member*.
disjoint(*lvalue-expression-list*)	Yields true if and only if no two objects in the expression list have overlapping storage. Typically used in preconditions to state that parameters passed by pointer or reference refer to distinct objects.
operator **over** *expression*	Left-fold *operator* over collection *expression*. Used to express e.g. summation of the elements of an array.
old(*expression*)	When used in a postcondition, this refers to the value of *expression* when the function was entered. When used in a loop invariant, it refers to the value of *expression* just before the first iteration of the loop.

Recursion is usually prohibited by safety-critical software standards, however it is sometimes useful to write recursive specifications. In particular, it is useful to be able to specify the return value of a function recursively, and it is useful to be able to write a loop invariant that calls the containing function. We therefore allow recursion in these two specification contexts and forbid it elsewhere. The recursion is constrained to be finite in the usual way by means of a variant expression.

We support the use of C union types to implement variant records, but not for conversion between different types. We give each variable of union type a ghost discriminant, which records the name of the union type member through which it was last initialized or assigned. The **holds** expression allows this ghost discriminant to be queried.

```cpp
#include "ecv.h"                        // for annotation macros
#include "stddef.h"                     // for size_t

const size_t capacity = 64;

template<class T> class Queue final
{
  T ring[capacity + 1u];                // storage for the data
  typedef size_t invariant(value <= capacity) RingPointer;
                                        // range-limited type for head and tail pointers
  RingPointer hd, tl;                   // indices of the first and last elements of the buffer

public:
  ghost(
  _ecv_seq<T> abstractData() const      // retrieve function for data in the queue
    returns(
        (tl >= hd) ? ring.take(tl).drop(hd)
                   : ring.drop(hd).concat(ring.take(tl))
    );
  )

  bool empty() const                    // test if the queue is empty
  returns(abstractData().lim == 0)
  {
    return hd == tl;
  }

  bool full() const                     // test if the queue is full
  returns(abstractData().lim == capacity)
  {
    return (tl + 1u) % (capacity + 1u) == hd;
  }

  void add(T x) writes(*this)           // add an element to the queue
  pre(!full())
  post(abstractData() == old(abstractData()).append(x))
  {
    ring[tl] = x;
    tl = (tl + 1u) % (capacity + 1u);
  }

  T remove() writes(*this)              // remove an element from the queue
  pre(!empty())
  returns(abstractData().head())
  post(abstractData() == old(abstractData()).tail())
  {
    T temp = ring[hd];
    hd = (hd + 1u) % (capacity + 1u);
    return temp;
  }

  explicit Queue(T initVal)             // constructor to build an empty queue
  post(empty())
  {
    // Dummy initialization to satisfy the complete-initialization rule
    for (size_t i = 0; i <= capacity; ++i)
    writes(i; ring)
    keep(i <= capacity + 1)
    keep(forall k in 0..(i - 1) :- ring[k] == initVal)
    decrease(capacity + 1 - i)
    {
      ring[i] = initVal;
    }
    hd = 0;
    tl = 0;
  }
};
```

Listing 1: Annotated C++ code example

A complication is that standard first-order logic requires that all functions are total, which is not the case in programming languages. One solution to this is to use three-valued logic and write a theorem prover to work with it. The more common solution (which we adopt) is to use classical two-valued logic and to prove separately that the preconditions of all calls to partial functions are met. Even this is not sufficient, because some transformations to quantified expressions that are valid in classical first-order predicate calculus are no longer valid if the quantified expression includes calls to partial functions, even when the precondition of the expression as a whole is satisfied.

Our reasons for using a theorem prover rather than a constraint solver are largely historical. A constraint solver has the advantage that when a verification condition cannot be shown to be true, the constraint solver will often generate a counter-example. This can be translated back to the programming language to help the user understand the problem. On the other hand, from failed proof attempts our prover is sometimes able to infer additional preconditions and loop invariants that would make a proof possible, and we feed these back to the user as suggestions.

For the example in Listing 1 our tool generates 68 verification conditions and proves them all in less than three seconds. The proofs are saved to file so that they could, in principle, be checked by an independent tool.

3. FUTURE WORK

3.1 Namespaces
Although our present subset of C++ is sufficient to overcome the main limitations of C, we plan to add a few more C++ features. For example, C++ supports namespaces to help partition large projects and to avoid clashes between identifiers with external linkage declared by different modules. Namespaces are popular with C++ developers and are used in the C++ standard library. We intend to add namespaces to our C++ subset, subject to the results of an analysis of the safety implications of the argument-dependent name lookup, which is triggered when namespaces are used.

3.2 Template Instantiation Preconditions
It is often the case that C++ templates can often only be meaningfully instantiated when the types with which they are instantiated have applicable operators with certain semantics. For example, a sorting function may require the type to implement **operator<** in a way that defines at least a partial ordering. Early drafts of C++ 0x included a proposal [11] to declare these instantiation preconditions in the form of "template concept" declarations, but this feature did not make it into the C++ 2011 standard. Therefore we intend to add our own syntax to express them. Not only do instantiation preconditions guard against incorrect instantiation of class and function templates, they are also essential to allow such templates to be verified using formal techniques.

3.3 Semantics of Volatile Variables
C and C++ both support the **volatile** qualifier in variable declarations. These are variables whose values may change in ways that are not predictable by the compiler, and for which the order in which they are read and written must be strictly preserved. Our verifier implements the semantics of **volatile** variables as defined in the C++ language standard. However, when we attempted to perform formal verification on one

particular embedded controller program, it became apparent that different sorts of volatile variables require different semantic treatment. For example, one use of **volatile** is to flag variables that are modified by an interrupt service routine and read by the main program thread. In the main program thread, these variables change unpredictably. Within the interrupt service routine, they do not, and it is desirable to treat them as normal variables so that their values can meaningfully be used within specifications. Another use of **volatile** is for variables that represent output ports. The value stored in the output port may be entirely predictable (unlike an input port) and it would be useful to refer to it in specifications; but the variable must still be declared **volatile** because the order in which it and other I/O ports are accessed must be preserved.

To resolve these issues, we plan to introduce some additional keyword macros, each of which expands to **volatile** but means something slightly different to our verifier. So we would be able to declare a variable that represents an output port whose value only changes when the program assigns it, and can therefore be used in specification expressions. Likewise, we would be able to declare a variable that is used to communicate between an interrupt service routine and the rest of the program. For such a variable, we would also provide a means to declare that it is effectively not volatile within a particular block of code, such as a block in which interrupts are disabled, or the interrupt service routine itself.

SPARK 2014 addresses a similar issue via the concept of external state [21].

3.4 Concurrency
Until recently, one of the biggest limitations of C and C++ was its lack of a standard for concurrency. The 2011 C++ language standard finally introduced concurrency primitives. The concurrency model has been formalized by Batty et al [12].

Shared-variable concurrency remains a big challenge for formal verification. We are delighted to be supporting the Taming Concurrency research project [22].

We have not yet attempted to model concurrency in our verification tool. This has not been a serious limitation so far. Developers generally apply formal verification only where the software has to meet the most demanding safety standards such as IEC61508 SIL 4, and such software typically runs single-threaded.

3.5 Floating Point Arithmetic
Target platforms for C++ and the associated libraries generally adopt the IEEE-754 floating-point standard [13]. From the perspective of formal verification, this standard defines the treatment of NaN (not-a-number) values in a very unhelpful way. In particular, a NaN is not equal to itself; so equational reasoning breaks down.

Our solution is to avoid allowing the program to generate NaNs. Our C++ subset forbids the use of the standard library functions that are provided to supply NaNs, and we put preconditions on functions such as *sqrt()* and inverse trigonometric functions so as to forbid input values that give rise to NaN outputs.

Another issue with floating point arithmetic is its inexact nature, which is at variance with the real arithmetic generally assumed by theorem provers. Our tool is currently unsound if floating-point arithmetic is used. For example, the theorem prover might consider that if x can be proved to be nonzero, then x * (1.0 / x) == 1.0, but this is not true at execution time when x = 3.0. It would be possible to model IEEE arithmetic more accurately in the theorem prover by removing axioms for real arithmetic that are not valid for practical floating point arithmetic, but this greatly reduces the ability to prove useful things about the program. Range arithmetic may provide a partial solution to this issue.

4. RELATED WORK

The Larch/C++ project [14] defines an alternative annotation language for C++ modules. It is supported by tools for syntax and type checking, but does not appear to have been used to perform formal verification of critical C++ programs.

Several tools are available for performing formal verification of annotated C programs. These include the Jessie plugin [15] for Frama-C, Vcc [16], our own Escher C Verifier [17], and VeriFast [18]. The Vcc tool supports multithreaded C programs with variables shared between threads. Some of these tools have been compared by Rainer-Harbach [19].

5. CONCLUSION

As a starting point for a programming language subset for developing high-integrity software, C++ is less suitable than Ada 2012 because of its language design deficiencies and lack of function contracts. Nevertheless, we have demonstrated that it is possible to define a subset of C++ that is based on the MISRA-C 2012 subset of C while at the same time enhancing safety by including sufficient features of C++ to provide object encapsulation, generics, and other useful facilities. Along with this we have designed an annotation language to express function contracts and other specifications, and implemented a tool to generate and prove the associated verification conditions.

We therefore believe that where political or other considerations force the use of C++ rather than Ada, this choice of programming language need not of itself compromise safety, at least in single-threaded programs.

6. REFERENCES

[1] Barnes, John. "SPARK - The Proven Approach to High Integrity Software". ISBN 978-0-957290-50-1, 2012.

[2] MIRA . "Guidelines for the Use of the C Language in Critical Systems", ISBN 978-1-906400-10-1 (paperback), ISBN 978-1-906400-11-8 (PDF), 2013.

[3] MIRA. "Guidelines for the Use of the C++ Language in Critical Systems", ISBN 978-906400-03-3 (paperback), ISBN 978-906400-04-0 (PDF), 2008.

[4] Lockheed Martin. "Joint Strike Fighter Air Vehicle C++ Coding Standards for the System Development and Demonstration Program", Document Number 2RDU00001 Rev C, December 2005.

[5] ISO/IEC 14882:2003, "Programming languages – C++", 2003.

[6] ISO/IEC 14882:2011, "Programming languages – C++", 2011.

[7] ISO/IEC TR 24772:2013 "Guidance to avoiding vulnerabilities in programming languages through language selection and use", second edition.

[8] Crocker, David, and Judith Carlton. "Verification of C programs using automated reasoning." Software Engineering and Formal Methods, 2007. SEFM 2007. Fifth IEEE International Conference on. IEEE, 2007.

[8] Crocker, David, and Judith Carlton. "Verification of C programs using automated reasoning." Software Engineering and Formal Methods, 2007. SEFM 2007. Fifth IEEE International Conference on. IEEE, 2007.

[9] RTCA. DO-332 Object-Oriented Technology and Related Techniques Supplement to DO-178C and DO-278A, RTCA, 2011.

[10] Liskov, Barbara H., and Jeannette M. Wing. "A behavioral notion of subtyping." ACM Transactions on Programming Languages and Systems (TOPLAS) 16.6 (1994): 1811-1841.

[11] Dos Reis & Stroustrup. "Specifying C++ concepts", Dos Reis, Gabriel, and Bjarne Stroustrup. ACM SIGPLAN Notices 41.1 (2006): 295-308.

[12] Batty, Mark, et al. "Mathematizing C++ concurrency." ACM SIGPLAN Notices. Vol. 46. No. 1. ACM, 2011.

[13] IEEE 754-2008, "IEEE Standard for Floating-Point Arithmetic", ISBN 978-0-7381-5752-8, 2008.

[14] Leavens, Gary T. "An overview of Larch/C++: Behavioral specifications for C++ modules." Object-Oriented Behavioral Specifications. Springer US, 1996. 121-142.

[15] Moy, Yannick, and Claude Marché. "The Jessie plugin for Deduction Verification in Frama-C—Tutorial and Reference Manual. INRIA & LRI, 2011."

[16] Dahlweid, Markus, et al. "VCC: Contract-based modular verification of concurrent C." Software Engineering-Companion Volume, 2009. ICSE-Companion 2009. 31st International Conference on. IEEE, 2009.

[17] Carlton, Judith, and David Crocker. "Escher Verification Studio: Perfect Developer and Escher C Verifier." Industrial Use of Formal Methods: Formal Verification: 155-193, 2013. ISBN 13: 9781848213630

[18] Jacobs, Bart, et al. "VeriFast: A powerful, sound, predictable, fast verifier for C and Java." NASA Formal Methods. Springer Berlin Heidelberg, 2011. 41-55.

[19] Rainer-Harbach, Marian. "Methods and Tools for the Formal Verification of Software", Technische Universität Wien, 2011. Retrieved from http://aragorn.ads.tuwien.ac.at/publications/bib/pdf/rainer-harbach_11.pdf, 12 June 2014.

[20] Crocker, David. "Safe object-oriented software: the verified design-by-contract paradigm." Proceedings of the Twelfth Safety-Critical Systems Symposium (ed. F.Redmill & T.Anderson) 19-41, Springer-Verlag, London, 2004. ISBN 1-85233-800-8

[21] Spark 2014 Reference Manual, section 7.1.2. Retrieved from http://docs.adacore.com/spark2014-docs/html/lrm/packages.html#external-state, 31 August 2014.

[22] http://www.ncl.ac.uk/computing/research/project/4519, retrieved 31 August 2014.

mbeddr - Extensible Languages for Embedded Software Development

Tamás Szabó
itemis AG
tamas.szabo@itemis.de

Markus Voelter
independent/itemis AG
voelter@acm.org

Bernd Kolb
itemis AG
bernd.kolb@itemis.de

Daniel Ratiu
Siemens AG
daniel.ratiu@siemens.com

Bernhard Schaetz
Fortiss
schaetz@fortiss.de

ABSTRACT

In this industrial presentation we will demonstrate mbeddr, an extensible set of integrated languages for embedded software development. After discussing the context of the talk, we will give details about the mbeddr architecture, which relies on the MPS language workbench. Then we will elaborate on the extension modules and show how they fit with safety-critical development processes. Finally we will point out how the existing languages can be extended by the user by giving some real-world examples, including a language construct that could have prevented the Apple "goto fail" bug as well as mathematical notations.

Keywords Domain Specific Languages and Tooling; Embedded Systems; Language Workbenches; Synthesis of Tailored Tools

1. CONTEXT

Todays' embedded systems are highly diverse, often very complex and many domains are safety-critical, where hardware or software failures may cost lives or a lot of money. An adequate language and tool can ease the development of such systems in many ways; it can ensure the well-formedness of the content and increase the productivity of the developer through the automation of many tedious and repetitive (thus error-prone) tasks, while it can also help in the verification of the critical properties of the system.

The C programming language is often used for the development of low-level control algorithms. On the plus side, the developer has precise control over memory management and it can be used to generate efficient binaries out of the source code. On the other hand, safety-critical domains often require the introduction of custom abstractions (e.g. for verification or requirements tracing), which can be problematic in C. Managing and extending large codebases without proper modularization and separation of specification from

implementation can also increase the accidental complexity of the development processes.

2. mbeddr OVERVIEW

The mbeddr project [7] is an industry-strength IDE for the C programming language, which aims to ease the design and development of embedded software. Its core idea is to use language engineering [6] to introduce additional language constructs into C. Extensions are modular, and additional language constructs can be added at any time, and also by the end user. This is a fundamental shift in the design of the tools because custom extensions can be created with minimal effort and without the need to invasively change the already existing languages. mbeddr relies on the MPS language workbench [3] to enable language and IDE extensibility and it exists as an open-source project [4]. Figure 1 shows the architecture of mbeddr. The figure also identifies the three concerns addressed by mbeddr: the implementation concern addresses the actual implementation of software, relying on existing C compilers for compilation. The analysis concern integrates existing verification tools to statically verify properties of C code. Finally, the process concern addresses integration into the development process.

The tight integration with external verification tools [5] also allows non-experts to benefit from the capabilities of the tools because (i) the input for the verification tool is automatically generated out of the edited contents and (ii) the results of the analysis is automatically lifted back to the abstraction level of the IDE (tracing information is also generated for the input of the analysis tools).This is a great benefit, because many people shy away from these tools due to the high gap between the abstraction levels of the used tools and because of the complexity of the interpretation of the results.

3. EXTENSIONS FOR HIGH-INTEGRITY LANGUAGES

mbeddr introduces many higher level abstractions to provide a more robust version of the C language, which makes it a good fit for the development of safety-critical systems:

Separation of specification from implementation Interfaces represent the specification and are essentially a set of operation signatures. The implementation of an interface is defined in a component, where the component can require other interfaces through ports. It then provides the

	Components	Physical Units	State Machines	State Machine Verification	Decision Tables	Contracts	Visualization	PLE Variability	Documentation	Requirements & Tracing
User Extensions	to be defined by users									
Default Extensions	Test Support	Decision Tables							Glossaries	Use Cases & Scenarios
	Components	Physical Units	State Machines	State Machine Verification	Decision Tables	Contracts				
Core	C core			Model Checking	SMT Solving	Dataflow Analysis	Visual-ization	PLE Variability	Documen-tation	Requirements & Tracing
Platform	JetBrains MPS									
Backend Tool	C Compiler, Debugger and Importer			NuSMV	Yices	CBMC	PlantUML			
	Implementation Concern			Analysis Concern			Process Concern			

Figure 1: Overview of the mbeddr architecture

implementation of the specification by making use of the required ports. Polymorphic behavior is also introduced with this approach, because a required port only specifies the interface, not the implementing component. This construct increases reusability and the developer can create more loosely-coupled software than in the standard version of C.

Testing and Verification The components mentioned above also improve testability because of the improved modularization. An extension supports the definition of mock components, further increasing the fidelity of tests. Interfaces also specify contracts (pre- and postconditions, protocol state machines) which can be verified statically or at runtime.

Physical Units mbeddr makes it possible to use physical units on types or literals (e.g. time [s], current [A] or voltage [V]). The type system has been extended with unit checks and computations (for example, adding V and A results in a type error and multiplying V and A results in W). It is also possible to define meta units for functions, which will be bound based on the units on the input parameters of a function call. The meta units that are used inside the function body in a return statement will then be checked with the specific binding. One can also create conversion rules between various unit definitions and invoke these conversions in the C code (conversion rules will be converted into macros in the generated C code). Beyond the benefits for type checking, this extension makes the code more readable and comprehensible.

Decision tables MPS supports notational flexibility within the IDE. This allows, for example, to insert a decision table inside the edited source code. Compared to a textual notation using nested if statements, decision tables are easier to edit and read. Decision tables can also be automatically verified for completeness and determinism directly from the IDE.

State machines Designing and implementing complex protocols can be cubersome in plain source code. Apart from the readability issues the verifiability of the algorithm is also an important concern. mbeddr helps here with the introduction of state machines. Interesting properties of the designed state machine can then be verified through model checking; counterexamples are lifted back to the abstraction level of the state machine if the verification finds an error.

Requirements tracing Development processes and certification standards emphasize the traceability between the implementation and the corresponding requirements. Many interesting impact analyses can be carried out if proper tooling is provided for the maintenance and update of traces. mbeddr makes it possible to easily specify requirements in the IDE and then link these requirements to corresponding implementation artifacts.

All of the extensions mentioned above are shipped with mbeddr and can be extended or enhanced even further to fully meet the requirements of the specific domain. In the end all of these constructs will be transformed to C99 source code, possibly in several steps. For example state machines embedded in components are first transformed to regular component implementations, those are then transformed to C, which is finally transformed to text for compilation.

4. CUSTOM EXTENSIONS

Apple has recently become "famous" for the *goto fail* bug, which was about a security flaw during the authentication of SSL certificates. A snippet of the corresponding C source code is shown on Figure 2 and the whole file can be found at [**?**]. The code tries to validate an SSL certificate using the multi-step error checking idiom where different kinds of validations are performed in a sequential order and the first failure will result in a jump to the error-handling routine (marked with the `fail` label here). As a consequence of the additional `goto` statement (marked in red) the program will immediately jump to the error-handling code instead of following the mentioned idiom. The `err` variable will not be set and the function will always return 0, indicating that the certificate is always valid.

This scenario could have been easily avoided in mbeddr with a small language extension for a `try-catch`-like construct (shown in Figure 3). The idea is to execute the separate branches of the multi-step error checking logic sequentially in the try block and free the developer from the need to write the individual return value checks. The construct will make

```
static OSStatus SSLVerifySignedServerKeyExchange(SSLContext *ctx,
bool isRsa, SSLBuffer signedParams, uint8_t *signature, UInt16 signatureLen)
{
    ...
    if ((err = ReadyHash(&SSLHashSHA1, &hashCtx)) != 0)
        goto fail;
    if ((err = SSLHashSHA1.update(&hashCtx, &clientRandom)) != 0)
        goto fail;
    if ((err = SSLHashSHA1.update(&hashCtx, &serverRandom)) != 0)
        goto fail;
    if ((err = SSLHashSHA1.update(&hashCtx, &signedParams)) != 0)
        goto fail;
        goto fail;
    if ((err = SSLHashSHA1.final(&hashCtx, &hashOut)) != 0)
        goto fail;

    err = ...
    if(err) {
        sslErrorLog("SSLDecodeSignedServerKeyExchange: sslRawVerify "
                    "returned %d\n", (int)err);
        goto fail;
    }

fail:
    SSLFreeBuffer(&signedHashes);
    SSLFreeBuffer(&hashCtx);
    return err;

}
```

Figure 2: The original goto fail bug

```
try-sequentially {
  verifyPartOneOfSSLConnection(connectionHandle, signature)
  dealWithPartTwoOfVerification(signature)
  andFinalizeWithPart3(connectionHandle)
} on fail (error) {
  authenticationFailed = true;
  lastError = error;
}
```

Figure 3: try-sequentially construct as a C language extension

sure that upon the presence of a non-zero return value, the logic in the catch block will be executed to handle the erroneous behavior. The generated C code will look exactly like the multi-step error checking in Apple's source code (with the if statements), but this low-level `goto` logic is automatically generated. This makes sure that errors such as the *goto fail* can be avoided. The extension code is more readable and less error prone. A modular extension such as this one can be built in 15 minutes; this is a nice example of the benefits of language extensions.

Another extension introduces mathematical notations to C (this functionality is part of mbeddr itself). Figure 4 shows an expression embedded in C code, which uses logarithm, fractions, summation and also muliplication. This seamless integration increases the readability of mathematical expressions and algorithms, making it easier to validate them (by simply looking a lot alike as they would do in a book or paper). A real-world project is using this language extension to implement complex calculation rules in the insurance domain.

```
double sumOfProductsOfLogs(int32[] arr, int32 size) {
```

$$\text{return } \sum_{k = 0}^{size} \frac{\prod_{i = 0}^{k} \log_2 arr[i]}{2} \;;$$

```
} sumOfProductsOfLogs (function)
```

Figure 4: Mathematical notation in the C code

5. CURRENT STATE AND OUTLOOK

mbeddr has been developed as part of a government-funded research project and it is now open-source software hosted at eclipse.org. Its continued development is ensured by itemis and fortiss; several other companies are interested and are investigating the use of mbeddr.

mbeddr is currently being used by itemis' French subsidiary to develop a commercial smart meter. It is currently ca. 100,000 lines of C code. Components, units and state machines have been used successfully, significantly improving the testability (and hence, reliability) of the overall system. In addition, a set of commercial mbeddr add-ons are currently being developed by Siemens PL. The extension languages include data flow diagrams as well as systematic management of controlled names.

In the future we will be working on adding specific support for functional safety, including languages for code-integrated fault-tree analyses [2] and failure mode and effects analyses [1].

6. REFERENCES

[1] *Failure mode and effects analysis - http://goo.gl/3CoKV (as on 21.07.2014).*
[2] *Fault tree analysis - http://goo.gl/XQBevA (as on 21.07.2014).*
[3] *Jetbrains MPS (Meta Programming System) - http://www.jetbrains.com/mps/.*
[4] *The mbeddr project - mbeddr.com.*
[5] D. Ratiu, B. Schaetz, M. Voelter, and B. Kolb. Language engineering as an enabler for incrementally defined formal analyses. In *Software Engineering: Rigorous and Agile Approaches (FormSERA), 2012 Formal Methods in*, pages 9–15, June 2012.
[6] Markus Voelter, Sebastian Benz, Christian Dietrich, Birgit Engelmann, Mats Helander, Lennart C. L. Kats, Eelco Visser, and Guido Wachsmuth. *DSL Engineering - Designing, Implementing and Using Domain-Specific Languages.* dslbook.org, 2013.
[7] Markus Voelter, Daniel Ratiu, Bernd Kolb, and Bernhard Schaetz. mbeddr: instantiating a language workbench in the embedded software domain. *Automated Software Engineering*, 20(3):339–390, 2013.

AADL and Model-based Engineering

Peter H. Feiler
Software Engineering Institute
4500 Fifth Ave
Pittsburgh, PA 15213
+1-412-268-7790
phf@sei.cmu.edu

ABSTRACT

Mission and safety critical software-reliant systems, aka. Cyber-physical systems, face the increasing challenges of exponential increase in verification related software rework cost. Industry studies show that 70% of defects are introduced in requirements and architecture design, while 80% are discovered post-unit test. The Architecture Analysis & Design Language (AADL) standard was targeted to address these issues through virtual system integration to analytically discover these system level issues regarding operational system properties early in the life cycle.

After a summary of the challenges, the presentation highlights the expressive, analytical, and auto-generation capabilities of the AADL core language as well as several of its standardized extensions. The presentation then illustrates the importance of the analytical virtual system integration capabilities on several realistic industrial examples. In this context we discuss the benefit of well-defined semantics of nominal and fault behavior, timing, semantics of the model in AADL over other MBD notations.

The presentation concludes by outlining a four part improvement strategy: architecture-led requirement specification to improve the quality of requirements, architecture refinement and incremental virtual system integration to discover issues early, compositional verification through static analysis to address scalability, and incremental verification and testing throughout the life cycle as assurance evidence.

Categories and Subject Descriptors

D.2.11 [**Software Architectures**] languages

Keywords

Architecture Analysis & Design Language (AADL); Virtual System Integration; Architecture-centric Software-reliant System Engineering

1. REFERENCES

[1] AADL and Model-based Engineering. *Software Engineering Institute (SEI) Research & Technology Highlight, Jan 2010.* http://www.sei.cmu.edu/library/assets/ResearchandTechnology_AADLandMBE.pdf.

[2] Feiler, P., Wrage, L., Hansson, J. *System Architecture Virtual Integration: An Industrial Case Study.* Technical Report. CMU/SEI-2009-TR-017. Software Engineering Institute. 2009. http://resources.sei.cmu.edu/asset_files/technicalreport/2009_005_001_15119.pdf.

[3] Feiler, P., Goodenough, J., Gurfinkel, A., Weinstock, C., Wrage, L. *Four Pillars for Improving the Quality of Safety-Critical Software-reliant Systems.* Software Engineering Institute, Technology Highlight, April 2013. http://resources.sei.cmu.edu/library/asset-view.cfm?assetid=47791.

Short Biography

Peter Feiler is a 29 year veteran and Principal Researcher of the Architecture Practice (AP) initiative at the Software Engineering Institute (SEI). His current research interest is in improving the quality of safety-critical software-reliant systems through architecture-centric virtual system integration and incremental life cycle assurance to reduce rework and qualification costs. Peter Feiler has been the technical lead and main author of the SAE Architecture Analysis & Design Language (AADL) standard. He has a Ph.D. in Computer Science from Carnegie Mellon.

DM-0001611

HILT 2014, October 18-21, 2014, Portland, Oregon, USA.
ACM 978-1-4503-3217-0/14/10.
http://dx.doi.org/10.1145/2663171.2663174

Resolute: An Assurance Case Language for Architecture Models

Andrew Gacek, John Backes,
Darren Cofer, Konrad Slind
Rockwell Collins
Advanced Technology Center
first.last@rockwellcollins.com

Mike Whalen
University of Minnesota
Computer Science Department
whalen@cs.umn.edu

ABSTRACT

Arguments about the safety, security, and correctness of a complex system are often made in the form of an assurance case. An assurance case is a structured argument, often represented with a graphical interface, that presents and supports claims about a system's behavior. The argument may combine different kinds of evidence to justify its top level claim. While assurance cases deliver some level of guarantee of a system's correctness, they lack the rigor that proofs from formal methods typically provide. Furthermore, changes in the structure of a model during development may result in inconsistencies between a design and its assurance case. Our solution is a framework for automatically generating assurance cases based on 1) a system model specified in an architectural design language, 2) a set of logical rules expressed in a domain specific language that we have developed, and 3) the results of other formal analyses that have been run on the model. We argue that the rigor of these automatically generated assurance cases exceeds those of traditional assurance case arguments because of their more formal logical foundation and direct connection to the architectural model.

Categories and Subject Descriptors

D.2.4 [**Software/Program Verification**]: Reliability;
D.2.11 [**Software Architectures**]: Languages

General Terms

Reliability; Security; Languages; Verification

Keywords

Assurance case; Avionics; Architecture models; AADL

HILT 2014, October 18–21, 2014, Portland, OR, USA.
Copyright is held by the owner/author(s). Publication rights licensed to ACM.
ACM 978-1-4503-3217-0/14/10 ...$15.00.
http://dx.doi.org/10.1145/2663171.2663177.

1. INTRODUCTION

The design of complex systems such as Unmanned Air Vehicles (UAVs) can be greatly improved through the use of advanced system and software architecting tools. In previous work, we have successfully used model checking to verify software components that have been created using model-based development (MBD) tools such as Simulink [27]. An objective of our current research is to build on this success and extend the reach of model checking and other formal methods to system design models.

The Architecture Analysis and Design Language (AADL) [12] is targeted for capturing the important design concepts in real-time distributed embedded systems. The AADL language can capture both the hardware and software architecture in a hierarchical format. It provides hardware component models including processors, buses, memories, and I/O devices, and software component models including threads, processes, and subprograms. Interfaces for these components and data flows between components can also be defined. The language offers a high degree of flexibility in terms of architecture and component detail. This supports incremental development where the architecture is refined to increasing levels of detail and where components can be refined with additional details over time.

One of our core innovations is to structure the formalizations and proofs by following the AADL descriptions of the system. In other work, we did this through the use of formal assume-guarantee contracts that correspond to the component requirements for each component [5]. Our current work on DARPA's High Assurance Cyber Military Systems (HACMS) program is focused on security properties of UAVs [8]. We have found that in assuring the cyber-security properties of aircraft designs we need to integrate a variety of evidence with varying levels of formality. This has been our motivation to explore assurance case approaches.

In this paper we report on *Resolute*, a new assurance case language and tool which is based on architectural models. In developing Resolute, we have followed the same approach of embedding the proof in the architectural model for the vehicle, tightly coupling terms in the assurance case with evidence derived directly from the system design artifacts. This ensures that we maintain consistency between the system design and its associated assurance case(s). Design changes that might invalidate some aspect of an assurance case can be immediately flagged by our tool for correction.

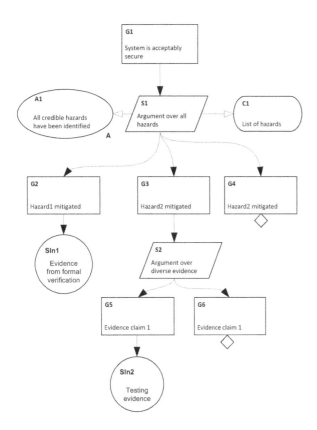

Figure 1: Example of GSN notation

2. ASSURANCE CASES

Using Resolute, the goal is to construct an *assurance case* [20, 21, 22] about a system specified in AADL. From [17], an assurance case is defined as:

> A reasoned and compelling argument, supported by a body of evidence, that a system, service or organization will operate as intended for a defined application in a defined environment.

Assurances cases are constructed to show that one or more *claims* about the system are acceptable; usually the claims are defined for an aspect of the system such as safety (*safety cases*) or security (*security cases*). For complex systems, these structured arguments are often large and complicated. In order to construct, present, discuss, and review these arguments, it is necessary that they are clearly documented. Several notations have been proposed to properly document assurance cases. The most popular notation is currently the Goal Structuring Notation (GSN) [17, 24], which is used in several assurance-case tool suites.

An example of the GSN notation is shown in Figure 1. In GSN, we have *goals* (G1..G6 in Figure 1) that represent claims about the system. When a claim is established through reasoning about subclaims, a *strategy* (S1, S2 in Figure 1) is used to describe the nature of how the subclaims establish the claim. Furthermore, strategies often rely on *assumptions* in order for the strategy to be reasonably applied. In the figure, we make an argument that the system is acceptably secure by enumerating the hazards that prevent it from being secure and demonstrating that these hazards are mitigated. An assumption of this strategy (A1 in Figure 1)

is that we have enumerated all reasonable security hazards. Also, it is often necessary to provide the *context* in which a strategy or goal occurs: in the case of the enumeration strategy, the context is the list of identified hazards. We terminate the argument either in goals that have no further decomposition, graphically notated by a diamond (shown in the figure by goals G4 and G6), or in *solutions* (Sln1, Sln2 in Figure 1) that describe evidence for the goal. GSN arguments form directed acyclic graphs; it is possible to use the same subclaim or evidence as part of the justification of a larger claim, but it is not well-formed to have a cyclic chain of reasoning within a GSN graph.

To be compelling, the argument must provide sufficient assurance in the claims made about the system. Constructing such arguments is quite difficult, even given appropriate notations. First, proper claims must be identified to define the objectives of the assurance case. Then appropriate argumentation must be constructed: such argumentation must often take into account the environment in which the system is used, the artifacts that are constructed during system design, implementation, and test, and the processes followed during the development and implementation cycle. There is a rich body of literature that describes proper processes and patterns for constructing assurance cases, *e.g.* [20, 21, 22, 23, 31, 10, 18, 16, 15].

3. AADL

Our domain of interest is distributed real-time embedded systems (including both hardware and software), such as comprise the critical functionality in commercial and military aircraft. Many aerospace companies have adopted MBD processes for production of software components, and we have successfully applied formal analysis at this level to verify component requirements. However, the system design process is often less rigorous: system-level descriptions of the interactions of distributed components, resource allocation decisions, and communication mechanisms between components are typically ad hoc and not based on analyzable models. Application of formal analysis methods at the system level requires 1) an abstraction that defines how components will be represented in the system model, and 2) selection of an appropriate formal modeling language.

In this approach, the architectural model includes interface, interconnections, and specifications for components but not their implementations. It describes the interactions between components and their arrangement in the system, but the components themselves are black boxes. The component implementations are described separately by the existing MBD environment and artifacts (or by traditional programming languages, where applicable). They are represented in the system model by the subset of their specifications that is necessary to describe their system-level interactions. This distinction between system architecture and component implementation is important to ensure the scalability of the analyses that we wish to perform.

We have selected AADL as a system modeling language for our work. AADL is described in SAE standard AS5506B and has a sufficiently precise definition to support formalization of its semantics [12]. It provides syntax for describing both hardware and software aspects of the system so that requirements related to resource allocation, scheduling, and communication between distributed elements can be addressed. Textual and graphical versions of the language are

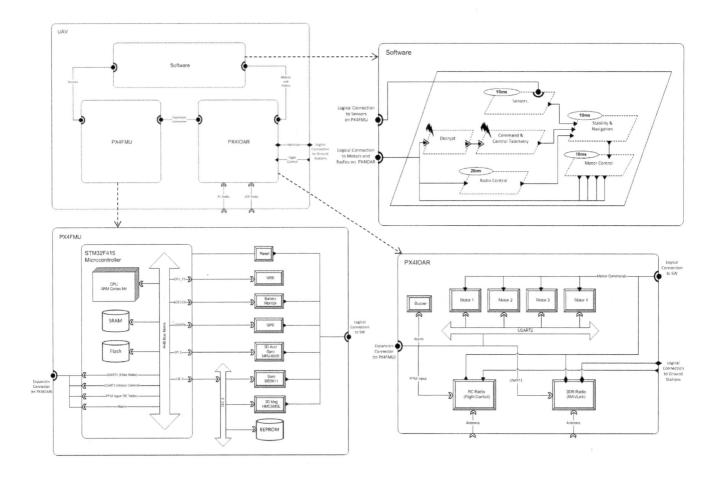

Figure 2: Simplified AADL model of HACMS quadcopter

available with tool support for each [30]. An important feature of the language is its extensibility via the annex mechanism. Language developers can embed new syntax into an AADL model to provide new features or to support additional analyses. Annex expressions have full access to the rest of the model providing the ability to refer to components and properties described in the base AADL language. We have used this annex mechanism to add behavioral contracts and assurance case rules to our system architecture models.

Figure 2 shows an example AADL system model (using the graphical syntax) that we have developed for the HACMS program. The model describes a UAV that includes a simplified version of the system software along with the processing hardware (PX4FMU) and an I/O board for motors and radios (PX4IOAR). The actual flight software model is over 7,000 lines of AADL and includes 35 computing threads, with a C implementation of over 50K lines of code.

In the HACMS project we are concerned primarily with cyber-security of UAVs. We are developing analysis tools based on the AADL language that allow us to verify important security and information flow properties for this kind

of system. We are also developing synthesis tools that allow us to generate glue code and system configuration data for the system. This data, along with the component implementations, provide everything needed to build the final flight binaries from the AADL model. To show that our results scale to real military systems, we are also transitioning these technologies for demonstration on Boeing's Unmanned Little Bird helicopter [4].

4. RESOLUTE

Resolute is a language and tool for constructing assurance cases based on AADL models. Users formulate claims and rules for justifying those claims, which Resolute uses to construct assurance cases. Both the claims and rules are parameterized by variable inputs which are instantiated using elements from the models. This creates a dependence of the assurance case on the AADL model and means that changes to the AADL model can result in changes to the assurance case. This also means that a small set of rules can result in a large assurance case since each rule may be applied multiple times to different parts of the architecture model.

Resolute is designed primarily to show the structure of an argument; in the GSN notation, it would define how a claim is provable from subclaims. In some ways, Resolute is richer than GSN; as shown below, it supports parametric goals and arbitrary Boolean relations between claims and subclaims rather than simple conjunctions or *m-of-n* relations. On the other hand, it does not currently provide specific placeholders for *context* and *assumption* information. In GSN, this information is explicit, but informal: it is documented to aid the readers and writers of the assurance case. Resolute currently does not have a placeholder for this information, but this could easily be remedied by adding string properties to document contextual aspects of claim/subclaim relationships. To define context and assumption ideas more formally is more challenging and something that we are considering for future work.

4.1 Claims and Rules

In Resolute, each claim corresponds to a first-order predicate. For example, a user might represent a claim such as "The memory of process `p` is protected from alteration by other processes" using the predicate `memory_protected(p : process)`. The user specifies rules for `memory_protected` which provide possible ways to justify the underlying claim. Logically, these rules correspond to global assumptions which have the form of an implication with the predicate of interest as the conclusion. For example, an operating system such as NICTA's secure microkernel seL4—which we are using in HACMS—might enforce memory protection on its own [25]:

```
memory_protected(p : process) <=
  (property_lookup(p, OS) = "seL4")
```

Here we query the architectural model to determine the operating system for the given process. Another way to satisfy memory protection may be to examine all the other processes which share the same underlying memory component. Note that in AADL a "process" represents a logical memory space while a "memory" represents a physical memory space.

```
memory_protected(p : process) <=
  forall (mem : memory). bound(p, mem) =>
    forall (q : process). bound(q, mem) =>
      memory_safe_process(q)
```

In the above rule, we are querying the architectural model via the universal quantification over memory and process components. Note that quantification is always finite since we only quantify over architectural components and other finite sets. The built-in `bound` predicate determines how software maps to hardware. In addition, we call another user defined predicate `memory_safe_process` to determine if a process is memory safe. In the resulting assurance case, the claim that a process `p` is memory protected will be supported by subclaims that all processes in its memory space are memory safe. Thus there will be one supporting subclaim for each process in the memory space.

The above rules for memory protection illustrate a couple of ways to justify the desired claim, but they do not constitute a complete description of memory protection nor a complete listing of sufficient evidence. This is a critical point in Resolute: rules are sufficient, but not complete. The negation of a claim can never be used in an argument (*i.e.*, in logic programming parlance, we do not make a closed world assumption). This is a manifestation of the traditional phrase "absence of evidence is not evidence of absence." Instead, if the user truly wants to use a claim in a negative context, that notion must be formalized as a separate positive

claim with its own rules for what constitutes sufficient evidence. For example, one may be interested in a claim such as `memory_violated` which has rules which succeed only when a concrete memory violation is detected.

4.2 Computations

Separate from claims, Resolute has a notion of *computations* which are complete and can thus be used in both positive and negative contexts. Usually these computations are based on querying the model. For example, the `bound` predicate above is a built-in computation which returns a Boolean value and is used in a negative context in the rule for `memory_protected`. Users may also introduce their own functions which are defined via a single equation such as

```
message_delay(p : process) =
  sum({thread_message_delay(t)
       for (t : thread) if bound(t, p)})
```

Here `sum` is a built-in function and `thread_message_delay` is another user-defined function.

Computations may contribute to an assurance case, but they do not appear in it independently since they do not make any explicit claim. Instead, a user may wrap claims around computations as needed, for instance a claim such as "message delay time for `p` is within acceptable bounds" using the `message_delay` function.

Since claims cannot be used negatively while computations can, claims may not appear within computations. This creates two separate levels in Resolute: the logical level on top and the computation level beneath it. The logical level determines the claims, rules, and evidence used in the assurance case argument, while the computation level helps determine which claims are relevant in a particular context and may directly satisfy some claims by performing computations over the model.

External analyses are incorporated in Resolute as computations. An external analysis is run each time the corresponding computation is invoked. This is useful for deploying existing tools for analyzing properties such as schedulability or resource allocation.

5. TOOL ENVIRONMENT

We have implemented Resolute as an AADL annex using the Open Source AADL Tool Environment (OSATE) [30] plug-in for the Eclipse IDE. Resolute itself is Open Source under a BSD License and available online [29]. Using OSATE, users are able to interact with Resolute in the same environment in which they develop their AADL models. In addition, the resulting framework provides on-the-fly syntactic and semantic validation. For example, references to AADL model elements in the Resolute annex are linked to the actual AADL objects in the same project so that undefined references and type errors are detected instantly.

The syntax of Resolute is inspired by logic programming. Each rule defines the meaning and evidence for a claim. The meaning of a claim is given by a text string in the rule which is parameterized by the arguments of the claim. The body of the rule consists of an expression which describes sufficient evidence to satisfy that claim. Claims may be parameterized by AADL types (e.g., threads, systems, memories, connections, etc.), integers, strings, Booleans, or sets.

Figure 3 shows an example of two Resolute rules. The meaning of the claim is given by the associated text, for

```
only_receive_decrypt(x : component) <=
  ** "The component " x " only receives messages that pass Decrypt" **
  forall (c : connection).
    (parent(destination(c)) = x) =>
      is_sensor_data(c) or only_receive_decrypt_connection(c)

only_receive_decrypt_connection(c : connection) <=
  ** "The connection " c " only carries messages that pass Decrypt" **
  let src : component = parent(source(c));
  unalterable_connection(c) and (is_decrypt(src) or only_receive_decrypt(src))
```

Figure 3: Example Resolute rules

```
bound(logical : component, physical : component) : bool =
  memory_bound(logical, physical) or
  connection_bound(logical, physical) or
  processor_bound(logical, physical)

memory_bound(logical : component, physical : component) : bool =
  has_property(logical, Deployment_Properties::Actual_Memory_Binding) and
  member(physical, property(logical, Deployment_Properties::Actual_Memory_Binding))

connection_bound(logical : component, physical : component) : bool =
  has_property(logical, Deployment_Properties::Actual_Connection_Binding) and
  member(physical, property(logical, Deployment_Properties::Actual_Connection_Binding))

processor_bound(logical : component, physical : component) : bool =
  has_property(logical, Deployment_Properties::Actual_Processor_Binding) and
  member(physical, property(logical, Deployment_Properties::Actual_Processor_Binding))
```

Figure 4: Definition of bound in the Resolute standard library

example only_receive_decrypt(x) means: "The component x only receives commands that pass Decrypt." An instantiated version of this string is what will appear in the corresponding assurance case. The built-in functions like destination and source return the feature to which a connection is attached, and the built-in parent then gives the component which holds that feature. These rules also make use of other user-defined claims such as is_sensor_data and unalterable_connection which talk about the content and integrity of connections. Note that the two claims shown in the figure are mutually recursive. Together, these claims walk over a model cataloging the data-flow and constructing a corresponding assurance case.

Many claims, rules, and functions will appear within a Resolute annex library which is typically a top-level file in an AADL project. These libraries define the rules for all claims in Resolute, but do not make any assertions about what arguments the claims should hold on. In addition, Resolute comes with a standard library of predefined functions for common operations. For instance, the bound predicate for determining if a logical component is bound to a specific physical component is part of the standard library and defined as in Figure 4.

An assurance case is initiated in Resolute by adding a *prove* statement to the Resolute annex for an AADL component. A prove statement consists of a claim applied to some concrete arguments. An example prove statement is shown in Figure 5 where the claim only_receive_ground_station is associated with the motor controller thread. When a Res-

```
process implementation Main_Loop.Impl
  subcomponents
    MC: thread Motor_Control

    ...

    annex resolute {**
      prove only_receive_ground_station(MC)
    **}
end Main_Loop.Impl;
```

Figure 5: Prove statements for Resolute claims

olute analysis is run on an AADL system instance, an assurance case is generated for every prove statement that appears in any component within that instance.

Figure 6 shows a portion of a successful assurance case generated by Resolute on our simplified UAV model. Each claim is shown on a single line. Supporting claims are shown indented one level beneath the claim they support. A check next to a claim indicates that it is proven. Figure 7 shows a portion of a failed assurance case. An exclamation point indicates that a claim has failed. In this case, the AADL model includes a safety controller which is allowed to bypass the Decrypt component and directly send messages to the UAV. This bypass is detected Resolute. In fact, the only difference between Figures 6 and 7 is the AADL model. The claims and rules are identical in both.

- ✔ only_receive_gs(ML : SOFTWARE::Main_Loop.Impl)
  - ✔ 'MC : SOFTWARE::Motor_Control' only receives messages from the Ground Station
    - ▷ ✔ Only the Ground Station can send messages that pass Decrypt
    - ✔ The component 'MC : SOFTWARE::Motor_Control' only receives messages that pass Decrypt
      - ✔ The connection 'SN.motor_commands -> MC.motor_commands' only carries messages that pass Decrypt
        - ▷ ✔ The connection 'SN.motor_commands -> MC.motor_commands' delivers data without alteration
        - ✔ The component 'SN : SOFTWARE::Stability_Navigation' only receives messages that pass Decrypt
          - ✔ The connection 'CCT.mavlink_out -> SN.mavlink' only carries messages that pass Decrypt
            - ▷ ✔ The connection 'CCT.mavlink_out -> SN.mavlink' delivers data without alteration
            - ✔ The component 'CCT : SOFTWARE::Command_Control_Telemetry' only receives messages that pass Decrypt
              - ▷ ✔ The connection 'DC.decrypt_out -> CCT.mavlink_in' only carries messages that pass Decrypt
          - ✔ The connection 'SS.sensors_out -> SN.sensors' only carries sensor data

Figure 6: Example of a successful assurance case from Resolute

- only_receive_gs(ML : SOFTWARE::Main_Loop.Impl)
  - 'MC : SOFTWARE::Motor_Control' only receives messages from the Ground Station
    - ▷ ✔ Only the Ground Station can send messages that pass Decrypt
    - The component 'MC : SOFTWARE::Motor_Control' only receives messages that pass Decrypt
      - The connection 'SN.motor_commands -> MC.motor_commands' only carries messages that pass Decrypt
        - ▷ ✔ The connection 'SN.motor_commands -> MC.motor_commands' delivers data without alteration
        - The component 'SN : SOFTWARE::Stability_Navigation' only receives messages that pass Decrypt
          - ▷ ✔ The connection 'CCT.mavlink_out -> SN.mavlink' only carries messages that pass Decrypt
          - The connection 'RC.commands_out -> SN.rc_commands' only carries messages that pass Decrypt
            - ▷ ✔ The connection 'RC.commands_out -> SN.rc_commands' delivers data without alteration
            - ▷ The component 'RC : SOFTWARE::Radio_Control' only receives messages that pass Decrypt

Figure 7: Example of a failed assurance cases from Resolute

The assurance case shown in Figure 6 is constructed over our simplified UAV model. We ported this assurance case to the true UAV model once the latter was available. Although the true UAV model contained seven times as many software components as the simplified model, very few of the Resolute rules needed to be changed. The most significant change was that the true UAV model has data-flow cycles, and therefore the simple recursive rules used in Figure 3 are insufficient. Instead, we created more sophisticated rules which recursively computed the set of components which were reachable prior to passing through the Decrypt component, and then we justified the claim that the given set was complete and did not have access to the motor control component.

Assurance cases as shown in Figures 6 and 7 are interactive in the Resolute user interface. The user can navigate through the assurance case and select a claim to navigate to locations in the model relevant to the claim. For example, the user can navigate to any of the AADL components referenced as input parameters to the claim or can navigate to the rule that defines the claim. This makes it much easier to figure out why an assurance case is failing or why a particular part of the assurance case has a given structure.

An assurance case generated by Resolute is also a stand-alone object. After construction, it no longer depends on Resolute or even the AADL model, though it of course still refers to elements of the model. This means the assurance case can be used as an independent certification artifact. In addition, Resolute allows assurance cases to be exported to other formats and assurance case tools such as CertWare [28].

6. FORMAL LOGIC

The Resolute language consists of both a logic and a computational sublanguage. The logic of Resolute is an intuitionistic logic similar to pure Prolog, but augmented with explicit quantification. The logic is parameterized by the computational sublanguage, and requires only that the sublanguage is deterministic. This allows the computational sublanguage to be customized to any domain (e.g. AADL in our context) and to be expanded and refined, without worrying about the logical consequences. In fact, we do not even require termination for the computational sublanguage, though in practice a non-terminating computation will lead to non-terminating proof search.

6.1 Syntax

Let the type of formulas be o. We assume the usual logical constants of $\wedge, \vee, \Rightarrow: o \to o \to o$ and $\forall, \exists : (\alpha \to o) \to o$ for every type α not containing o. Let the type of Booleans be *bool* with constants *true* and *false*. We use the constant $\langle \cdot \rangle : bool \to o$ to inject Booleans into formulas. We assume a notion of evaluation $e \Downarrow v$ read "e evaluates to v". We assume evaluation is deterministic. The full set of types and terms is left unspecified, but would typically be determined by the computational sublanguage.

6.2 Sequent Rules

We define a judgment $\Gamma \vdash G$ where Γ is a set of formulas called assumptions and G is a formula called the goal. This judgment holds when the goal G is a consequence of assumptions Γ in the Resolute logic. The rules for this judgment are presented in Figure 8.

$$\frac{\Gamma \vdash G_1 \quad \Gamma \vdash G_2}{\Gamma \vdash G_1 \wedge G_2} \wedge \mathcal{R} \qquad\qquad \frac{\Gamma \vdash G_i}{\Gamma \vdash G_1 \vee G_2} \vee \mathcal{R}_{i=1,2} \qquad\qquad \frac{\Gamma, G_1 \vdash G_2}{\Gamma \vdash G_1 \Rightarrow G_2} \Rightarrow \mathcal{R}$$

$$\frac{\Gamma \vdash G(t_1) \quad \cdots \quad \Gamma \vdash G(t_n)}{\Gamma \vdash \forall x : \alpha. \; G(x)} \forall \mathcal{R} \qquad\qquad \frac{\Gamma \vdash G(t_i)}{\Gamma \vdash \exists x : \alpha. \; G(x)} \exists \mathcal{R}_{i=1\ldots n}$$

$$\text{where } \alpha = \{t_1, \ldots, t_n\}$$

$$\frac{\Gamma \vdash G(\bar{t})}{\Gamma \vdash A(\bar{t})} \text{ backchain}$$

$$\text{where } \forall \bar{x}. A(\bar{x}) \Leftarrow G(\bar{x}) \in \Gamma.$$

$$\frac{e \Downarrow \text{false}}{\Gamma, \langle e \rangle \vdash G} \text{ eval-}\mathcal{L} \qquad\qquad \frac{e \Downarrow \text{true}}{\Gamma \vdash \langle e \rangle} \text{ eval-}\mathcal{R}$$

Figure 8: Resolute logic rules

The rules for $\wedge$, $\vee$, and $\Rightarrow$ are standard. The quantification rules apply only to types with finitely many inhabitants since the rules work via explicit enumeration. This simplistic treatment of quantification means that proof search only needs to consider ground terms. Moreover, finiteness is appropriate for our domain where we want to quantify over types such as all threads in a model or all processes within a particular system. The rule for backchain allows the assumptions in Γ to be used in constructing a proof of an atomic goal. Note that in the backchain rule, A stands for an atomic formula, *i.e.*, a predicate applied to arguments. Finally, the rules for evaluation allow a proof to be finished by finding an assumption which evaluates to *false* or a conclusion that evaluates to *true*.

User specified claims in Resolute are treated as predicates in the logic, and the rules for claims are treated as initial assumptions. Each prove statement in the AADL model is translated to a goal G while all the Resolute rules are translated into the initial context Γ. Then proof search is performed on $\Gamma \vdash G$. If a proof is found, that proof is transformed into an assurance case by replacing each intermediate sequent of the form $\Gamma \vdash A(\bar{t})$ by the instantiated version of the claim text for the claim $A(\bar{x})$. Thus, for us, an assurance case is a proof in the Resolute logic, and browsing the assurance case means traversing the proof tree.

6.3 Customizing the Resolute Logic for AADL

The Resolute logic we use in our implementation is a customization of the general Resolute logic. In particular, we allow quantification over all AADL model types (threads, process, etc) and over all user computed sets. Our computational sublanguage is based on the Requirements Enforcement Analysis Language [13]. Our sublanguage includes all the AADL model types and more traditional types of integers, reals, strings, ranges, and sets. There are pre-defined functions for common operations (e.g. sum, union, member) or queries against the AADL model properties and components. Users may also define their own functions even using recursion, and thus our computational sublanguage is Turing complete. Moreover, our sublanguage allows calls out to external tools for richer analyses such as scheduling or model checking.

Users may specify any rules or meanings for claims, and thus Resolute can make no judgment about how valid the resulting argument is. Resolute only ensures that the constructed assurance cases are valid with respect to the user specified claims and rules. Ultimately, the acceptability of an assurance case generated by Resolute must depend on traditional assurance case techniques such as expert review. Resolute provides a way of keeping an assurance case synchronized with an architecture model, but the quality of that assurance case is still dependent on the user.

7. RELATED WORK

As discussed in Section 2, assurance cases have a large and well-developed literature. Patterns for assurance case argumentation have been considered in [23, 31, 10, 18], and common fallacies in assurance cases are considered in [16]. An approach to apply and evolve assurance cases as part of system design is found in [15], which is similar to the process we have used in applying the Resolute tools. A comparison of assurance cases to prescriptive standards such as DO178B/C is provided by [19]. Recent work on *confidence cases* as a means of assessing assurance case arguments is found in [14].

Several commercial and research tools support the development of assurance cases. ASCE [1] from Adelard is currently the most widely used commercial tool for constructing assurance cases. ASCE supports integration with commercial requirements management tools such as DOORS, constructing confidence cases with assurance cases, and integration with a variety of tools through its plug-in architecture. Other assurance case tools include AdvoCATE [11] from NASA Ames, CertWare [28] from NASA Langley, D-Case [26], and NOR-STA [7]. These tools provide structured editing, visualization, metrics, and reasoning tools for safety arguments but are not tied into a system architectural model.

In [3], a safety case in ASCE involving a combination of mechanized proof, testing, and hand-proofs is used to argue that the maximum error introduced in the computation of a monotonic function is within some tolerance of the actual value of the function. This is similar to how we use Resolute in the example in Section 5; we assemble disparate evidence from different verification techniques towards an argument. Unlike our work, the ASCE safety case is not directly integrated into the software/system architecture. Similar work in [9] describes patterns for using proofs within a safety case and automation for generating portions of the proof as a part of the safety case.

The Evidential Tool Bus (ETB) [6] is very similar in syntax and semantics to Resolute. It is supported by a Datalog-style logic and is designed to combine evidence from a variety of sources. However, the focus of the ETB is on distribution and on *provenance*—that is, to log the sequence of tool invocations that were performed to solve the query. It uses timestamps to determine which analyses are out of date with respect to the current development artifacts and to only re-run those analyses that are not synchronized with the current development artifacts. In addition, it is designed to perform distributed execution of analyses. Analysis tool plug-ins are used to execute the analysis tools within ETB. ETB is designed to be tool and model agnostic, and is therefore not integrated with a model of the system architecture.

The work in [2] ties together an assurance case with a model-based notation (Simulink) for the purpose of demonstrating that the Simulink-generated code meets its requirements. This work has many similarities to ours, in that the assurance case is closely tied to the hierarchical structure of the model. It is more rigorous (in that the assurance case is derived from a formal proof) but also much more narrow, corresponding to a component in the system assurance cases that we create. The two approaches could perhaps be integrated to provide more rigorous safety cases for a wider class of software developed in a model-based environment.

8. FUTURE WORK

We have generated a number of assurance cases with Resolute for the design of a UAV in the HACMS project. Specifically, we have generated assurance cases that reason about the flow of information through the vehicle and the availability of resources under different operating modes. The tool has been useful for modeling requirements of the architecture at early phases of the design, and verifying that they still hold in later phases. In future work we plan to make the assurance cases generated by Resolute exportable to more assurance case tools. In order to support this, we may extend Resolute with a more complete set of standard assurance case constructs. For example, we may introduce strategies as first-class constructs by augmenting Resolute rules with explicit textual descriptions that would then appear in the assurance case. We also plan to improve the grammar to support more features of AADL.

9. ACKNOWLEDGMENTS

The work presented here was sponsored by DARPA as part of the HACMS program under contract FA8750-12-9-0179.

10. REFERENCES

[1] Adelard. ASCE. http://www.adelard.com/asce/.
[2] N. Basir, E. Denney, and B. Fischer. Deriving safety cases for hierarchical structure in model-based development. In E. Schoitsch, editor, *Proceedings of the 2010 International Conference on Computer Safety, Reliability, and Security (SAFECOMP)*, volume 6351 of *Lecture Notes in Computer Science*, pages 68–81. Springer, 2010.
[3] P. Bishop, R. Bloomfield, and L. Cyra. Combining testing and proof to gain high assurance in software. In *ISSRE 2013*, November 2013.
[4] Boeing. Unmanned Little Bird. http://www.boeing.com/boeing/rotorcraft/military/ulb/.
[5] D. D. Cofer, A. Gacek, S. P. Miller, M. W. Whalen, B. LaValley, and L. Sha. Compositional verification of architectural models. In A. E. Goodloe and S. Person, editors, *Proceedings of the 4th NASA Formal Methods Symposium (NFM 2012)*, volume 7226, pages 126–140, Berlin, Heidelberg, April 2012. Springer-Verlag.
[6] S. Cruanes, G. Hamon, S. Owre, and N. Shankar. Tool integration with the evidential tool bus. In R. Giacobazzi, J. Berdine, and I. Mastroeni, editors, *Verification, Model Checking, and Abstract Interpretation*, volume 7737 of *Lecture Notes in Computer Science*, pages 275–294. Springer Berlin Heidelberg, 2013.
[7] L. Cyra and J. Górski. Supporting compliance with security standards by trust case templates. In *2007 International Conference on Dependability of Computer Systems (DepCoS-RELCOMEX 2007), June 14-16, 2007, Szklarska Poreba, Poland*, pages 91–98. IEEE Computer Society, 2007.
[8] Defense Advanced Research Projects Agency. High-Assurance Cyber Military Systems. http://www.darpa.mil/Our_Work/I2O/Programs/High-Assurance_Cyber_Military_Systems_(HACMS).aspx.
[9] E. Denney and G. Pai. Evidence arguments for using formal methods in software certification. In *IEEE International Workshop on Software Certification (WoSoCer 2013)*, November 2013.
[10] E. Denney and G. Pai. A formal basis for safety case patterns. In *Proceedings of the 2013 International Conference on Computer Safety, Reliability and Security (SAFECOMP)*, September 2013.
[11] E. Denney, G. Pai, and J. Pohl. AdvoCATE: An assurance case automation toolset. In *Proceedings of the 2012 International Conference on Computer Safety, Reliability, and Security (SAFECOMP)*, pages 8–21, Berlin, Heidelberg, 2012. Springer-Verlag.
[12] P. H. Feiler and D. P. Gluch. *Model-Based Engineering with AADL: An Introduction to the SAE Architecture Analysis & Design Language*. Addison-Wesley Professional, 1st edition, 2012.
[13] O. Gilles and J. Hugues. Expressing and enforcing user-defined constraints of AADL models. *Engineering of Complex Computer Systems, IEEE International Conference on*, 0:337–342, 2010.
[14] J. Goodenough, C. Weinstock, and A. Klein. Toward a theory of assurance case confidence. Technical Report CMU/SEI-2012-TR-002, Software Engineering Institute, Carnegie Mellon University, September 2012.
[15] P. Graydon, J. Knight, and E. Strunk. Assurance based development of critical systems. In *2007 International Symposium on Dependable Systems and Networks (DSN)*, June 2007.
[16] W. Greenwell, J. Knight, C. M. Holloway, and J. Pease. A taxonomy of fallacies in system safety

arguments. In *24th International System Safety Conference*, August 2006.

[17] GSN. GSN community standard version 1.
`http://www.goalstructuringnotation.info/documents/GSN_Standard.pdf`, November 2011.

[18] R. Hawkins, K. Clegg, R. Alexander, and T. Kelly. Using a software safety argument pattern catalogue: Two case studies. In *Proceedings of the 2011 International Conference on Computer Safety, Reliability and Security (SAFECOMP)*, September 2011.

[19] R. Hawkins, I. Habli, T. Kelly, and J. McDermid. Assurance cases and prescriptive software safety certification: A comparative study. *Safety Science*, 59:55 – 71, 2013.

[20] R. D. Hawkins and T. P. Kelly. A Systematic Approach for Developing Software Safety Arguments. In *Proceedings of the 2009 International System Safety Conference (ISSC)*, 2009.

[21] T. Kelley. Concepts and principles of compositional safety case construction. Technical Report COMSA/2001/1/1, The University of York, 2001.

[22] T. Kelly. *Arguing Safety – A Systematic Approach to Managing Safety Cases*. PhD thesis, University of York, 1998.

[23] T. Kelly and J. McDermid. Safety case construction and reuse using patterns. In *Proceedings of the 1997 International Conference on Computer Safety, Reliability, and Security (SAFECOMP)*, 1997.

[24] T. Kelly and R. Weaver. The goal structuring notation – a safety argument notation. In *Proceedings of the Dependable Systems and Networks 2004 Workshop on Assurance Cases*, July 2004.

[25] G. Klein, K. Elphinstone, G. Heiser, J. Andronick, D. Cock, P. Derrin, D. Elkaduwe, K. Engelhardt, R. Kolanski, M. Norrish, T. Sewell, H. Tuch, and S. Winwood. seL4: Formal verification of an OS kernel. In *Proceedings of the ACM SIGOPS 22nd Symposium on Operating Systems Principles*, SOSP '09, pages 207–220, New York, NY, USA, 2009. ACM.

[26] Y. Matsuno, H. Takamura, and Y. Ishikawa. A dependability case editor with pattern library. In *HASE*, pages 170–171. IEEE Computer Society, 2010.

[27] S. P. Miller, M. W. Whalen, and D. D. Cofer. Software model checking takes off. *Commun. ACM*, 53(2):58–64, Feb. 2010.

[28] NASA. Certware. `http://nasa.github.io/CertWare/`.

[29] Rockwell Collins. Resolute. `https://github.com/smaccm/smaccm`.

[30] Software Engineering Institute, Carnegie Mellon University. OSATE. `http://www.aadl.info/aadl/currentsite/tool/osate.html`.

[31] L. Sun, O. Lisagor, and T. Kelly. Justifying the validity of safety assessment models with safety case patterns. In *Proceedings of the 6th IET System Safety Conference*, September 2011.

Hybrid Annex: An AADL Extension for Continuous Behavior and Cyber-Physical Interaction Modeling

Ehsan Ahmad
School of Computer Science
Northwestern Polytechnical
University,
State Key Lab. of Comput.
Sci. Inst. of Software
Chinese Academy of Sciences
ehah@ios.ac.cn

Brian R. Larson
Computing and Information
Systems
Kansas State University
Manhattan, KS 66506
brl@ksu.edu

Stephen C. Barrett
Computing and Information
Systems
Kansas State University
Manhattan, KS 66506
scbarrett@ksu.edu

Naijun Zhan
State Key Lab. of Comput.
Sci. Inst. of Software
Chinese Academy of Sciences
Beijing, 100190
znj@ios.ac.cn

Yunwei Dong
School of Computer Science
Northwestern Polytechnical
University
Xi'an, 710129
yunweidong@nwpu.edu.cn

ABSTRACT

Correct design, and system-level dependability prediction of highly-integrated systems demand the collocation of requirements and architectural artifacts within an integrated development environment. Hybrid systems, having dependencies and extensive interactions between their control portion and their environment, further intensify this need.

AADL is a model-based engineering language for the architectural design and analysis of embedded control systems. Core AADL has been extended with a mechanism for discrete behavioral modeling and analysis of control systems, but not for the continuous behavior of the physical environment. In this paper, we introduce a lightweight language extension to AADL called the Hybrid Annex for continuous-time modeling, fulfilling the need for integrated modeling of the computing system along with its physical environment in their respective domains. The Isolette system described in the FAA Requirement Engineering Management Handbook is used to illustrate continuous behavior modeling with the proposed Hybrid Annex.

Categories and Subject Descriptors

D.2.2 [**Software Engineering**]: Design Tools and Techniques—*continuous behavioral modeling*

General Terms

Design, Languages, Reliability

Keywords

AADL annex; continuous behavior modeling; cyber-physical; hybrid annex; Hybrid CSP; hybrid systems

1. INTRODUCTION

Integrated dynamical systems, where computing units of discrete dynamics interact with a physical world possessing continuous dynamics are known as *hybrid systems*. Such systems interact with their external environment so as to monitor and control those physical quantities necessary for ensuring correct system functionality. These physical quantities are often termed *controlled variables* in the parlance of embedded-systems engineers.

The behavior of a computing unit is described by its responses to discrete events within a countable set of *states* $\{s_1, s_2, ...s_n\}$ where $n \in \mathbb{Z}$. Ordered events along with certain real-time properties are used to model the behavior of a hybrid system's computing units. Behavior of the physical portion, on the other hand, concerns a Euclidean space $\mathbb{R}^n$ where $n \geq 1$, and is specified using continuous domain differential equations. Obtaining these equations can make the definition of critical issues related to physical quantities a challenging task.

Hybrid systems complicate the matter further with external changes in the environment's continuous domain introducing behavior variation into the computing unit's discrete domain, and vise-versa: evolution of physical quantities on the continuous side of the system can trigger events on the discrete side, while events can, in turn, interrupt the evolution of continuous physical quantities by replacing one set of specifying differential equations with another. This circular dependency greatly increases the difficulty of correct hybrid system design and development, especially with regard to timing, safety, and reliability related properties.

Model-Based Engineering (MBE) is considered to be an effective way of developing correct, complex safety-critical systems, and has been successfully employed to that end in the embedded-systems industry [11, 20]. We contend that in order to formally specify, model, and take full advantage of advancements in MBE for dependability prediction and hybrid system certification, the requirements related to both discrete and continuous behaviors need to be collocated in a single, integrated development environment. The Architecture Analysis & Design Language (AADL)—a description language for embedded systems based on the MBE paradigm—is a strong candidate for the modeling of highly-integrated systems.

AADL provides abstractions for *components* and their *connections*. Additionally, it supports precise behavior modeling with extensive analysis at various architectural levels. Static architectures are specified as hierarchical compositions of interconnected components, the internal structures of which are themselves formed from interconnected (sub)components. A dynamic architecture, on the other hand, is modeled by presenting the *modal* behavior of the system. Modes contain the component and connection configurations for different operational and error states. Due to its extensive support for modeling (abstraction, reusability, composition, etc.) and its substantial analysis capabilities, AADL is being successfully used by embedded system designers in aircraft manufacturing.

Unfortunately, core AADL only provides mechanisms for modeling the discrete behavior of a computing unit (i.e., the control software and the platform on which it runs), and nothing at all related to the behavior of the physical process to be controlled. Hence, to equip AADL for hybrid system modeling and analysis, the core language needs to be extended. A predefined language extension mechanism makes the specification of such an *annex* possible.

In this paper, we propose a *Hybrid Annex* for AADL, a lightweight language extension for specifying the continuous behavior of model components. Based on the idea of Hybrid CSP (Communicating Sequential Processes) [9, 26, 24], the annex allows for the modeling of the continuous behavior of physical processes external to the system being designed with which the system's sensors and actuators interact.

The next section presents AADL and motivates the need for a dedicated continuous behavior modeling annex. Section 3 introduces the example system used to illustrate the Hybrid Annex specification for continuous time modeling. The proposed sublanguage and its grammar are discussed in Section 4, with the example system used to detail its constructs. Section 5 demonstrates behavior constraint specification using BLESS Assertions. Section 6 presents related work, while Section 7 concludes the study.

2. BACKGROUND AND MOTIVATION

Architecture describes how a system is decomposed into constituent parts and the ways in which those parts interact. It is a "prudent partitioning of a whole into parts, with specific relations among the parts" [5]. Traditionally, it has fallen to informal box-and-arrow drawings to communicate a system's decomposition. Despite their failings, such elementary notations served their purpose, but flourishing research in the area of software documentation has pointed to better ways. One promising line of inquiry has resulted in domain-specific architecture description languages, of which AADL is an exemplar.

2.1 Overview of AADL

AADL is an SAE International standard language for the architectural description of embedded systems [16]. It is an architecture-centric, model-based engineering approach that was introduced to cope with embedded system design challenges. AADL strives to minimize model inconsistency, decrease mismatched assumptions between stakeholders, and support dependability predictions through analyzable architecture development [7]. Several safety-critical industrial case studies in domains like medical and aerospace engineering have used AADL for system architecture design and analysis.

The important collaborative System Architecture Virtual Integration (SAVI) project for designing complex distributed aerospace systems has selected AADL as its lingua franca [8]. SAVI emphasizes an *"Integrate, Then Build"* approach—the key concept being to verify virtual integration of architectural components *before* implementing their internal designs. AADL supports virtual integration with an effective mechanism for component contract specification based on interfaces and interactions, and through well defined semantics for extensive formal analysis at different architecture levels.

2.1.1 System Architecture Modeling

Architectural modeling in AADL is realized through the component specification of both the *application software* and the *execution platform* it is to run on. Component *Type* and *Implementation* declarations, or classifiers, corresponding to system entities are instantiated and then connected together to form the system architecture model.

Component interface elements, called *ports*, are specified in the *features* section of a type classifier. AADL provides *data*, *event* and *event data* ports to transmit and receive data, control, and combined control and data signals, respectively. Port communication is typed and directional. The externally observable attributes of a component are specified in the *properties* section of its type.

An implementation classifier defines a particular internal structure of the component by specifying its subcomponents and the connections between them. Application software may contain *process*, *data*, *subprogram*, *thread*, and *thread group* components. The process component represents a protected memory space shared among thread subcomponents. A data component represents a type, local data subcomponent, or parameter of a subprogram, i.e., callable code. A thread abstracts sequential control flow.

The execution platform is made up of computation and communication resources, consisting of *processor*, *memory*, *bus*, and *device* components. The processor represents the hardware and software responsible for thread scheduling and execution. The memory abstraction is used for describing code and data storage entities. Devices can represent either physical entities in the external environment, or interactive system components like actuators and sensors. Physical connections between execution platform components are accomplished via a bus component.

2.1.2 System Behavior Modeling

AADL core language is extendable: additional sublanguages for modeling and analysis can be added through its *annex* mechanism. For example, standardized Data Modeling and Error Modeling annexes have been introduced to associate architectural components with data and error models, respectively, and an ARINC653 annex was added for defining ARINC653-compliant system architectures.

The component and connection constructs of AADL are sufficient for modeling the structure of a system architecture. However, the extensive formal analysis needed for dependability prediction requires detailed behavior modeling, which AADL lacks. The Behavior Annex (BA) and BLESS were introduced to address this shortcoming [13, 18]. They both use state transition mechanisms with guards and actions to model the discrete behavior of control systems. To prove correctness, BLESS adds a tool for the automatic generation of proof obligations and interactive theorem proving, based on temporal logic formulas specified with *Assertions*[1].

2.2 Motivation

Most systems exist to control *something*. Any system controller, whether human or automated, must know the current state of the process being controlled, and be able to judge the effect on that state of any control actions it might take. For this kind of awareness, a controller must either be, or contain, a model of the entirety under consideration: that is, the process being controlled and the controller's role in doing so.

This so-called *process model* is what supplies a snapshot of the system's condition. It can vary from having one or two variables, to defining control laws, to being a very complex model with a large number of state variables and transitions. A valid process model is essential to the proper and safe operation of a controller. According to Levenson, "...many accidents have been caused by the controller incorrectly assuming the controlled system was in a particular state and imposing a control action (or not providing one) that led to a loss" [22]. Causality and hazard analyses like STAMP and STPA also rely extensively on knowing about the process.

As most digital controllers interact with, or try to control some aspect of the physical world, they are, by definition, hybrid systems. Realizing the promise of MBE (system analysis, code generation, implementation transformation, etc.) necessitates an ability to describe the behavior of the process model. In a hybrid system, this entails enumeration of discrete events for the controlling part, and continual evaluation of differential equations for the real process.

So much for a system's realization, what about its design? According to Heimdhal et al. [10], approaching the "Twin Peaks" design activities of requirements and architecture through modeling can uncover, and help better understand the requirements (e.g., rate of change, settling time, cumulative error propagation) needed to adequately constrain desired system behavior. Again, we see the need for behavior modeling.

Additionally, in the case of a hybrid system, extensive interaction between the embedded computing unit and its environment, and their mutual dependence on each other intensifies the need for *integrated* requirements specification and design modeling. The contributions of such an integration at the requirements specification and early design (i.e., architecture) stages are twofold. Firstly, it supports requirement identification for both discrete and continuous variables. And secondly, correct operation of the physical portion of the system can be assessed through several dependability related analyses, allowing for the systems level correctness certification of a hybrid system.

Capturing system requirements and providing controller

process models establishes the need for being able to model the behavior of real world entities (i.e., continuous domain), while describing system architectures requires an ability for modeling computing unit behavior (i.e., discrete domain). To fully understand how the behaviors in one domain influence those in the other demands an integrated approach to the modeling of the computing units and the physical environment of the respective domains. It is for this purpose that we propose the Hybrid Annex to AADL.

3. EXAMPLE SYSTEM

In the Requirement Engineering Management Handbook (REMH) [21], its guide to managing requirements for embedded systems, the Federal Aviation Administration (FAA) describes an infant incubator known as an *isolette*. Because the specification is simple enough to grasp, yet rich enough to highlight the need for our proposed annex, we use it to demonstrate application of the Hybrid Annex notation to modeling the continuous dynamics of interactions between a control system and its environment.

The isolette example has previously been used to introduce important research efforts, and to advocate for AADL-based development and new annexes. It has been used by Blouin to illustrate the Requirements Annex [3], by Larson to explain detailed behavior modeling with the BLESS Annex [18], and to demonstrate hazard analysis techniques using the Error Model Annex(v.2) [19].

3.1 Isolette Operation

The context diagram of Figure 1 depicts a classical control loop with controller, actuator, controlled process, and sensor units. The system exists to maintain the temperature of the *Air* in the Isolette—a physical process—for the benefit of the infant, within a desired range as set by the Nurse through the *Operator Interface* and controlled by the *Thermostat*. We focus on modeling the continuous behavior of the Air, and its interactions with the *Heat Source* and *Temperature Sensor* units. The internals of the controller (i.e., the Thermostat and Operator Interface) are not considered.

The Thermostat monitors the Air temperature through the Temperature Sensor, and attempts to manipulate it with the Heat Source actuator. The *control strategy* followed by the Thermostat, is derived from a process model that is implicit in the interpretations it gives to the current Air information coming from the sensor, and the commands it has previously issued to the actuator. Making any part of this loop digital makes the overall system a hybrid.

The amount of heat required of the Isolette Heat Source depends on the rate at which the Air component cools. Observations about the environment in which the system is to operate, and upon which its correct operation depends are termed *environmental assumptions*. Other relevant properties about the environment for this relationship might include construction material and dimensions of the incubator, and body size and skin temperature of the infant.

The continuous behavior of the Air's changing temperature, which the Heat Source must work to balance can most easily be assumed to follow the differential equation known as Newton's law of cooling (or heating).[2]

$$\dot{T}_o = -k \cdot (T_o - T_e)$$

---

[1]The capital 'A' proper noun signifies temporal logic formulas used by BLESS

[2]The effect of heat transfer between the Isolette and the

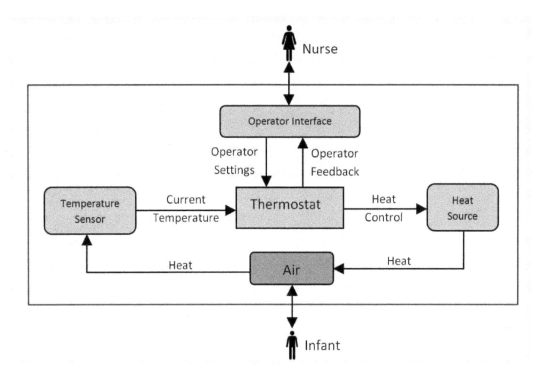

Figure 1: Isolette Context Diagram with Controller (Thermostat) and Physical Environment (Air)

The law states that the rate of change in temperature of an object $\dot{T}_o$ at time t is directly proportional to the difference in temperature between the object T_o and its environment T_e. Proportionality constant k is the thermal conductivity of the object, which depends on the physical properties of the object i.e., more environmental assumptions. The sign of the constant indicates whether the object is cooling down (-), or warming up (+).

The specification in Section A.5.1.3 of the REMH [21] provides us with two environmental assumptions concerning the continuous behavior of Air temperature change in the Isolette:

EA-IS1: *When the Heat Source is turned on and the Isolette is properly shut, the Current Temperature will increase at a rate of no more than 1°F per minute.*

EA-IS2: *When the Heat Source is turned off and the Isolette is properly shut, the Current Temperature will decrease at a rate of no more than 1°F per minute.*

The continuous change in current Air temperature $\dot{c}$ (i.e., heating or cooling of the Isolette) depends on the current status of the Heat Source, and, if **on**, the heat q being produced by it. Assumptions **EA-IS1** and **EA-IS2** lead us to set the change in q equal to a rate of 1°F per unit time, as summarized here:

$$\begin{cases} \dot{c} & = & -0.026 \cdot (c - q) \\ \dot{q} & = & 1 \quad \text{if heater is on} \\ \dot{q} & = & -1 \quad \text{if heater is off} \end{cases}$$

infant's body can be modeled by using Fourier's law of conduction: $\dot{Q} = -kA\frac{dT}{dx}$.

where c is the current temperature of the Air, 0.026 its thermal conductivity k, and q the temperature of the heater.

An initial plot of Air temperature behavior can be seen in the graph of Figure 2(a) with the vertical axis denoting the temperature of the Air (c), and the horizontal axis the temperature being output by the Heat Source (q). With the system quiescent, both c and q are equal to the room temperature, assumed to be a constant 73°F. However, when the system controller turns on the Heat Source, the resulting rise in q forces a consummate rise in c.

The observed effects of the Isolette operating as intended are given by Figure 2(b). Starting from the extreme *Upper Desired Temperature* of 100°F as mentioned in Section A.3.4 of the REMH, curve 'm' exhibits first the cooling of the Air, since the Heat Source is **off**, and then, once the heat goes **on**, the subsequent rise in its temperature. Conversely, curve 'n' tracks the heating of the Air from the minimum *Lower Desired Temperature* of 97°F, only to cool when the initially **on** Heat Source is turned **off**.

The control strategy of the Thermostat is to turn the Heat Source **on** or **off**, depending on the desired direction of temperature change, at the points where the 'm' and 'n' curves intersect. This gives the system the time needed to overcome the Heat Source *latency* (Section A.5.1.3 of the REMH) and thereby keep the current temperature c within the desired temperature range (in this case [97°..100°F]) as set by the clinician through the Operator Interface.

Modeling the just described physical behavior of the Isolette example with the proposed Hybrid Annex is detailed in Section 4 along with an AADL *implementation*. As an introduction, the Air AADL *type* is first presented here.

The type classifier of Listing 1 declares the interface of the Air component as an AADL *abstract* component. The **hss** *in data port* is used to get the current status of the Heat Source

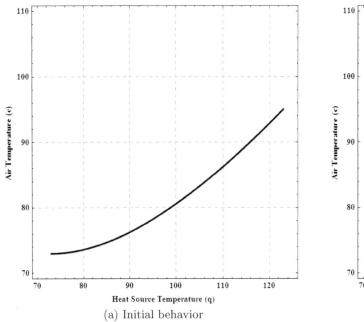

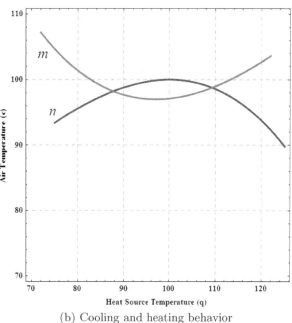

(a) Initial behavior   (b) Cooling and heating behavior

Figure 2: Physical Behavior of the Air Component

while the `hin` port is used to get a measure of the amount of heat being produced. The Heat Source is linked to `hss` and `hin` through appropriate port connections. The `tout` *out data port* communicates the heat energy in the Air to the Temperature Sensor for measurement. Type `Heat` references an AADL Data Model Annex component defined in package `Iso_Variables` that specifies the range of possible values a variable of this type can take on, and its unit of measure. The corresponding implementation classifier for the Air type is given in Listing 2 and will be considered in the next section in the context of the Hybrid Annex.

Listing 1: AADL Air Component Type

```
abstract Air
  features
  hss: in data port Iso_Variables::on_off;
  hin: in data port Iso_Variables::Heat;
  tout: out data port Iso_Variables::Heat;
end Air;
```

4. HYBRID ANNEX

In order to equip AADL for hybrid system modeling and analysis, we propose a lightweight extension to the language named the Hybrid Annex (HA). The annex brings with it the ability to model those physical, real-world elements, or processes, that the system must interact with to achieve its goals of monitoring and controlling one or more of those processes. The annex subclause grammar and semantics are inspired by an extension of CSP known as Hybrid Communicating Sequential Processes (HCSP) [9, 26] with the added intention of impartially supporting other continuous behavior modeling tools and methodologies. Formal syntax and operational semantics of HCSP are detailed in [24].

In use, HA subclauses annotate either AADL *device* component implementations in order to model the continuous behavior of sensors and actuators, or *abstract* component

implementations so as to model the continuous behavior of physical processes.

An HA specification may consist of up to six sections: `assert`, `invariant`, `variables`, `constants`, `channels`, and `behavior` to specify: assertions, or predicates; a single assertion that must hold throughout operation of the continuous behavior model; local variables; constants; communication channels; and continuous behavior, respectively.

HA was first presented to the SAE International AADL Standards Committee AS-2C at Santa Barbara, on April 14-17, 2014 [6]. The first draft of the proposed HA annex standard document was considered, line-by-line, in committee at Orlando on July 7-10, 2014.

4.1 Continuous Behavior Modeling

What follows are details for completing the various sections of an HA behavior specification, examples of which appear in Listing 2 where they are expressed in standard AADL notation [16]. For each section, the Extended Backus-Naur Form (EBNF) of the HA grammar is also given, in which: literals are printed in **bold**; alternatives are separated by a pipe |; groupings are enclosed with parentheses ( ); square braces [ ] delimit optional elements; and the closures { }+ and { }* are used to signify one-or-more, and zero-or-more of the enclosed element, respectively.

4.1.1 Assert Section

HA provides an `assert` section for declaring predicates applicable to the intended continuous behavior of the annotated AADL component. These predicates take the form of BLESS Assertions, and may be used later in defining the invariant (see the next subsection). The grammar and semantics for BLESS Assertions may be found in [17].

4.1.2 Invariant Section

The `invariant` section is used in conjunction with the declarations made in the assert section to define a condition of operation that must hold true throughout the model's execution lifetime. Note that there is only *one* invariant, but it can be logically complex, having as many terms as needed.

The HA assert and invariant sections are touched upon again in Section 5.

4.1.3 Variables Section

Local variables in the scope of an Hybrid Annex subclause are declared in the `variables` section along with their data types. Depending on which AADL component the HA subclause has been applied to, a variable will hold either a discrete or continuous value. Following is the grammar for the HA `variables` section:

```
variable_declaration ::=
variable_identifier
{ , variable_identifier }* :
data_component_classifier_reference
```

A data type is assigned by a classifier reference to the appropriate AADL data component. The referenced external data component must either be part of the package containing the component being annotated, or must be declared within the scope of another package that has been imported using the AADL keyword, `with`.

The `variables` section of the HA specification for the example Isolette system appears in Listing 2. The variables were identified through consideration of environmental assumptions drawn from those system requirements that relate to the continuous behavior of the physical processes the Isolette is meant to interact with, namely, the Air. Variable `c` represents the monitored variable *Current Temperature*, variable `h` is either `0` or `1` to represent the **off** or **on** state of the *Heat Control* controlled variable, and `l` and `u` represent the *Lower Desired Temperature* and *Upper Desired Temperature* controlled variables, respectively, as defined in the REMH [21]. Variable `q` holds the value of the heat, if any, being generated by the Heat Source.

4.1.4 Constants Section

Similar to local variables, constants in the scope of an HA subclause are declared in the `constants` section. Adhering to standard convention: constants can only be initialized at declaration, and cannot be assigned another value afterwards. The grammar for the `constants` section is as follows:

```
constant_declarations ::=
behavior_constant
{ , behavior_constant }*

behavior_constant ::=
behavior_constant_identifier =
( integer_literal | real_literal )
[ unit_identifier ]
```

A constant must be initialized with either an integer, or a real value, and may include a description of its unit of measure.

The `constants` section of Listing 2 contains declarations for the constants `r` and `k` that represent the room temperature and the thermal conductivity of the substance being modeled, which of course is the air in the room. The room

is assumed to be held at a constant temperature of $73°F$. Keeping in mind that the value of the monitored *Current Temperature* variable can vary from $68°F$ to $105°F$ lets us assign a value of 0.026 as the average air thermal conductivity to constant `k` of the Air implementation.

HA also supports the specification of measuring units that have been defined using the AADL Unit Relation Annex [4]. As a result, common constants like the mathematical ratio π and the physical gravitational attractive force g can be easily declared in HA with `pi = 3.14159` (no units) and `g = 9.81` `mpss` (*meters per second*^{2}), respectively. In our model, the measuring unit for temperature is $°F$, indicated in the model with an `f`, and the measuring unit of thermal conductivity is *watts per meter kelvin* ($W/(mK)$), denoted for the constant `k` as `wpmk`.

4.1.5 Behavior Section

The `behavior` section of the HA subclause is used to specify the continuous behavior of the annotated AADL component in terms of concurrently-executing processes. Thus, a behavior declaration has process declarations, which in turn, may contain several predefined executing processes of various topologies (sequential, concurrent, repetitive, etc.). The process algebra notation that models reactive system behavior as communication flows is documented below.

```
behavior_declaration ::=
behavior_identifier ::=
process_declaration
{ & process_declaration }*

process_declaration ::=
skip | wait time_value | assignment
| communication | sequential_composition
| concurrent_composition | choice
| continuous_evolution | repetition
```

Behavior of a physical controlled variable of a hybrid system is specified by continuous evolution—a differential expression controlled optionally by a Boolean expression. Differential expressions consist of several derivative expressions combined with standard multiplication ($*$), addition ($+$) and subtraction operators ($-$). A derivative expression is indicated using the keyword DE followed by the order of the differential equation, then the dependent variable, and finally the independent variable. For example, the rate of change of variable y with respect to x, denoted $\frac{dy}{dx}$, a first order equation, is specified as `DE 1 y x`, while the second order equation $\frac{d^2y}{dx^2}$ is specified with `DE 2 y x`. A similar notation is defined for time derivation, a frequently encountered concept in real-time systems. Here the keyword is DT, and the independent variable, always being time, is not needed. Thus, the rate of change of y with respect to time t, $\frac{dy}{dt}$, is stated `DT 1 y`. The grammar for the continuous evolution process is defined as follows.

```
continuous_evolution ::=
'differential_expression =
differential_expression'
[ < boolean_expression > ] [ interrupt ]
```

Listing 2: AADL Air Component Implementation with Hybrid Annex Specifications

```
abstract implementation Air.impl
annex hybrid {**
  assert
    <<NORMAL: : (c@now < (u+Iso_Properties::Tolerance)) and    --air temp normal range
      (c@now > (l-Iso_Properties::Tolerance))>>
    <<EA_IS_1: : forall x:BLESS_Types::Time in 0.0 ,, now are   --limit rate of heating
      (c@now - c@x) <= Iso_Properties::Heat_Rate*(now-x)>>
    <<EA_IS_2: : forall x:BLESS_Types::Time in 0.0 ,, now are   --limit rate of cooling
      (c@now - c@x) >= Iso_Properties::Cool_Rate*(now-x)>>
  invariant
    <<NORMAL() and EA_IS_1() and EA_IS_2()>>
  variables
    h :  Iso_Variables::on_off   -- heat control command value
    q :  Iso_Variables::Heat     -- heat source energy value
    c :  Iso_Variables::Heat     -- current Air heat energy value
    l :  Iso_Variables::LdtTemp  -- lower desired temperature value
    u :  Iso_Variables::UdtTemp  -- upper desired temperature value
  constants
    r = 73.0 f   -- constant room temperature
    k = 0.026 wpmk  -- average thermal conductivity of air
  behavior
    Heating ::= 'DT 1 c = -k*(c - q)' & 'DT 1 q = 1' [[> tout!(c) ]]> Continue
    Cooling ::= 'DT 1 c = -k*(c - q)' & 'DT 1 q = -1' [[> tout!(c) ]]> Continue
    AirTemp ::= hss?(h) & (h=on) -> Heating [] (h=off) -> Cooling
    Continue ::= skip
    WorkingIsolette ::= repeat(AirTemp)
**};
end Air.impl;
```

```
differential_expression ::=
differential
| differential { * differential }+
| differential { + differential }+
| differential - differential

differential ::=
numeric_literal
| variable_identifier [^ numeric_literal ]
| derivative_expression
| derivative_time
| ( differential_expression )

derivative_expression ::=
DE order_integer_literal
dependent_variable_identifier
independent_variable_identifier

derivative_time ::=
DT order_integer_literal variable_identifier
```

Boolean expressions are composed of Boolean terms combined with the binary **and**, **or**, and **xor** operators, and may be negated with the unary **not** operator. A term must either be a Boolean value, **true** or **false**, or an expression or relation that evaluates to a Boolean value. A relation is defined using numeric expressions combined with the standard relational operators $=, <>, >, <=, >=$, and $>$. The complete grammar for Boolean expressions is given below.

```
boolean_expression ::=
boolean_term
| boolean_term { and boolean_term }+
| boolean_term { or boolean_term }+
| boolean_term { xor boolean_term }+

boolean_term ::=
[ not ] ( true | false |
( boolean_expression ) | relation )

relation ::=
[ numeric_expression relation_symbol
numeric_expression ]

numeric_expression ::=
numeric_term | numeric_term - numeric_term
| numeric_term / numeric_term
| numeric_term mod numeric_term
| numeric_term { + numeric_term }+
| numeric_term { * numeric_term }+

numeric_term::=
[-] ( numeric_literal | variable_identifier
| numeric_expression )

numeric_literal ::=
integer_literal | real_literal

relation_symbol ::= = | <> | > | <= | >= | >
```

In our running example, the continuous behavior of the Air component has been captured as a repeating **AirTemp** process in the **WorkingIsolette** process of the behavior section in Listing 2. On each iteration, process **AirTemp** obtains the status of the Heat Source through its **hss?(h)** communication event, and chooses between **Heating** or **Cooling** processes based on the communicated value of variable **h**. If the Boolean expression (**h=on**) is true then the behavior is as specified by process **Heating**, otherwise as specified by process **Cooling**.

Continuous evolution of current temperature c, when the Heat Source is **on**, is specified by 'DT 1 c = -k*(c - q)' & 'DT 1 q = 1' with the ampersand acting as a separator having no semantics. As explained in Section 3, changes in current temperature c depend on the amount of heat being generated by the Heat Source. This physical behavior is modeled by the 'DT 1 q = 1' term, where q is the rate of change in Heat Source output. When the Heat Source is switched **off** by the Thermostat the rate of change in q becomes negative and the Air behavior is then governed by the **Cooling** process, 'DT 1 c = -k*(c - q)' & 'DT 1 q = -1'. The **Heating** and **Cooling** processes define the continuous evolution of c under different conditions. Either can be preempted by a communication interrupt delivered along the Air *out data* port, **tout**.

In addition to modeling the constructs described above, HA supports both sequential and concurrent composition. Sequential composition defines consecutively-executing behaviors. For example, a sequentially composed process P;Q behaves as P first and after its successful termination, behaves as Q. A parallel compose S1||S2 behaves as if S1 and S2 were running independently, except that all interactions occur through communication events. The grammar for sequential and concurrent compositions, and choice and repetition constructs is as follows.

```
SequentialComposition ::=
{ behavior_identifier
{ ; behavior_identifier }+ }

ConcurrentComposition ::=
{ behavior_identifier
{ || behavior_identifier }+ }

choice ::=
alternative { [] alternative }*

alternative ::=
( boolean_expression ) -> process_identifier

repetition ::=
repeat [ [ ( integer_literal
| integer_variable_identifier ) ] ]
( process_identifier )
```

Several primitive processes like skip to model successful execution termination; x:=e to model variable assignment; and wait to model time delay, can also be specified using HA. The grammar for these primitive processes is quite simple and is not specified here.

4.2 Cyber-Physical Interaction Modeling

A computing unit's extensive interactions with, and strong dependence on its physical environment makes precise specification of the system's cyber-physical interaction (communication between computing units and the physical environment) an essential part of hybrid system modeling.

Extensive support for interaction and continuous evolution preemption due to timed and communication interrupts is a major innovation of our proposed HA. Communication between physical processes uses the channels declared in the channels section of the respective behavior specifications, while communication with an AADL component relies on the ports that are declared in the component's type. Communication channels must be paired in complementary directions, e.g., an *out* channel with an *in* channel. The grammar for the channels section and communication events is defined below.

```
channel ::=
channel_identifier {, channel_identifier }*
: data_component_classifier_reference

communication ::=
port_communication | channel_communication

port_communication ::=
port_identifier (?|!)
( [variable_identifier] )

channel_communication ::=
channel_identifier (?|!)
[ variable_identifier ]
```

Communication events hss?(h) and tout!(c) of Listing 2 enable cyber-physical interactions involving data ports of AADL components and variables of the physical process. An event can result from either a port input (?) or a port output (!) action. In this case, the Air component (Listing 1) declares input port **hss** and output port **tout**, while quantities h and c are declared in the variables section of the component's HA specification (Listing 2).

Continuous process evolution may be terminated after a specific time or on a communication event. These are invoked through timed and communication interrupts, respectively. A timed interrupt preempts continuous evolution after a given amount of time whereupon the process then assumes the behavior specified by the interrupt. A communication interrupt preempts continuous evolution whenever communication takes places along any one of the named ports or channels. The grammar for interrupts follows.

```
interrupt ::=
timed_interrupt | communication_interrupt

timed_interrupt ::=
[> time_value ]> { behavior_identifier }+

time_value ::=
time_variable_identifier |
real_literal time_unit

communication_interrupt ::=
[[> port_or_channel_identifier
{ , port_or_channel_identifier }*
]]> { process_identifier }+
```

Listing 2 defines a communication interrupt that preempts the continuous evolution of the current temperature process quantity, c with [[> tout!(c)]]> Continue. The only port named is **tout**, and no channels named. Thus, whenever a value is sent out of the Air's **tout** port, the evolution of c will cease, and the **Continue** process will be adopted as the subsequent behavior for the process.

5. BEHAVIOR CONSTRAINTS

In addition to continuous-time differential equations, HA accommodates the use of BLESS as a behavior interface specification language (BISL). Then, BLESS Assertions may be used to express constraints on any HA defined behavior. Assertion are more fully explained in [17].

Two sections of an HA subclause permit the application of BLESS Assertion constraints to a component's continuous-time behavior: the `invariant` section may contain a single Assertion that always hold true for aspects of the component's behavior; and the `assert` section may declare Assertions either for later inclusion as terms in the `invariant` section, thereby making it more concise, or for expressing exceptional conditions.

The HA specification in Listing 2 uses Assertions in both the `assert` and `invariant` sections to constrain the continuous behavior of the Air in the Isolette. The intent is to keep the Air temperature within a normal range, `NORMAL`, and to limit the rates of heating, `EA_IS_1`, and cooling, `EA_IS_2`. Statements within an AADL property set, `Iso_Properties` (not shown), puts the tolerance for the temperature range at 0.5°F, and sets the Air heating and cooling rates to be 1°F per minute.

6. RELATED WORK

In order to enhance its extensive capabilities for system modeling and analysis, AADL supports extensions to its core language by way of properties and annexes. The Hybrid Annex presented in this paper, takes advantage of the latter to extend AADL with capabilities suitable for modeling the continuous behavior of physical environments. Major existing work related to the language extension (i.e., annex definition) of AADL consists of numerous dedicated annexes defined to fulfill specific modeling and analysis needs. Some of these annexes have already been standardized while others are currently undergoing the standardization process.

Standardized annexes include the Error Model Annex [12] for conducting safety and reliability analyses that specify the fault behavior of components and connections on identified paths, or *flows*, along with their propensity for error propagation; the Data Modeling Annex [14] to enable the creation of complicated data types in an architectural model; and the ARINC653 Annex [15] used to enforce standard ARINC653 compliant modeling and analysis. One of the important annexes presently undergoing standardization is the Requirements Definition and Analysis Annex [3] for the association of system requirements with elements of an AADL model.

The works most closely related to ours, in terms of providing AADL with behavior modeling support, are the Behavior Annex (BA) and BLESS [13, 18]. Both BA and BLESS use state transition systems with guards and actions to model the discrete behavior of control systems. To prove correct behavior, BLESS includes a means for the automatic generation of proof obligations, as well as an interactive theorem proving tool based on temporal logic formulas, specified with BLESS Assertions.

The modeling of cyber-physical systems with AADL presented in [25] is based on networks of timed automata with use of the UPPAAL model checker for property analysis. Another approach to modeling hybrid systems with AADL has been proposed by Qian [23], but it is not expressive enough to model constants with measuring units, and has difficulty modeling complex continuous behavior expressed with differential equations. In [2], Banerjee, et al. discuss the modeling of Body Area Networks (BAN) with AADL based on intentional and un-intentional interactions between human body and the BAN devices. These interactions are modeled using the concepts of the region of impact and the region of interest, with identified parameters.

Compared to the above mentioned related works, our proposed Hybrid Annex is more expressive in specifying the primitives of hybrid system models, e.g., variables with data types, constants with measuring units, and behavior with complex Boolean expressions. It also provides extensive support for cyber-physical interaction modeling through use of timed and communication interrupts—an essential element of hybrid system modeling not provided for to such an extent by related efforts. Exclusive support for behavior constraints and the definition of component invariants with BLESS Assertions is a novel feature of our Hybrid Annex.

7. CONCLUSION AND FUTURE WORK

To facilitate the continuous behavior modeling of the physical portion of a hybrid system, and to integrate this with discrete behavior modeling activities, we have proposed a Hybrid Annex for AADL. We have demonstrated its use by modeling the physical environment of the FAA's well-known isolette example, and illustrated how this continuous model interacts with a more conventional AADL model of the system's discrete components, thus opening the door to truly integrated modeling of cross-domain interactions within cyber-physical systems. The EBNF grammar of the proposed sublanguage was also provided.

The Hybrid Annex language extension provides a means for the AADL community to engage in the full modeling of hybrid systems: One which includes the behavior of critical environmental and continuous-time elements, like, for example, the process model required for proper functioning of a control system. And furthermore, to do so in an integrated manner where the artificial separation between discrete and continuous domains has been erased. Finally, we showed how the modeled behavior can be constrained through the use of BLESS Assertions and invariants in two sections of a Hybrid Annex subclause.

Being a first step towards continuous behavior and cyber-physical interaction modeling with AADL, this study has opened up new opportunities for research and development. An important future contribution will be the implementation of a Hybrid Annex plug-in for the Open-Source AADL Tool Environment (OSATE) modeler. A plug-in planned to verify the correctness of Hybrid Annex specifications will leverage ongoing work with an in-house Hybrid Hoare Logic (HHL) theorem prover [27]. Formalizing the semantics of AADL models augmented with Hybrid Annex specifications is another topic for immediate research [1].

Acknowledgements

The first and fourth authors are supported by the National Basic Research Program of China under Grant No. 2014CB340700, by Natural Science Foundation of China under Grant No. NSFC-91118007 and NSFC-6110006, and by the CAS/SAFEA International Partnership Program for Creative Research Teams, and the last author is supported by the National Infrastructure Software Plan under Grant

No.2012ZX01041-002-003. The second and third authors are supported in part by the US National Science Foundation (NSF) (#0932289, #1239543), and the NSF US Food and Drug Administration Scholar-in-Residence Program (#1065887, #1238431).

8. REFERENCES

[1] Ehsan Ahmad, Yunwei Dong, Shuling Wang, Naijun Zhan, and Liang Zou, *Adding formal meanings to aadl with hybrid annex*, accepted for publication, The 11th International Symposium on Formal Aspects of Component Software, FACS'14, 2014.

[2] Ayan Banerjee, Sailesh Kandula, Tridib Mukherjee, and Sandeep K. S. Gupta, *Band-aide: A tool for cyber-physical oriented analysis and design of body area networks and devices*, ACM Transactions on Embedded Computing Systems vol:11, no. S2, pp. 49:1–49:29, ACM, 2012.

[3] Dominique Blouin, Eric Senn, and Skander Turki, *Defining an annex language to the architecture analysis and design language for requirements engineering activities support*, Model-Driven Requirements Engineering Workshop (MoDRE), pp. 11–20, 2011.

[4] Denis Buzdalov, Alexey Khoroshilov, and Eugene Kornykhin, *Unit relations annex*, (draft, progress update) https://wiki.sei.cmu.edu/aadl/images/c/c5/201309-ispras-unit-relations-annex.pdf, 2013.

[5] Paul Clements, Felix Bachmann, Len Bass, David Garlan, James Ives, Reed Little, Robert Nord, and Judith Stafford, *Documenting software architecture: Views and beyond*, SEI Series in Software Engineering, Pearson Education, Inc., Boston, MA, 2003.

[6] AADL Standard Committee, *Aadl user days website*, https://wiki.sei.cmu.edu/aadl/index.php/AADL_User_Days, 2014.

[7] Peter Feiler and David Gluch, *Model-based engineering with AADL: An introduction to the SAE architecture analysis & design language*, Addison-Wesley, 2012.

[8] Peter Feiler, Jörgen Hansson, Dionisio de Niz, and Lutz Wrage, *System architecture virtual integration: An industrial case study*, Tech. Report CMU/SEI-2009-TR-017, SEI, CMU, 2009.

[9] Jifeng He, *From CSP to hybrid systems*, A Classical Mind, Essays in Honour of C.A.R. Hoare, Prentice Hall International (UK) Ltd., pp. 171–189, 1994.

[10] Mats Heimdahl, Lian Duan, Anitha Murugesan, and Sanjai Rayadurgam, *Modeling and requirements on the physical side of cyber-physical systems*, Second International Wokshop on the Twin Peaks of Requirements and Architecture, ICSE'13, IEEE, 2013.

[11] Thomas A. Henzinger and Joseph Sifakis, *The embedded systems design challenge*, FM'06, LNCS, pp. 1–15, 2006.

[12] SAE International, *Architecture analysis & design language (AADL) annex volume 1: Annex e: Error model annex*, 2006.

[13] SAE International, *Architecture analysis & design language (AADL) annex volume 2: Annex d:behavior model annex*, 2011.

[14] SAE International, *Architecture analysis & design language (AADL) annex volume 2: Annex b:data modeling annex*, 2011.

[15] SAE International, *Architecture analysis & design language (AADL) annex volume 2: Annex f:arinc653 annex*, 2011.

[16] SAE International, *SAE as5506b, architecture analysis & design language (AADL)*, 2012.

[17] Brian R. Larson, *Behavior Language for Embedded Systems with Software: Language Reference Manual*, info.santoslab.org/research/aadl/bless, 2014.

[18] Brian R. Larson, Patrice Chalin, and John Hatcliff, *BLESS: Formal specification and verification of behaviors for embedded systems with software*, NASA Formal Methods, LNCS, vol. 7871, Springer Berlin Heidelberg, pp. 276–290, 2013.

[19] Brian R. Larson, John Hatcliff, Kim Fowler, and Julian Delange, *Illustrating the AADL error modeling annex (v.2) using a simple safety-critical medical device*, Proceedings of the 2013 ACM SIGAda Annual Conference on High Integrity Language Technology, HILT '13, ACM, pp. 65–84, 2013.

[20] Edward A. Lee, *What's ahead for embedded software?*, IEEE Computer, pp. 18–26, 2000.

[21] David L. Lempia and Steven P. Miller, *Requirement engineering management handbook*, Tech. Report DOT/FAA/AR-08/32, Federal Aviation Administration, 2009.

[22] Nancy Levenson, *Engineering a safer world*, MIT Press, Cambridge, MA, 2011.

[23] Qian Yuqing, Liu Jing, and Chen Xiaohong, *Hybrid aadl: A sublanguage extension to aadl*, Proceedings of the 5th Asia-Pacific Symposium on Internetware, Internetware '13, ACM, pp. 27:1–27:4, 2013.

[24] Naijun Zhan, Shuling Wang, and Hengjun Zhao, *Formal modelling, analysis and verification of hybrid systems*, Unifying Theories of Programming and Formal Engineering Methods, LNCS, pp. 207–281, 2013.

[25] Yu Zhang, Yunwei Dong, Fan Zhang, and Yunfeng Zhang, *Research on modeling and analysis of cps*, Proceedings of the 8th International Conference on Autonomic and Trusted Computing (Berlin, Heidelberg), ATC'11, Springer-Verlag, pp. 92–105, 2011.

[26] Chaochen Zhou, Ji Wang, and Anders P. Ravn, *A formal description of hybrid systems*, Hybrid systems, LNCS, vol. 1066, pp. 511–530, 1996.

[27] Liang Zou, Jidong Lv, Shuling Wang, Naijun Zhan, Tao Tang, Lei Yuan, and Yu Liu, *Verifying chinese train control system under a combined scenario by theorem proving*, VSTTE, LNCS, vol. 8164, pp. 262–280, 2013.

Leveraging Ada 2012 and SPARK 2014 For Assessing Generated Code From AADL Models

Jérôme Hugues
Université de Toulouse, ISAE
10 avenue E. Belin
31055 Toulouse, France
jerome.hugues@isae.fr

Christophe Garion
Université de Toulouse, ISAE
10 avenue E. Belin
31055 Toulouse, France
christophe.garion@isae.fr

ABSTRACT

Modeling of Distributed Real-time Embedded systems using Architecture Description Language provides the foundations for various levels of analysis: scheduling, reliability, consistency, etc.; but also allows for automatic code generation. A challenge is to demonstrate that generated code matches quality required for safety-critical systems. In the scope of the AADL, the Ocarina toolchain proposes code generation towards the Ada Ravenscar profile with restrictions for High-Integrity. It has been extensively used in the space domain as part of the TASTE project within the European Space Agency.

In this paper, we illustrate how the combined use of Ada 2012 and SPARK 2014 significantly increases code quality and exhibits absence of run-time errors at both run-time and generated code levels.

Categories and Subject Descriptors

D.2.4 [**Software/Program Verification**]: Correctness proofs, Formal methods, Programming by contract; I.6.5 [**Model Development**]: Modeling methodologies

General Terms

Design, Languages, Verification

Keywords

AADL; Ada 2012; SPARK 2014; Ocarina

1. INTRODUCTION

The Model-Based System Engineering (MBSE) paradigm allows for a high-level description of a system, its analysis and eventually its automatic generation. Significant efforts have been undertaken to design modeling frameworks that support this view with a sufficient level of expression and fidelity towards the system being built. Besides, MBSE already demonstrated capability for scheduling and reliability

assessment in combination with analysis tools . This provides foundations for a wide support for the engineering of safety-critical systems.

The Architecture Analysis and Design Language, standardized by SAE International [10], provides such an integrated framework for the modeling of safety-critical systems. Combined with the Ocarina code generation toolchain, it allows for the automatic code generation towards Ada runtimes using a restricted middleware: PolyORB-HI/Ada. Both generated code and runtime were initially written in Ada95, with significant effort done to ensure compatibility with both the Ravenscar profile and High-Integrity restrictions such as absence of dynamic features (object-orientation, memory allocation, streams, etc.). This greatly reduces the benefit of code generation compared to traditional hand coding strategies in the context of safety-critical systems: the only strategy to ensure absence of run-time errors was through careful code review and testing of the generated code on the target.

The advent of Ada 2012 programming-by-contract approach, and the availability of SPARK 2014 language and toolset to assess a) that contracts are true, and b) the absence of runtime errors promise to increase confidence in source code, and stronger link with formalized specifications of programs. In the following, we illustrate how the use of these two technologies allows us to streamline code generation and analysis effort by providing easier access to code quality assessment.

In section 2 we present the AADL and some existing tools to support the model-based engineering of embedded systems. In section 3, we outline the basic principles of the PolyORB-HI/Ada runtime, inherited from the schizophrenic middleware architecture deployed in the PolyORB middleware, and the code generation strategies used in the Ocarina toolchain. In section 4, we discuss modernization of the initial code base to take advantage of Ada 2012's new constructs, and how we had to overcome some existing limitations in the current SPARK2014. In section 5 we show how SPARK 2014 allows us to demonstrate absence of run-time errors of the middleware components. Finally, we provide some elements for future works.

2. A BRIEF OVERVIEW OF AADLV2

The "Architecture Analysis and Design Language" (AADL) [10] is a textual and graphical language for model-based engineering of embedded real-time systems. AADL is used to design and analyze software and hardware architectures of embedded real-time systems.

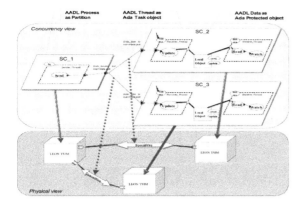

Figure 1: IST-ASSERT demonstrator

The AADL allows for the description of both software and hardware parts of a system. It focuses on the definition of clear block interfaces, and separates the implementations from these interfaces. From the separate description of these blocks, one can build an assembly of blocks that represents the full system. To take into account the multiple ways to connect components, the AADL defines different connection patterns: subcomponent, connection, binding. For example, figure 1 provides the graphical description of a case study used in the scope of the ASSERT project.

An AADL model can incorporate non-architectural elements: non-functional properties (execution time, priority, scheduler, ...) and behavioral or fault descriptions. It is hence possible to use AADL as a backbone to describe all the aspects of a system. Let us review these elements in the following.

An AADL description is made of *components*. Each component category describes well-identified elements of the actual architecture, using the same vocabulary of system or software engineering. The AADL standard defines software components (`data`, `thread`, `thread group`, `subprogram`, `process`) and execution platform components (`memory`, `bus`, `processor`, `device`, `virtual processor`, `virtual bus`) and hybrid components (`system`) or imprecise (`abstract`).

Component declarations have to be instantiated into subcomponents of other components in order to model an architecture. At the top-level, a system contains all the component instances. Most components can have subcomponents, so that an AADL description is hierarchical. A complete AADL description must provide a top-most level system that will contain certain kind of components (*processor*, *process*, *bus*, *device*, *abstract* and *memory*), thus providing the root of the architecture tree. The architecture in itself is the instantiation of this system: the *root system*.

The interface of a component is called *component type*. It provides *features* (e.g. communication ports). Components communicate one with another by *connecting* their *features*. A given component type correspond zero or several implementations. Each of them describes the internal structure of the components: subcomponents, connections between those subcomponents, and refine non-functional properties.

The AADL defines the notion of *properties*. They model non-functional properties that can be attached to model elements (components, connections, features, instances, etc.). Properties are typed attributes that specify constraints or characteristics that apply to the elements of the architecture such as clock frequency of a processor, execution time of a thread, bandwidth of a bus. Some standard properties are defined, e.g. for timing aspects; but it is possible to define new properties for different analysis (e.g. to define particular security policies). Besides, the language is defined by a companion standard document that defines legality rules for component assemblies, its static and execution semantics.

AADL's initial requirement document mentions analysis as the key objective. AADL is backed with a large set of analysis tools[1], covering many different domains: scheduling analysis like Cheddar [11] and MAST [5]; dependability assessment: AADL provides an annex for modeling propagation of error, like COMPASS project [3], or ADAPT [6]; behavioral analysis: mapping to formal methods and associated model checkers have been defined for Petri Nets [9], RT-Maude [8] and many others code generation: Ocarina implements Ada and C code generators for distributed real-time embedded systems [7].

3. CODE GENERATION FROM AADL

Automatic code generation from AADL models require first a comprehensive definition of a versatile middleware. Versatility is required so as to ensure a consistent mapping from AADL concerns (multiplicity of schedulers, transport protocols) to well-defined implementable services. Such versatility has been captured in the schizophrenic middleware architecture and later used in the Ocarina code generation toolset.

3.1 Schizophrenic middleware architecture

In previous projects, we defined the "schizophrenic middleware architecture" [13]. It separates concerns between distribution model, API, communication protocols, and their implementation by refining the definition and role of personalities.

The schizophrenic architecture consists of 3 layers: *application-level* and *protocol-level* personalities built around a *neutral core*. The user's application interacts with application personalities; protocol personalities operate with the network.

Application personalities constitute the adaptation layer between application components and the middleware through a dedicated API or code generator. They provide APIs to interface application components with the core middleware; they interact with the core layer in order to allow the exchange of requests between entities. Application personalities can either support specifications such as CORBA, JMS, etc. or dedicated API for specific needs.

Protocol personalities handle the mapping of personality-neutral requests (representing interactions between application entities) onto messages exchanged using a chosen communication network and protocol. Protocol personalities can instantiate middleware protocols such as IIOP (for CORBA), SOAP (for Web Services), etc.

The neutral core acts as an adaptation layer between application and protocol personalities. It manages execution resources and provides the necessary abstractions to transparently pass requests between protocol and application per-

---

[1]An updated list of supporting tools, projects and papers can be found on the official AADL web site `http://www.aadl.info`.

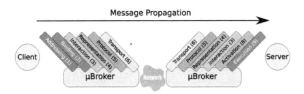

Figure 2: Services of a schizophrenic middleware

sonalities in a neutral way. It is completely independent from both application and protocol personalities.

The neutral core layer enables the selection of any combination of application and/or protocol personalities. Several personalities can be collocated and cooperate in a given middleware instance, leading to its "schizophrenic" nature.

The middleware core provides neutral services that correspond to the identification of the key functions involved in request processing. In figure 2, we define the canonical operations performed by any middleware.

The *μbroker* is the core component that provides support for interaction between the canonical services:

- *addressing* manages references of entities connected to the middleware,

- *binding* handles a connection with the remote nodes,

- *representation* takes care of marshaling and unmarshaling when necessary,

- *interaction* manages the liaisons between connected entities in the application,

- *protocol* supports the transmission between two nodes thanks to the network link,

- *typing* manages the typing system in the application (sophisticated when it comes to CORBA *any* mechanism for instance),

- *transport* handles the physical line,

- *activation* ensures that a concrete entity is available to execute requests,

- *execution* assigns resources to process the requests.

In [13], we presented PolyORB, our implementation of a schizophrenic middleware. PolyORB is a free software middleware framework. We assessed its suitability to build middleware platforms to support multiple heterogeneous specifications (CORBA, Ada Distributed Systems Annex, Web Applications, Ada Messaging Service close to Sun's JMS, OMG DDS) and as a COTS for industry projects.

3.2 Code generation with Ocarina

Our code generation strategy consists in using AADL to describe the user requirements as well as the deployment information. We reuse the schizophrenic architecture and its canonical functions to automatically generate most of them in order to implement an AADL distribution model restricted to those features required by the application. We take advantage of the deployment information to statically instantiate the policies needed. To do so, we had to revisit PolyORB implementation as its initial version was based

on design patterns. The new schizophrenic middleware, PolyORB-HI, is composed of a minimal middleware core and several automatically generated functions.

PolyORB-HI strictly follows restrictions set by High-Integrity applications on object orientation, scheduling, use of memory. It was developed in Ada95. It is compliant with both the Ravenscar profile and the High-Integrity system restrictions (Annexes D and H of the Ada standard). High-Integrity system restrictions are facilities provided by the Ada standard to help developers understanding their program, reviewing its code and restricting the language constructs that might compromise (or complicate) the demonstration of program correctness. Most of these restrictions are enforced at compile time (no dispatching, no floating point, no allocator, etc.). This simply yet efficiently enforces no unwanted features are used by the middleware, increasing the confidence in the code generated while limiting its complexity.

We defined our distribution model as a set of *sender/receiver* tuples that interact through asynchronous oneway messages. This allows for clean support of the Ravenscar model of computation. It is supported by an AADL architectural model that defines the location of each node, and the payload of the message exchanged as a thread-port name plus possible additional data. From a system's AADL description, we compute required resources, then generate code for each logical node. We review the elements supporting this distribution model:

1. Naming table lists one entry per remote node that can be reached, and one entry per opened communication channel on this node. We build one static table per node, computed from the topology of the interactions described in the AADL model. It is indexed by an enumeration affecting one tag per logical node, resulting in $O(1)$ access time to communication handlers (e.g. sockets, SpaceWire).

2. Marshallers handle type conversion between network streams and actual application data. They are derived from data components and thread interfaces, they describe the structure of data to be exchanged. This is computed beforehand from the AADL models, code has $O(payload)$ complexity.

3. Stubs and skeletons handle the construction and analysis of network messages. Stubs transform a request for an interaction into a network stream, skeletons do the opposite operation. Both elements are built from AADL components interface and actual interaction between threads. We exploit this knowledge to have $O(payload)$ components.

4. Protocol instances are asynchronous communication channels, set up at node initialization time. The complexity of the action performed by these instances depends on the underlying transport low-level layer (e.g. sockets, SpaceWire).

5. Concurrent objects handle the execution logic of the node. We build one task per periodic or sporadic AADL thread. Subsequent tasks are built for the management of the transport low-level layer (at least one additional task to handle incoming network messages). Finally, we build one protected object (mutex-like entity) to allow for communication between tasks. Let

us note all these objects strictly follow the Ravenscar Computation Model.

These elements will be later refined in section 5.

The generated code provides a framework that will call directly user code when necessary. This relieves the user from the necessity to know an extensive API, and allows a finer control of the behavior of the system that is under the sole responsibility of the code generation patterns. The generated code can be interfaced with the user code attached to AADL threads.

4. LEVERAGING ADA 2012 AND SPARK 2014

Ada 2012 [12] is the latest revision of the Ada programming language. One of the most interesting features in the context of code generation is the capability to attach contracts to subprograms as pre and post-conditions, or invariants applied to types. This brings to Ada a feature that existed in other languages like Fortran, Eiffel, and SARK. Ada 2012 rationale [2] lists all details of this feature. Other new additions related to expressions, iterators or multi-core processing are noticeable, but not relevant to our experiments. These will not be discussed here

SPARK 2014 [1] is built on top of Ada 2012 well-defined semantics and definition of run-time errors, as well as programming-by-contract constructs to bring to the user evidence his code will under no circumstances raise a runtime error or that all contracts are true. SPARK 2014 relies on the same concepts as the initial SPARK language and toolset: definition of a sound subset of Ada, combined with a Ada processor that generates Verification Conditions (VCs). VCs denotes boolean predicates that should be proved correct (or discharged) based on the current context of a call, or on existing hypothesis such as assertions or pre and post-conditions.

4.1 Adapting for Ada 2012

Updating PolyORB-HI/Ada to Ada 2012 requires first capturing the relevant features that deserve attention. Being implemented in Ada95 and regular restrictions, compiling the existing code base under Ada 2012 language definition does not require any modification thanks to backwards compatibility. Yet, the current code base makes extensive usage of assertions in the form of pragma Assert in the implementation code to assess the validity of input parameters. These can be re-implemented as pre-conditions, attached to subprogram signatures as shown in this example:

```
package PolyORB_HI.Messages is
   --  ...
   function Sender (M : Message_Type)
      return Entity_Type
      with Pre => (Valid (M));
      --  Ensure M is valid

private
   subtype PDU_Index is Stream_Element_Count
      range 0 .. PDU_Size;
   subtype PDU is Stream_Element_Array
      (1 .. PDU_Index'Last);

   Empty_PDU : constant PDU := (others => 0);

   type Message_Type is record
      Content : PDU := Empty_PDU;
      First   : PDU_Index := 1;
      Last    : PDU_Index := 0;
```

```
end record;

function Valid (M : Message_Type)
   return Boolean is
   (M.First >= M.Content'First
      and then M.First < M.Last
      and then M.Last <= M.Content'Last);
```

Such adaptations are truly minor adaptations of the existing code base, and do not require excessive rewritings.

4.2 Introducing SPARK 2014

Adaptations towards SPARK2014 require a more complex reengineering of the existing code base. First, one needs to understand in-depth the additional requirements of SPARK2014, and adapt to these. Luckily enough, SPARK2014 is a much more extensive language subset than its ancestor SPARK2005. In the context of PolyORB-HI, this means

- *contracts:* No need for extensive additions of SPARK-specific contracts for global variables, package visibility, etc. All these are now deduced when need to be, and not necessary for checking for the absence of runtime errors, or validity of pre- and post-conditions;

- *generics:* Ada generic packages are allowed. They are used extensively in PolyORB-HI/Ada to support code-generation driven instantiations of message queues, message marshallers or task artifacts;

- *access types:* Use of access types is explicitly forbidden. The runtime does not use access types for dynamic memory allocation. Yet, a few occurrences of access type are present in the generated code for the implementation of routing matrix. For each thread, we need a structure that holds the destinations associated to each outgoing ports. In the initial design of the runtime, these were encoded as static arrays following this pattern: For each port, an array encoding all destinations is generated; its address is used in an array indexed by the port type. This was to circumvent the limitation in Ada in creating non-rectangular 2D arrays, so as to limit memory consumption, as shown in this example:

```
Foo_Destinations :
   constant Foo_Destinations_Array :=
   Foo_Destinations_Array'
   (1 => Foo_Signal_K);

Task_Foo_Destinations :
   constant Foo_Address_Array :=
   (Foo_Port => Foo_Destinations'Address);
```

We changed this code pattern to implement a function that returns this array, avoiding the need for an Address attribute, at the expense of a slight memory consumption increase.

Let us note SPARK2014 has other restrictions we had to mitigate. We discuss them in section 5. These restrictions correspond to situation where we need bindings to C function or unchecked conversions. These functions are required for the proper operation of the middleware and have been kept as-is. We made usage of the **SPARK_Mode** aspect to hide some elements of the implementation, and kept those as minimal as possible.

4.3 Addressing concurrency

More problematic to the current definition of SPARK2014 and associated implementations is the lack of support for concurrency constructs. PolyORB-HI/Ada uses the Ravenscar model of computation, it thus needs tasks and protected objects. Yet, we may work-around this issue.

4.3.1 Revisiting the Ravenscar Profile

Let us recall that the intent when moving to SPARK2014 is to demonstrate the absence of run-time errors. Considering we are under the restrictions of the Ravenscar profile, we can make the following statements:

- *Use of tasks:* A task has no entry, it can either execute sequential code, or makes use of a protected object. To demonstrate that a task cannot cause a runtime-error, it is therefore sufficient to demonstrate that the sequential code is correct, and the pre-conditions for calling entries or procedures on protected object are met;

- *Use of protected object procedures* Protected object procedures cannot block as a consequence of the pragma Detect_Blocking. Furthermore, in PolyORB-HI/Ada they do not call any other protected objects. As a consequence, these are equivalent to sequential code. The conditions for a run-time error in such procedures are therefore reduced to runtime error in sequential code, or violation of the Ceiling policy. The latter can be assessed through external code reviews by reviewing accessors of the protecting object;

- *Use of protected object entries* By symmetry with the previous case, entries share the same considerations. Besides, they cannot use the requeue mechanism. Hence, these are limited to sequential code encapsulated in an entry block.

Hence, per construction of the Ravenscar profile, concurrency constructs can induce run-time errors only in a limited number of situations, namely violations of the ceiling protocol or blocking inside a protected object procedure or entry. We take advantage of this to revisit our code generation strategy.

4.3.2 Updating code generation strategies

From the previous considerations, we may now update code generation strategies implemented in Ocarina:

- *Management of tasks* Tasks are used for implementing one of the AADLv2 dispatching policy: periodic, sporadic, background, timed, hybrid or aperiodic. The generated code instantiates one generic package that implements the corresponding task skeleton.

  In the context of SPARK2014, we revisited this pattern, and decided to diverge from the Ravenscar profile and introduce a Round-Robin non-preemptive scheduler. Under this scheduling policy, we instantiate a reduced task skeleton that is limited to an infinite loop executing user code, without usage of Ada tasking. This skeleton is a simple function that represents an AADLv2 thread automata, made of initialization code and a call to the user code.

- *Management of queues* Protected objects are used to support message exchanges between tasks. We split the implementation of this package in two separate packages: one package implementing the management of the message queue; another being the implementation of the protected message queue. Under the Round-Robin non-preemptive scheduler, we use the non-protected variant; under the Ravenscar implementation, we use the protected variant.

As a consequence, we can now generate SPARK2014 compliant code from AADL models under the hypothesis of tasks being scheduled under a non-preemptive Round-Robin scheduler. Should we achieve formal proof of this code, then we have arguments to derive similar results in the case of a Ravenscar-compliant model through additional review or testing.

- Correct usage of Ceiling protocol is reduced to external review of the control flow of the program. In our setting, each protected object is associated with a ceiling priority set to the maximum value. Hence violations are not possible.

- Correct implementation of the task skeletons used in the Ravenscar-compilant case. We rely on existing well-known patterns from [4], these are validated from extensive usage.

Other potential errors due to the use of Ravenscar profile are yet to be determined, yet we are confident those will be limited to simple cases.

5. DEMONSTRATING ABSENCE OF RUN-TIME ERRORS

Having adapted code generation strategies for Ada2012 and SPARK2014, we now discuss in this section the application of the SPARK2014 toolset to demonstrate the absence of runtime errors in both the PolyORB-HI/Ada middleware and generated code.

For this study, we considered the usage of the GNATProve GPL 2014 edition. The input AADL model used is from [7], and is derived from the case study from [4]. This model exhibits a set of periodic threads interchanging data. We simply adapted it to use the non-preemptive Round Robin scheduler we introduced instead of a Ravenscar preemptive one. Although the functional code is relevant, we will focus only on the proof of absence of runtime errors of the generated code and the underlying middleware.

In our setting, GNATProve generates Verification Conditions (VCs) based on possibility of a runtime error (and an exception being raised), or due to pre-conditions. Thanks to the GNAT front-end technology, GNATProve generated VCs only for the non-trivial cases that cannot be eliminated by the front-end. Hence, several potential VCs, per strict compliance to the Ada Reference Manual, are discharged internally and not shown to the user.

5.1 PolyORB-HI/Ada code

We first review each package of the current distribution, and discuss how to prove absence of runtime errors.

- `PolyORB_HI`, `PolyORB_HI.Errors`, `PolyORB_HI.Streams`: these packages only define types, there is no code associated, hence no generation of Verification Conditions;

- `PolyORB_HI.Port_Kinds`: this package defines enumeration types for ports and basic test function. Although code exists, it is simple enough to not require any generation of Verification Conditions;

- `PolyORB_HI.Utils`: this package defines basic conversion function, bounded string manipulation API. All 21 functions are considered, 16 VCs are generated and fully discharged;

- `PolyORB_HI.Output`: this package defines basic output function that emulates Ada.Text_IO.Put_Line using a thin binding over the C function `write`, along with basic formatting.

  Let us note that we take advantage of the `SPARK_Mode` aspect to hide from the toolset code that make thread-safe calls to the print functions. Similarly, the binding to the C function `write()` is hidden from the toolset, as it uses C pointers.

  Only the functions in charge of formatting text are "seen" by the toolset. The 14 associated functions yields to 13 VCs fully discharged;

- `PolyORB_HI.Protocols`: this package provides a single function, which is a wrapper that simply calls generated corresponding function from generated code in `PolyORB_HI.Generated.Transport` to send requests. It does not have proper VCs generated

- `PolyORB_HI.Suspenders`: this package provides a mechanism to support a synchronized start of all tasks. It relies on two Ada runtime packages (`Ada.Real_Time` and `Ada.Synchronous.Task_Control`) to either suspend the environment task (using a delay until) or awake all tasks.

  Although SPARK2014 does not fully support these packages, the way primitives operations are used is compatible with the supported toolset. Since the code simply iterates through bounded arrays (denoting tasks to be awaken), it does not cause any VC to be generated.

- `PolyORB_HI.Messages`: this package is in charge of the request life cycle: building, marshalling elements, encapsulation of message destination, etc. This package makes heavy usage of arrays to represent the underlying message, and copying to perform marshalling and encapsulation of data.

  This package has 16 functions, generating 35 VCs. We note 5 VCs are not discharged. These are related to the usage of slicing operation, for which the toolset requires some enhancements.

- `PolyORB_HI.Port_Type_Marshallers` and `PolyORB_HI.Time_Marshallers`: these packages instantiate the generic package `PolyORB_HI.Marshallers_G`. This package provides generic marshalling functions based on performing an unchecked conversion from a base type to a corresponding array of Stream_Elements.

  To date, this package cannot be proved as the toolset does not support the `Size` attribute. More problematic, `SPARK_Mode`, as of GNATProve GPL2014, is inoperant on generic packages: these are systematically considered for proof. These instances have been isolated in a package, and hidden from the toolset.

- The generic packages `PolyORB_HI.Null_Periodic_Task` and `PolyORB_HI.Thread_Interrogators` support respectively the task skeleton and the message queue used for our Round-Robin scheduling strategy. Being generic packages, these can only be proved at instance-level. The generic package cannot be proved alone.

Let us note that the following packages were outside of this study: all packages implementing task skeletons and protected queues, `PolyORB_HI.Scheduler` (used for task migration) and `PolyORB_HI.Transport_Low_Level` (used in a distributed setting). This code requires support for tasking, or access to networking APIs that are currently not available.

From this first round of analysis, we conclude that the toolset is able to proof a significant portion of the code of the runtime. This can be explained by the extensive usage of simple patterns compatible with High-Integrity requirements: no dynamicity, basic transformations, etc. Handling slice operations is a known-issue, this is likely to be addressed by enhancing the GNATProve toolset.

5.2 Generated code

We now review code generated from the AADL model, and bound to the PolyORB-HI/Ada runtime.

- `PolyORB_HI.Generated.Types`: this package defines types mapped from AADL types. There is no code and no VC associated;

- `PolyORB_HI.Generated.Deployment`: this package defines types derived from the deployment information from the AADL model: name of threads, processes. There is no code, but 17 VCs associated. They correspond to elaboration code to build an id-to-string correspondance table.

- `PolyORB_HI.Generated.Marshallers`: this packages defines per-type marshaller/unmarshaller functions. All 32 functions, 23 VCs could be discharged completely;

- `PolyORB_HI.Generated.Transport`: this package implements the send/receive operation used by AADL threads to communicate. In a local setting, these functions simply dispatch the request to the local message queue. 8 functions are generated, 3 VCs out of 4 could not be proved. They relate to pre-conditions that cannot be fullfilled: similarly to the `PolyORB_HI.Messages` package, the corresponding code performs slicing operations, for which support at proof-level is incomplete;

- `PolyORB_HI.Generated.Activity`: this package instantiates task skeletons and message queues from the set of threads and ports of the AADL model. Proof of the task skeleton is trivial, and leads to no VC generation as we simply call in sequence two functions. Proof of the message queue in a non-protected case is a bit more complex, as it involved 50 VCs, of which 7 are not discharged. As stated previously, slicing is again the main issue.

5.3 Lessons learnt

In this experiment, we were mostly interested in demonstrating the absence of runtime errors. We used GNATProve GPL2014 as an oracle to report on potential issues. Surprisingly, the process went smoothly: most of the VCs could be proved at the first round. A few were discharged after rewriting part of the code to cover some corner cases (e.g. non-initialized variable, potential out-of-bound execution, etc.). These were corrected and integrated in PolyORB-HI/Ada.

Although GNATProve allows one to use an IDE to discharge proof manually, we note it was not necessary in our case. On the one hand, the code complexity is quite small, despite the services being made. The runtime mostly transforms data, and moves it to queues. On the other hand, some code patterns like slicing cause troubles. We decided not to change them with manual copies through loops: reports on SPARK2014 forums indicate this is being addressed. Hopefully, the full code base will soon be fully proved in the next iteration of the SPARK2014 toolset.

Finally, time to run the toolset in an automatic way to discharge VCs is reasonably low. The full analysis of code generated + runtime is less than 3 minutes to cover the corresponding 5 kSLOCs.

6. CONCLUSION

In this paper, we aimed at leveraging both Ada 2012 and SPARK 2014 to assess the absence of run-time errors in a restricted middleware that is used for code generation from AADL models using Ocarina and PolyORB-HI/Ada. The initial implementation already includes many restrictions for both the Ravenscar profile, and the High-Integrity domain.

We first introduced how we updated the existing code base to use Ada 2012 pre- and post-conditions, and then adaptation to work-around restrictions of SPARK 2014. We also discussed a few corner cases when this was not possible (bindings to C functions, unchecked conversion). Noting the strong restriction set by the absence of concurrency constructs, we introduced a restricted non-preemptive scheduler in the runtime to evaluate sequential code with a good level of coverage. We also introduced arguments to exploit results in a Ravenscar-context by translating some of the results, combined with careful code review.

Future work will consider two directions: impact of the code refactoring on time and memory performances; further definition of the contracts to demonstrate the code implemented matches the actual semantics as defined in the AADLv2 standard. The second item is likely to stretch SPARK2014 limits in terms of proof of complex contracts.

Acknowledgments

The authors wish to thank Yannick Moy from AdaCore for his insightful comments and suggestions when discussing adaptation of the initial code base to SPARK2014 and in our effort to prove it using the GNATProve GPL2014 toolset.

7. REFERENCES

[1] AdaCore and Altran. SPARK 2014 Reference Manual. Technical report, 2011-2014.

[2] J. Barnes. Ada 2012 Rationale, Chapter 1: Contracts and Aspects. Technical report, 2014.

[3] M. Bozzano, A. Cimatti, J.-P. Katoen, V. Y. Nguyen, T. Noll, and M. Roveri. The COMPASS Approach: Correctness, Modelling and Performability of Aerospace Systems. In *Proceedings of the 28th International Conference on Computer Safety, Reliability, and Security*, SAFECOMP '09, pages 173–186, Berlin, Heidelberg, 2009. Springer-Verlag.

[4] B. Dobbing, A. Burns, and T. Vardanega. Guide for the use of the of the Ravenscar Profile in High Integrity Systems. Technical report, 2003.

[5] M. González Harbour, J. Gutiérrez García, J. Palencia Gutiérrez, and J. Drake Moyano. MAST: Modeling and Analysis Suite for Real Time Applications. In *13th Euromicro Conference on Real-Time Systems*, pages 125–134. IEEE, 2001.

[6] M. Hecht, A. Lam, and C. Vogl. A Tool Set for Integrated Software and Hardware Dependability Analysis Using the Architecture Analysis and Design Language (AADL) and Error Model Annex. In I. Perseil, K. Breitman, and R. Sterritt, editors, *ICECCS*, pages 361–366. IEEE Computer Society, 2011.

[7] G. Lasnier, B. Zalila, L. Pautet, and J. Hugues. OCARINA: An Environment for AADL Models Analysis and Automatic Code Generation for High Integrity Applications. In *Reliable Software Technologies'09 - Ada Europe*, volume LNCS, pages 237–250, Brest, France, June 2009.

[8] P. C. Ölveczky, A. Boronat, and J. Meseguer. Formal Semantics and Analysis of Behavioral AADL Models in Real-Time Maude. In J. Hatcliff and E. Zucca, editors, *FMOODS/FORTE*, volume 6117 of *Lecture Notes in Computer Science*, pages 47–62. Springer, 2010.

[9] X. Renault, F. Kordon, and J. Hugues. Adapting models to model checkers, a case study : Analysing AADL using Time or Colored Petri Nets. In *IEEE/IFIP 20th International Symposium on Rapid System Prototyping* , Paris, France, June 2009.

[10] SAE. Architecture Analysis and Design Language (AADL) AS-5506A. Technical report, The Engineering Society For Advancing Mobility Land Sea Air and Space, Aerospace Information Report, Version 2.0, January 2009.

[11] F. Singhoff, A. Plantec, P. Dissaux, and J. Legrand. Investigating the usability of real-time scheduling theory with the Cheddar project. *Journal of Real-Time Systems, Springer Verlag*, 43(3):259–295, November 2009.

[12] S. T. Taft, R. A. Duff, R. Brukardt, E. Ploedereder, P. Leroy, and E. Schonberg. *Ada 2012 Reference Manual. Language and Standard Libraries - International Standard ISO/IEC 8652/2012 (E)*, volume 8339 of *Lecture Notes in Computer Science*. Springer, 2013.

[13] T. Vergnaud, J. Hugues, L. Pautet, and F. Kordon. PolyORB: a Schizophrenic Middleware to Build Versatile Reliable Distributed Applications. In *Proceedings of the 9th International Conference on Reliable Software Techologies Ada-Europe 2004 (RST'04)*, volume NCS 3063, pages 106–119, Palma de Mallorca, Spain, June 2004. Springer Verlag.

Formal Semantics for the PACEMAKER System Specification

Brian R Larson
Computing and Information Sciences
Kansas State University
Manhattan, KS 66506
brl@ksu.edu

ABSTRACT

This paper formally expresses the timing behavior of a cardiac pacemaker as defined in the PACEMAKER System Specification as understood by its principal author.

The PACEMAKER System Specification was publicly released by Boston Scientific to provide a real-world subject for application of formal methods in response to Jim Woodcock's request at FM2006 for an industrial Grand Challenge problem. PACEMAKER's use for purposes other than formal methods has been surprising in its variety. Most ambitious is the Software Certification Consortium's mock regulatory submission, PACEMAKER Grand Challenge, to show that a product with safety-critical software is in fact safe. McMaster University is designing a second-generation hardware platform to execute formally-verified software during system feature test validation with an electrical heart simulator to show correct behavior.

This paper uses first-order predicates, extended with a simple temporal operator, to formally express what the principal author understands to be "correct" behavior defined in PACEMAKER.

Categories and Subject Descriptors

D.2.1 [**Software Engineering**]: Requirements/Specifications—*specification formalizes requirements*

General Terms

Languages, Theory

Keywords

AADL annex; assertion; BLESS; pacemaker;

1. INTRODUCTION

During re-writing of a company-confidential system specification for a cardiac pacemaker into the *PACEMAKER System Specification* [6], the author tried to formally express

the crucial timing behavior with every temporal logic that he could find, especially Duration Calculus [7] and Temporal Logic of Actions [2], without success. Formal specification of pacemaker timing needs to define what is true at particular instants of time, and also during periods with specified endpoints. Eventually, an @ operator was conceived to express when a first-order predicate was defined: predicate@time.

The natural language requirements for pacemaker timing in the *PACEMAKER System Specification* are transliterations of formulas written with first-order predicates extended with the @ operator. The @ operator appears able to declaratively specify the intricate timing of cardiac pacing, with clear correspondence to natural language requirements.

This paper walks through Chapter 5 of the *PACEMAKER System Specification* specifying requirements for cardiac pacemaker timing, and comparing the natural language expression with its formalization using the @ operator.

The purpose of this paper is two fold:

- formally define the timing behavior of the *PACEMAKER System Specification*

- show the @ operator is capable of expressing intricate timing

2. PACEMAKER

The natural-language expression of the requirements for cardiac pacing comes from the *PACEMAKER System Specification* [6] publicly-released by Boston Scientific in 2007, specifically for the application of formal methods in assuring safety-critical properties. Names for devices early in their development were all capital letters.

Formal definition of the *PACEMAKER System Specification* timing using the @ operator was first presented at Dagstuhl Seminar 14062: "The Pacemaker Challenge: Developing Certifiable Medical Devices" [4], devoted to use of the *PACEMAKER System Specification* as a subject for formal methods for certification of medical-device safety and effectiveness. The Dagstuhl Report for the seminar is available at http://www.dagstuhl.de/dagrep.

For those unfamiliar with pacemaker behavior, the order of the *PACEMAKER System Specification* requirements can be confusing, because they are grouped by function rather than beginning with simple behavior and incrementally adding complexity. That order is largely followed because an intent of this paper is to show formalization of requirements–not teach pacemaker function.

Figure 1 shows the block diagram of the PACEMAKER pulse generator system created from its Architecture Anal-

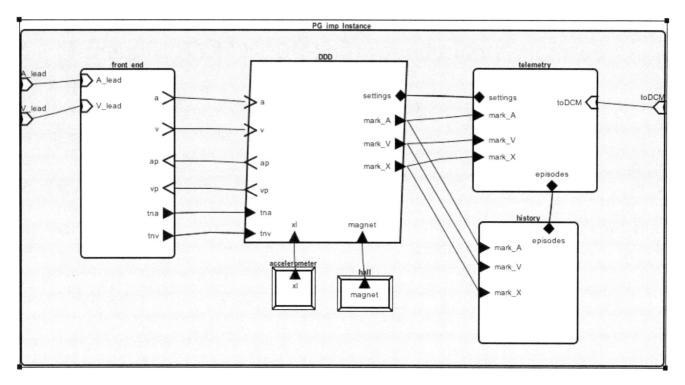

Figure 1: PACEMAKER Block Diagram

ysis and Design Language (AADL) model. Leads from the pulse generator to the patient's right atrium and ventricle connect to A_lead and V_lead respectively.

The analog *front end* connects to the leads through which it senses cardiac activity (a and v) and applies paces when commanded (ap and vp). The front end also indicates when electromagnetic interference (noise) overwhelms intrinsic cardiac signals (tna and tnv).

The *pacing control* subsystem determines when to pace (ports ap and vp), and determines markers (mark_A, mark_V and mark_X) displayed in real-time on a DCM or recorded in the history. Its behavior is the principal subject of this paper.

An *accelerometer* measures patient motion used by rate responsive modes to pace faster according to patient activity.

A *Device Controller-Monitor* (DCM) connects to the *telemetry* subsystem to allow clinicians to set pacing parameters, and extract recordings of cardiac episodes for analysis recorded by the *history* subsystem. A *Hall-effect switch* detects strong magnetic fields. These subsystems' behavior is not considered in this paper, which focuses on crucial pacing behavior.

3. THE @ OPERATOR

The @ operator defines a time reference, at which a predicate holds. Similarly, the @ operator can be used in expressions to define when a value is valid, but is neither needed, nor used, here.

Grammar for first order predicates follow *The Science of Programming* [1], which should be familiar to most readers, so BNF grammar is unnecessary in understanding the formal expression of natural language requirements, and is thus omitted. For those interested, complete grammar with detailed semantics can be found in the *Behavior Language for Embedded Systems with Software (BLESS) Language Refer-*

ence Manual [3], which uses the @ operator in logic formulas called "Assertions".[1] Assertion predicates are enclosed in angle brackets, << >>, and may include a label and formal parameters, <<label:formals:predicate>>, which can then be used by other Assertions as label(actuals), meaning the substitution of actual values for formal variables in its predicate. The @ operator may not be nested; the expression for time used by the @ operator must evaluate to a real value, and have a time type.

4. MODELING PACEMAKER WITH AADL

For context, an Architecture Analysis and Design Language (AADL) [5] system component will be used to give names to the signals used in the *PACEMAKER System Specification*.

AADL is a domain-specific language, designed for safety-critical electronic systems, that use software. Complex functionality is recursively decomposed into simpler subsystems.

Here, only a single system component is needed to show how its behavior is *specified* with BLESS Assertion properties of ports.

4.1 Pacing Modes

Modes are defined by what chambers (right atrium or ventricle) are paced, what chambers are sensed, and how the sensing influences the pacing. For example, VVI mode paces the ventricle (first-V), senses the ventricle (second-V), and inhibits pacing (third-I) when the heart is beating fast enough on its own. DDD mode paces both chambers (first-D), senses both chambers (second-D), and both inhibits and tracks atrial senses with ventricular paces (third-D). If ac-

---

[1]The capital-A proper noun signifies temporal logic formulas used by BLESS.

tivity is detected and pacing rate increased accordingly, and R is appended to the mode to indicate rate response.

All therapeutic pacing modes are some subset of DDDR. Turning-off atrial sensing and pacing and rate response makes DDDR behavior into VVI; turning-off ventricular sensing and pacing makes AAIR mode. Therefore, formal semantics for DDDR mode suffice for all other therapeutic modes.

The triggering modes, VVT, AAT, and DDT, defined in the *PACEMAKER System Specification* are non-therapeutic diagnostic modes, unnecessary today with real-time telemetry that shows device operation. Triggering modes provide visible evidence the device is working when pacing is inhibited by sufficiently-fast intrinsic rate. Triggering modes are not subsets of DDDR; they are not formally defined here.

4.2 Assertion Properties of Ports

One of the strengths of AADL is the ability to attach your own properties to architectural entities. Here, BLESS Assertion properties attached to ports are AADL strings, interpreted as BLESS Assertions. BLESS Assertion properties of an AADL component event port specifies what is true at the moment an event is received or issued by the port. BLESS Assertion properties of ports, plus a thread invariant much like a loop invariant, formally specify component behavior.

The following box shows port declarations of the AADL system type DDD.

```
system DDD
  features
  a: in event port; --atrial sense
  v: in event port; --ventricular sense
  --atrial pace
  ap: out event port  {BLESS::Assertion=>
    "<<AP(now)>>";};
  --ventricular pace, but not too soon
  vp: out event port  {BLESS::Assertion=>
    "<<VP(now) and URL(now)>>";};
  --non-refractory atrial sense
  as: out event port  {BLESS::Assertion=>
    "<<NRAS(now)>>";};
  --non-refractory ventricular sense
  vs: out event port  {BLESS::Assertion=>
    "<<NRVS(now)>>";};
  . . .
end DDD;
```

The system DDD has two in event ports for signals from the front end indicating either an atrial signal (a) or a ventricular signal (v). Whether or not the signals are interpreted as "senses" of contractions makes DDD behavior interesting. When an event on in port a is deemed to be an atrial sense, an event is issued on 'out' port as. Similarly, when an event on in port v is deemed to be a ventricular sense, an event is issued on out port vs.

When the system decides the atrium needs to be paced, it issues an event on out port ap which causes the front end to pace the atrium with a short (0.4 ms) single-digit voltage pulse (2V). Similarly, pacing the ventricle issues an event on out port vp.

All the out event ports have BLESS::Assertion that define what must be true when an event is issued from the port. These Assertions will be defined in following sections.

4.3 Dynamic Behavior Parameters

The *PACEMAKER System Specification* defines DDD mode behavior, and then augments it with rate modifiers like rate-response so as to act as DDDR mode does.

Formal semantics are defined when all the rate modifiers are used together. Because individual features can be turned-off by choosing parameters appropriately, the all-inclusive semantics define behavior for every smaller combination of rate modifiers.

There are some parameters expressing a patient's prescription that are effectively constant. The following parameters are dynamic, changing to achieve required behavior of pacemaking functions beyond DDD behavior.

MaxCCI maximum cardiac cycle interval (like a lower rate limit interval)

MinCCI minimum cardiac cycle interval (like an upper rate limit interval)

DAV dynamic AV delay

FB ATR fall-back: temporarily ignore all atrial senses

Hysteresis increases MaxCCI

Rate Response shortens MaxCCI during activity

All of the rate modifiers beyond DDD mode control dynamic parameters to cause their effect.

5. LOWER RATE LIMIT

The Lower Rate Limit expresses the fundamental effectiveness property for bradycardia therapy: a minimum heart rate, corresponding to the longest interval allowed between heartbeats.

> **§5.1 Lower Rate Limit (LRL)** The Lower Rate Limit is the number of generator pace pulses delivered per minute (atrium or ventricle) in the absence of
>
> - Sensed intrinsic activity.
> - Sensor-controlled pacing at a higher rate.

Expressing this rate-based requirement in equivalent an interval-based manner: a heartbeat occurred in the previous LRL interval, either an intrinsic contraction was electrically sensed, or it was caused by an electrical pace. Let

- the Lower Rate Limit interval be L
- an intrinsic ventricular contraction sensed at time t be $\mathfrak{M}_t[\![vs]\!]$
- a paced ventricular contraction caused at time t be $\mathfrak{M}_t[\![vp]\!]$

then for an arbitrary time x, the predicate $LRL(x)$ is defined as

$$LRL(x) \equiv \exists t \in [(x - L) .. x] \mid (\mathfrak{M}_t[\![vs]\!] \vee \mathfrak{M}_t[\![vp]\!])$$

This means that $LRL(x)$ is true, for times x of concern, when there is a non-refractory sense or pace in the Lower Rate Limit interval preceding x, and false otherwise.

Lower Rate Limit as Assertion:

```
<<LRL:x:  --Lower Rate Limit
    --there was a moment
  exists t:T
    --within the LRL interval before time x
  in x-L..x
    --with a ventricular pace or
    --non-refractory ventricular sense
  that (vs@t or vp@t) >>
```

The most recent heartbeat occurring within the most-recent LRL interval can be expressed as <<LRL(now)>>, where now refers to the present instant.

6. UPPER RATE LIMIT

The Upper Rate Limit is the fundamental safety property for dual-chamber pacing.

§5.2 **Upper Rate Limit (URL)** The Upper Rate Limit (URL) is the maximum rate at which the paced ventricular rate will track sensed atrial events. The URL interval is the minimum time between a ventricular event and the next ventricular pace.

Let

- the upper rate limit interval be u

- a non-refractory ventricular sense occurring at time t be $\mathfrak{M}_t[\![vs]\!]$

- a ventricular pace caused at time t be $\mathfrak{M}_t[\![vp]\!]$

then the upper rate limit safety property is [2]

$$URL(x) \equiv \neg\exists t \in [(x-u),,x] \mid (\mathfrak{M}_t[\![vs]\!] \vee \mathfrak{M}_t[\![vp]\!])$$

This means that $URL(x)$ is true, for times x of concern, when no ventricular event (paced or sensed) occurred in the previous URL interval, and false otherwise.

Upper Rate Limit as Assertion:

```
<<URL:x:
    --at no time
  not (exists t:T
    --within the Upper Rate Interval
    in x-u,,x
    --with a ventricular pace or
    --non-refractory ventricular sense
    that (vs@t or vp@t)) >>
```

To safely pace a ventricle, there must be no ventricular sense or pace in the previous URL interval. This is expressed by the URL(now) term of the BLESS::Assertion property of port vp:

```
  --pace ventricle, but not too soon
vp: out event port {BLESS::Assertion=>
  "<<VP(now) and URL(now)>>";};
```

---

[2]The open interval (excluding endpoints) between $x-u$ and x is expressed using commas as $[(x-u),,x]$.

7. ATRIAL-VENTRICULAR DELAY

The Atrial-Ventricular (AV) delay defines the maximum time after which an atrial event must be followed by a ventricular event. The *sensed* AV delay following an atrial sense, can be programmed to be a little shorter than the *paced* AV delay following an atrial pace.

§5.3 **Atrial-Ventricular (AV) Delay** The AV delay shall be the programmable time period from an atrial event (either intrinsic or paced) to a ventricular pace. In atrial tracking modes, ventricular pacing shall occur in the absence of a sensed ventricular event within the programmed AV delay when the sensed atrial rate is between the programmed LRL and URL. AV delay shall either be

1. Fixed (absolute time)
2. Dynamic

7.1 Paced AV Delay

§5.3.1 **Paced AV Delay** A paced AV (PAV) delay shall occur when the AV delay is initiated by an atrial pace.

Let

- the AV delay interval be av

- an atrial pace occurring at time t be $\mathfrak{M}_t[\![ap]\!]$

then the paced AV delay property is

$$PAV(x) \equiv \exists t \in [(x-av)..x] \mid \mathfrak{M}_t[\![ap]\!]$$

This means that $PAV(x)$ is true, for times x of concern, when an atrial pace occurred in the previous (paced) AV delay interval, and false otherwise.

Paced AV Delay expressed as an Assertion:

```
<<PAV:x:
    --there was a time
  exists t:BLESS_Types::Time
    --in the paced AV delay before x
    in x-av..x
    --with an atrial pace
    that ap@t >>
```

7.2 Sensed AV Delay

§5.3.2 **Sensed AV Delay** A sensed AV (SAV) delay shall occur when the AV delay is initiated by an atrial sense.

Let

- the AV delay interval be av
- the (negative) sensed AV offset be o
- the Upper Rate Limit interval be u
- a non-refractory atrial sense occurring at time t be $\mathfrak{M}_t[\![as]\!]$

then the sensed AV delay property is

$$SAV(x) \equiv \exists t \in [x - (av + o)..x] \mid \mathfrak{M}_t[\![as]\!]$$

Sensed AV Delay expressed as an Assertion:

```
<<SAV:x:
  --there has been a time
  exists t:T
  --in the sensed AV delay (av+o) before x
  in x-(av+o)..x
  --with an atrial sense
  that as@t >>
```

7.3 Dynamic AV Delay

The AV delay can be made dynamic by shortening it in proportion to shorter cardiac cycle intervals (faster heart rates).

---

§5.3.3 **Dynamic AV Delay** If dynamic, the AV delay shall be determined individually for each new cardiac cycle based on the duration of previous cardiac cycles. The previous cardiac cycle length is multiplied by a factor stored in device memory to create the dynamic AV delay.

The AV delay shall vary between

1. A programmable maximum paced AV delay
2. A programmable minimum paced AV delay

Let

- fixed AV delay be av
- minimum dynamic AV Delay be m
- Lower Rate Limit interval be L
- Upper Rate Limit interval be u
- dynamic AV delay be dav
- cardiac cycle interval at time x be $CCI(x)$

then the dynamic AV delay at time x is

$$DAV(x) \equiv \left(\frac{av - m}{L - u} \right) \times CCI(x) + m$$

Dynamic AV delay expressed as an Assertion-function:

```
<<DAV:x:= (CCI(x)*((av-m)/(L-u))) + m>>
```

Note: when fixed (av) and minimum (m) AV delays are the same, then dynamic AV delay becomes fixed.

Assertions for paced and sensed AV delay can be made dynamic by substituting `DAV(x)` for `av`:

```
<<PAV:x:   --dynamic
   exists t:T in x-DAV(x)..x that ap@t>>
<<SAV:x:   --dynamic, with offset
   exists t:T in x-(DAV(x)+o)..x that as@t>>
```

---

§5.3.4 **Sensed AV Delay Offset** The Sensed AV Delay Offset option shall shorten the AV delay following a tracked atrial sense. Depending on which option is functioning, the sensed AV delay offset shall be applied to the following:

1. The fixed AV delay
2. The dynamic AV delay

The sensed AV delay offset is the 'o' appearing in the above formulas and Assertions.

8. REFRACTORY PERIODS

During refractory periods, senses are ignored. These inhibit inherent electrical noise following events (contractions), either sensed or paced, in either the atrium or ventricle. Refractories following events, in the same chamber as the event, are *same-chamber* refractory periods.

---

§5.4 **Refractory Periods** To avoid false sensing, refractory periods follow events during which senses in the affected chamber are ignored. To show that a sense was ignored due to refractory, its marker is displayed in parentheses.

8.1 Ventricular Refractory Period

Electrical chaos follows contraction. Therefore a pacemaker is *refractory* (unresponsive) to millivolt (mV) heart signals immediately after heartbeats. A ventricular sense will be non-refractory when the most-recent beat, whether intrinsic or paced, occurred further in the past than the Ventricular Refractory Period.

---

§5.4.1 **Ventricular Refractory Period (VRP)** The Ventricular Refractory Period shall be the programmed time interval folowing a ventricular event during which time ventricular senses shall not inhibit nor trigger pacing.

Let

- the time of the most recent heartbeat be *lb* (for last-beat)

- $\mathfrak{M}_x[\![vs]\!]$ be an intrinsic heartbeat occurring at time x,

- $\mathfrak{M}_x[\![vp]\!]$ be a heartbeat paced at time x

- r be the Ventricular Refractory Period

- *now* be the present instant

then ventricular senses will be non-refractory, NR, when the last beat occurred earlier than the previous Ventricular Refractory Period

$$NR(x) \equiv \neg \exists t \in [(x-r)..x] \mid (\mathfrak{M}_t[\![vs]\!] \vee \mathfrak{M}_t[\![vp]\!])$$

```
<<NR:x:  --time x is non-refractory VRP
  --at no time
  not exists t:T
  --in VRP before time x
  in [x-r..x]
  --with a ventricular sense or pace
  that (vs@t or vp@t)>>
```

8.2 Atrial Refractory Period

§5.4.2 Atrial Refractory Period (ARP)
For single chamber atrial modes, the Atrial Refractory Period (ARP) shall be the programmed time interval following an atrial event during which time atrial events shall not inhibit nor trigger pacing.

Let

- the atrial refractory period be *arp*

- an atrial pace occurring at time t be $\mathfrak{M}_t[\![ap]\!]$

- a non-refractory atrial sense occurring at time t be $\mathfrak{M}_t[\![as]\!]$

then the atrial refractory period property is

$$ARP(x) \equiv \exists t \in [(x-arp),,x] \mid (\mathfrak{M}_t[\![as]\!] \vee \mathfrak{M}_t[\![ap]\!])$$

```
<<ARP:x:   --time x is in ARP
  --at some time t
  exists t:T
  --in the ARP before x
   in x-arp,,x
  --with an atrial sense or pace
   that (as@t or ap@t) >>
```

8.3 Refractory During SAV and PAV

Atrial senses are ignored during AV delay.

§5.4.5 Refractory During AV Interval
The PG shall also be in refractory to atrial senses during the AV interval. In this context, refractory means the pacemaker does not track or inhibit based on the sensed activity.

8.4 Post-Ventricular Atrial Refractory Period

After a ventricular event, atrial senses must be ignored during the following Post-Ventricular Atrial Refractory Period (PVARP). This is called a *cross-chamber* refractory. Inhibiting atrial senses after ventricular contractions ignores inherent electrical noise caused in the ventricle, but detected in the atrium.

The *tracking* of atrial senses by ventricular paces, and *inhibiting* pacemaker action when beating normally, rely on being able to sense all the real contractions, and ignoring spurious "over" sensing, caused by anything other than a contraction *in that chamber*. PVARP inhibits cross-chamber over-sensing.

In section 15, Extended PVARP, will lengthen the duration of refractory, in certain, unusual circumstances.

§5.4.3 Post Ventricular Atrial Refractory Period (PVARP) The Post Ventricular Atrial Refractory Period shall be available in modes with ventricular pacing and atrial sensing. The Post Ventricular Atrial Refractory Period shall be the programmable time interval following a ventricular event when an atrial cardiac event shall not

1. Inhibit an atrial pace.
2. Trigger a ventricular pace.

Let

- the post-ventricular, atrial refractory period be *pvarp*

- an ventricular pace occurring at time t be $\mathfrak{M}_t[\![p]\!]$

- a non-refractory ventricular sense occurring at time t be $\mathfrak{M}_t[\![vs]\!]$

then the PVARP property is

$$PVARP(x) \equiv \exists t \in [(x-pvarp),,x] \mid (\mathfrak{M}_t[\![vs]\!] \vee \mathfrak{M}_t[\![vp]\!])$$

```
<<PVARP:x:
  exists t:T
   in x-pvarp,,x
   that (vs or vp)@t >>
```

9. NOISE RESPONSE

Electromagnetic interference (EMI) can overwhelm the mV signals from chamber contraction. The analog front end that extracts heart signals from expected noise also must detect when EMI swamps heart signals (**tna** and **tnv**). Noise response suppresses all senses reverting to asynchronous pacing (AOO VOO or DOO) at the Lower Rate Limit.

> **§5.5 Noise Response** In the presence of continuous noise the device response shall be asynchronous pacing.

Noise response is included in definition of atrial and ventricular senses below.

10. VENTRICULAR SENSE

Ventricular senses are suppressed (made refractory) by noise and Ventricular Refractory Period.
Let

- ventricular signal at time x be $\mathfrak{M}_x[\![v]\!]$

- ventricular noise at time x be $\mathfrak{M}_x[\![tnv]\!]$

- whether time x is not in a ventricular refractory period be $NR(x)$

then a non-refractory atrial sense is

$$VS(x) \equiv \mathfrak{M}_x[\![v]\!] \wedge \neg \mathfrak{M}_x[\![tnv]\!] \wedge NR(x)$$

```
<<VS:x:
  v@x    --ventricular signal from front end
  and not tnv@x  --no noise on V-channel
    --not ventricular refractory period
  and NR(x)>>
```

11. ATRIAL SENSE

The *PACEMAKER System Specification* doesn't explicitly say when an atrial signal from the front end is to be considered to be a 'sense'. Instead, five extra conditions are added.

Atrial senses are suppressed (made refractory) for noise, atrial refractory period, post-ventricular atrial refractory period, paced or sensed AV delay, and ATR fall-back.
Let

- atrial signal at time x be $\mathfrak{M}_x[\![a]\!]$

- atrial noise at time x be $\mathfrak{M}_x[\![tna]\!]$

- whether time x is in an atrial refractory period be $ARP(x)$

- whether time x is in a post-ventricular atrial refractory period be $PVARP(x)$

- whether time x is in a paced AV delay be $PAV(x)$

- whether time x is in a sensed AV delay be $SAV(x)$

- whether time x is in an atrial tachycardia response fall-back be $FB(x)$

then a non-refractory atrial sense is

$$AS(x) \equiv \begin{aligned}&\mathfrak{M}_x[\![a]\!]\\ \wedge &\neg\mathfrak{M}_x[\![tna]\!] \wedge \neg ARP(x) \wedge \neg PVARP(x)\\ \wedge &\neg(PAV(x) \vee SAV(x)) \wedge \neg FB(x)\end{aligned}$$

```
--non-refractory atrial sense
<<AS:x: --atrial sense at time x
  a@x   --atrial signal from front-end
    --no noise on A-channel
  and not tna@x
    --not atrial refractory period
  and not ARP(x)
    --not post-ventricular atrial refractory
  and not PVARP(x)
    --not paced or sensed AV delay
  and not (PAV(x) or SAV(x))
    --not ATR fall-back
  and not FB(x)>>
```

12. RATE-ADAPTIVE PACING

Rate-adaptive pacing is an attempt to mimic the normal increase in heart rate with activity. A Sensor Indicated Rate (SIR) is calculated from activity measured by the accelerometer.

> **§5.7 Rate-Adaptive Pacing** The device shall have the ability to adjust the cardiac cycle in response to metabolic need as measured from body motion using an accelerometer.

Cardiologist can choose parameters to customize response:

Maximum Sensor Rate (MSR) maximum pacing rate based on accelerometer-detected activity

Activity Threshold minimum milliG[3] for rate increase

Response Factor how much activity increases pacing rate

Reaction Time minimum time to increase pacing rate from LRL to MSR

Recovery Time minimum time to decrease pacing rate from MSR to LRL

12.1 Maximum Sensor Rate

The Maximum Sensor Rate (MSR) is the fastest pacing rate due to patient activity detected by the accelerometer.

> **§5.7.1 Maximum Sensor Rate (MSR)**
> The Maximum Sensor Rate is the maximum pacing rate allowed as a result of sensor control. The Maximum Sensor Rate shall be
>
> 1. Required for rate adaptive modes
> 2. Independently programmable from the URL

---

[3]1/1000 of acceleration of gravity on Earth (G)

The Maximum Sensor Rate must be less than the Upper Rate Limit, $MSR < URL$. The Sensor Indicated Rate (SIR) is at most Maximum Sensor Rate, $SIR \leq MSR$

12.2 Activity Threshold

Activity Threshold prevents slight activity from increasing pacing rate.

> **§5.7.2 Activity Threshold** The activity threshold is the value the accelerometer sensor output shall exceed before the pacemaker's rate is affected by activity data.

Activity Threshold may be V-Low, Low, Med-Low, Med, Med-High, High, V-High. There is no mention in the *PACEMAKER System Specification* of how many milliG for each threshold level.

Acceleration values assumed in this paper (in milliG):

Table 1: Activity Threshold

	V-Low	Low	Med-Low	Med
milliG	10	15	20	25
	Med-High	High	V-High	
milliG	35	50	75	

12.3 Response Factor

The Response Factor determines how much pacing rate is increased when activity is greater than the Activity Threshold.

> **§5.7.3 Response Factor** The accelerometer shall determine the pacing rate that occurs at various levels of steady state patient activity. Based on equivalent patient activity:
>
> 1. The highest response factor setting (16) shall allow the greatest incremental change in rate.
>
> 2. The lowest response factor setting (1) shall allow a smaller change in rate.

The *PACEMAKER System Specification* provides no definition of what Response Factors 1 through 16 mean, just that a larger number causes a greater increase in pacing rate for the same activity.

Response Factor f together with Activity Threshold th (from Table 1), Lower Rate Limit interval L and accelerometer xl determine Sensor Indicated Rate interval $SIRi$ which can be no shorter than Maximum Sensor Rate interval $MSRi$.

For activity greater than the threshold, $xl > th$:

$$SIRi = max(MSRi, L - f \times (xl - th))$$

```
<<SIRI:x:= MAX(m,l-(f*(xl-th)))>>
```

12.4 Reaction Time

Upon commencement of vigorous activity, normal hearts gradually increase heart rate. Rate response pacing also gradually increases pacing rate due to activity. Reaction Time (10, 20, 30, 40, 50 sec) is the minimum time to increase pacing rate from LRL to MSR due to activity.

> **§5.7.4 Reaction Time** The accelerometer shall determine the rate of increase of the pacing rate. The reaction time is the time required for an activity to drive the rate from LRL to MSR.

Reaction Time restricts how much the pacing rate can be increased each cardiac cycle. Because increasing rate is reducing cardiac cycle interval (CCI), Reaction Time limits the number of milliseconds consecutive CCI can be shortened.

A bit of algebra is needed determine the maximum number of ms to shorten CCI, such that the time between pacing at the Lower Rate Limit and the Maximum Sensor Rate takes Reaction Time seconds.

Let L be the Lower Rate Limit interval, and M be the Maximum Sensor Rate interval. Each of the k cardiac cycles from pacing at LRL to pacing at MSR is z ms shorter than the previous one:

$$z = \frac{(L - M) \times (\frac{L+M}{2})}{rt - L}$$

$$MaxCCI = max((CCI - z), SIRi)$$

Where `CCI(x)` is the cardiac cycle interval at time `x`, and `SIRi(x)` is the Sensor Indicated Rate interval at time `x`, the maximum cardiac cycle interval due to reaction time is `MaxCCI(x)`:

```
<<Z:= ((L-M)*(L+m)) / (2*(rt-L))>>
<<MaxCCI:x:= max((CCI(x)-Z()), SIRi(x))>>
```

12.5 Recovery Time

Recovery time is time for pacing rate to decrease from MSR to LRL after exercise.

> **§5.7.5 Recovery Time** The accelerometer shall determine the rate of decrease of the pacing rate. The recovery time shall be the time required for the rate to fall from MSR to LRL when activity falls below the activity threshold.

Let y be the maximum increase in CCI to recover from maximum sensor rate interval m to Lower Rate Limit interval l, in recovery time ct,

$$y = \frac{(l - m) \times (\frac{l+m}{2})}{ct - l}$$

When $SIRi > CCI$ sensor indicated rate interval is longer than previous cardiac cycle interval,

$$MinCCI = min((CCI + y), SIRi)$$

```
<<Y:= ((1-m)*(1+m)) / (2*(ct-1))>>

<<MinCCI:x:= min((CCI(x)+Y()), SIRi())>>
```

13. HYSTERESIS PACING

Hysteresis pacing attempts to encourage intrinsic contractions, by extending the Lower Rate Limit interval (delaying the next pace) following non-refractory senses.

§5.8 **Hysteresis Pacing** When enabled, hysteresis pacing shall result in a longer period following a sensed event before pacing. This encourages self-pacing during exercise by waiting a little longer to pace after senses, hoping that another sense will inhibit the pace.

To use hysteresis pacing:

1. Hysteresis pacing must be enabled (not Off).

2. The pacing mode must be inhibiting or tracking.

3. The current pacing rate must be faster than the Hysteresis Rate Limit (HRL), which may be slower than the Lower Rate Limit (LRL).

4. When in AAI mode, a single, non-refractory sensed atrial event shall activate hysteresis pacing.

5. When in an inhibiting or tracking mode with ventricular pacing, a single, non-refractory sensed ventricular event shall activate hysteresis pacing.

Hysteresis pacing re-defines LRL property to have variable maximum cardiac cycle interval (HyLRL)

```
  --Lower Rate Limit with Hysteresis
<<LRL_Hy:x:
  --there was a moment
  exists t:T
  --within the previous hysteresis interval
  in x-HyLRL(x)..x
  --with a ventricular pace or sense
  that (vs@t or vp@t) >>
```

The Hysteresis Rate Limit interval (HyLRL) is dependent on whether last ventricular event was a sense or pace. Lengthen the Hysteresis Rate Limit if last ventricular event was a sense.

```
<<HyLRL:x:=     --lengthen LRL upon VS
  --if last V was VS.
  (LAST_V_WAS_VS(x) ?? 1+h : 1) >>
```

```
<<LAST_V_WAS_VS:x:
  --there was a time t in LRLi before  x
  exists t:T in x-1..x that
  --with a ventricular sense
  (vs@t and
  --and, there has been no vs or vp since
    not exists t2:T in t,,x that
    (vs@t2 or vp@t2)) >>
```

14. RATE SMOOTHING

Rate smoothing limits the change in pacing rate for any reason, but particularly when ventricular paces track atrial senses.

§5.9 **Rate Smoothing** Rate Smoothing shall limit the pacing rate change that occurs due to precipitous changes in the intrinsic rate. Two programmable rate smoothing parameters shall be available to allow the cardiac cycle interval change to be a percentage of the previous cardiac cycle interval:

1. Rate Smoothing Up

2. Rate Smoothing Down

The increase in pacing rate shall not exceed the Rate Smoothing Up percentage. The decrease in pacing rate shall not exceed the Rate Smoothing Down percentage.

Up- and down-rate smoothing may be set independently. May interfere with sensor rate if too strict (3%). Next CCI will only slow drs percent

$$cci \leq MaxCCI \leq cci \times (1 + drs)$$

Next CCI will only quicken urs percent

$$cci \times (1 - urs) \leq MinCCI \leq cci$$

```
--down rate smooth limits CCI lengthening
<<DOWN:x:= CCI(x)*(1.0+drs)>>
  --maximum CCI is shortest of,
<<MaxCCI:x:=
  min((CCI(x)+Y()), --recovery time
  SIRI(),  --sensor-indicated rate interval
  DOWN(x))>> --down rate smoothing
  --up rate smooth limits CCI shortening
<<UP:x:= CCI(x)*(1.0-urs)>>
  --minimum CCI is longest of,
<<MinCCI:x:=
  max((CCI(x)-Z()), --response time
  SIRI(),  --sensor-indicated rate interval
  UP(x))>>  --up rate smoothing
```

15. EXTENDED PVARP

Extended PVARP makes the period after ventricular events during which atrial senses are ignored, longer in some circumstances.

For some patients, using the extended PVARP, only following premature ventricular contractions, their inherent cardiac noise will not be mis-sensed as an atrial contraction. A cardiologist can adjust the refractories during which atrial senses are ignored, following an infrequent cardiac event, the pacemaker won't be fooled by the longer-duration heart signals of premature ventricular contractions. However, PVARP may not be extended twice in a row.

---

§5.4.4 Extended PVARP The Extended PVARP works as follows:

1. When Extended PVARP is enabled, an occurrence of a premature ventricular contraction (PVC) shall cause the pulse generator to use the Extended PVARP value for the post-ventricular atrial refractory period following the PVC.

2. The PVARP shall always return to its normal programmed value on the subsequent cardiac cycle regardless of PVC and other events. At most one PVARP extension shall occur every two cardiac cycles.

Let

- the extended, post-ventricular, atrial refractory period be *ex_pvarp*

- an ventricular pace occurring at time t be $\mathfrak{M}_t[\![p]\!]$

- a non-refractory ventricular sense occurring at time t be $\mathfrak{M}_t[\![vs]\!]$

then the extended PVARP property is

$$ExPVARP(x) \equiv \exists t \in [(x-ex\_pvarp),,x] \mid (\mathfrak{M}_t[\![vs]\!] \vee \mathfrak{M}_t[\![vp]\!])$$

($ExPVARP(x)$ means a ventricular event occurred in the *ex_pvarp* time before x)

However, extended PVARP may not be used in consecutive cardiac cycles. Extended PVARP must be enabled by having a value larger than PVARP, be triggered by a premature ventricular contraction (PVC), and previous PVARP was not extended.

$$UseExPVARP(x) \equiv \begin{array}{l} ex\_pvarp > pvarp \ \wedge \\ PVCinCC(x) \ \wedge \\ \neg XPlastCC(x) \end{array}$$

where

- enabling the extended, post-ventricular, atrial refractory period be $ex\_pvarp > pvarp$

- occurrence of pre-mature ventricular contraction (PVC) during previous cardiac cycle be $PVCinCC(x)$

- PVARP was extended previous cardiac cycle be $XPlastCC(x)$

```
<<PVARP:x:
  exists t:T
    in x-
--use extended pvarp in some circumstances
```

```
  (UseExPVARP(x) ?? ex_pvarp : pvarp)
    ,,x
  that (vs or vp)@t >>
--use extended PVARP when
<<UseExPVARP:x:   --longer ex_pvarp enabled
  (ex_pvarp>pvarp)
    and     --PVC in previous cardiac cycle
    PVCinCC(x)
    and   --not extended PVARP last CC
    not XPlastCC(x)>>
```

Extended PVARP depends on the definition of Premature Ventricular Contraction (PVC).

So the definition of Extended PVARP must take a detour to define when a ventricular sense is deemed to be premature.

A Premature Ventricular Contraction (PVC) is a ventricular sense not caused by an atrial sense or pace.

---

§4.8.2 A ventricular sense is deemed to be a premature ventricular contraction if there has been no atrial event since the previous ventricular event.

PVC occurs when there is a non-refractory ventricular sense at time x, with some time y earlier than x with a ventricular event, but no atrial event since.

$$PVC(x) \equiv \begin{array}{l} \mathfrak{M}_x[\![vs]\!] \\ \wedge \neg VRP(x) \\ \wedge \exists y : T \mid y < x \wedge (\mathfrak{M}_y[\![vs]\!] \vee \mathfrak{M}_y[\![vp]\!]) \\ \wedge \neg \exists t : T \in [y..x] \mid (\mathfrak{M}_t[\![as]\!] \vee \mathfrak{M}_t[\![ap]\!]) \end{array}$$

```
<<PVC:x:   --v-sense is premature when
  VS(x)   --a ventricular sense occurred
  and   --previously v-pace or sense
  (exists y:T in y<x that (vs or vp)@y
    and   --no intervening a-sense or pace
    not (exists t:T in y..x
      that (as or ap)@t))>>
```

Having defined PVC, its occurrence in the previous cardiac cycle can be defined.

$$PVCinCC(x) \equiv \exists t : T \in [(x-l),,x] \mid PVC(t)$$

```
<<PVCinCC:x:   --in prior LRL interval
  exists t:T in x-l,,x
    --had premature ventricular contraction
  that PVC(t)>>
```

Finally, definition of when PVARP was extended during the previous cardiac cycle.

$$XPlastCC(x) \equiv \exists t : T \in [(x-l),,x] \mid ExPVARP(t)$$

```
<<XPlastCC:x: exists t:T in x-l,,x
  that UseExPVARP(t)>>
```

To re-cap extended PVARP:

- PVARP uses a value for length of duration controlled by a complex predicate

- When enabled

- Following premature ventricular contraction (PVC)

- But not twice in a row

16. ATRIAL TACHYCARDIA RESPONSE

Atrial Tachycardia Response (ATR) changes pacing mode from DDD to VVI or from DDDR to VVIR when the rate of atrial sensing has been too-fast for too-long.

Sometimes, patients have "atrial storms" in which the atrial rate is abnormally fast, so will be ignored by switching to VVI-mode (first-V pace ventricle, second-V sense ventricle, third-I inhibit pacing when intrinsic rate exceeds Lower Rate Limit, fourth-(R) optional rate response).

When atrial storms subside, the pacing mode switches back to DDD or DDDR, as before.

ATR has four phases: Detection, Duration, Fall-back, and Cessation.

Detection detect when atrial senses have been abnormally fast

Duration wait to determine whether fast atrial senses are sustained

Fall-back switch to VVI(R)-mode, but slowly reduce pacing rate from URL to LRL

Cessation switch back to DDD(R)-mode when atrial rate returns to normal

---

§5.6 Atrial Tachycardia Response (ATR) The Atrial Tachycardia Response prevents long term pacing of a patient at unacceptably high rates during atrial tachycardia. When Atrial Tachycardia Response is enabled, the pulse generator shall declare an atrial tachycardia if the intrinsic atrial rate exceeds the URL for a sufficient amount of time.

16.1 ATR Detection and Cessation

The text in the *PACEMAKER System Specification* defining atrial tachycardia detection deliberately obscures the actual algorithm in the company-confidential document from which the *PACEMAKER System Specification* was re-written for public release by Boston Scientific. All company-specific terms were changed. The company-specific algorithm for ATR detection was genericized to "predominately, but not exclusively".

There are also two (known) errors in the *PACEMAKER System Specification*. The text defining ATR detection has one of them: Item 2, below, should be 'slower' rather than 'faster'.

---

§5.6.1 Atrial Tachycardia Detection
The atrial tachycardia (AT) detection algorithm determines onset and cessation of atrial tachycardia.

1. AT onset shall be detected when the intervals between atrial senses are predominately, but not exclusively, faster than URL.

2. AT cessation shall be detected when the intervals between atrial senses are mostly, but not exclusively, faster (**slower**) than URL.

3. The detection period shall be short enough so ATR therapy is not unnecessarily delayed nor continued.

4. The detection period shall be long enough that occasional premature atrial contractions do not cause unnecessary ATR therapy, nor cease necessary ATR therapy upon occasional slow beats.

For the purposes of demonstration, we define detection and cessation as

Detection: 5 (or more) of 7 atrial senses (AS) are faster than Upper Rate Limit (URL)

Cessation: 3 (or fewer) of 7 AS are faster than URL.

ATR is detected when of the most recent 7 atrial senses, AS were there at least 5 that were faster than URL.

Define an atrial sense (AS) to be atrial-tachycardia (AT) when duration since last atrial sense less than URL interval. AT events are just AS events that happen to be faster than URL.

Determine ATR detection (`ATR_DETECT`) by counting AT events versus AS events. If at least 5 of the last 7 AS events were also AT events, then ATR detection is met.

```
--at least 5 of 7 lA-events were AT
<<ATR_DETECT:x:
  --there is time s, earlier than x
  exists s:T in s<x that
  --of the previous 7 atrial senses
  ((7=numberof t:T in s..x of as@t)
   and --five or more were faster than URL
   (5<=numberof t:T in s..x of at@t))>>
```

ATR ceases (`ATR_END`) when of the most recent 7 atrial senses, AS were there at most 3 that were faster than URL.

```
--at most 3 of 7 A-events were AT
<<ATR_END:x:
  --there is an earlier time s
  exists s:T in s<x that
  --of the previous 7 atrial senses
  ((7=numberof t:T in s..x of as@t)
   and --at most 3 were faster than URL
   (3>=numberof t:T in s..x of at@t))>>
```

16.2 ATR Duration

Once detected, fast atrial rates must continue for ATR Duration before switching from DDD mode to VVI (or DDDR to VVIR). This inhibits inappropriate mode switching.

---

§5.6.2 **ATR Duration** ATR Duration works as follows:

1. When atrial tachycardia is detected, the ATR algorithm shall enter an ATR Duration state.

2. When in ATR Duration, the PG shall delay a programmed number of cardiac cycles before entering Fallback.

3. The Duration delay shall be terminated immediately and Fallback shall be avoided if, during the Duration delay, the ATR detection algorithm determines that atrial tachycardia is over.

Once detection is met (at least 5 of 7 atrial senses is faster than), duration continues until programed CC count, or fast beats fall to 3 out of 7 or fewer.

let

- `dur` be the prescribed number of cardiac cycles to stay fast

- met ATR detection (put out "ATR-Dur" marker) at time `d`

```
<<ATR_DURATION:d x:    --duration at time x
  --when detection met at time d
ATR_DETECT(d) and
  --when at least dur heartbeats
dur<=(numberof t:T in d..x
    that (vs@t or vp@t))
and   --which ATR didn't end
all t2:T in d..k are not ATR_END(t2) >>
```

16.3 ATR Fall-Back

After duration is met, the device falls-back to VVI(R) mode, ignoring atrial activity.

---

§5.6.2 **ATR Fall-Back** If the atrial tachycardia condition exists after the ATR Duration delay is over, the following shall occur:

1. The PG enters a Fallback state and switches to a VVIR Fallback Mode.

2. The pacing rate is dropped to the Lower Rate Limit. The fallback time is the total time required to drop the rate to the LRL.

3. During Fallback, if the ATR detection algorithm determines that atrial tachycardia is over, the following shall occur:

- Fallback is terminated immediately
- The mode is switched back to normal

4. ATR-related mode switches shall always be synchronized to a ventricular paced or sensed event.

---

let

- `dur` be the prescribed number of cardiac cycles to stay fast before switching to single-chamber pacing mode

- `CC(x)` be the cardiac cycle at time x

- met ATR detection (put out "ATR-Dur" marker) on cardiac cycle `d`

When starting ATR fall-back, have been tracking at or near URL. Therefore when mode switching to fall-back, pacing pacing rate must be slowly reduce to LRL.

Let the time when duration met be t_d, and fall-back time to decrease pacing rate from URL to LRL be t_{fb}.

Then the maximum cardiac cycle interval during ATR fallback for time x between t_d and $t_d + t_{fb}$ is:

$$FB\_MaxCCI(x) = (x - t_d) \times \left(\frac{l - u}{t_{fb}} \right)$$

```
<<FB_MaxCCI:d x:= (x-d)*((l-u)/fb_time)>>
```

After $t_d + t_{fb}$ until ATR ceases the maximum cardiac cycle interval is the Lower Rate Limit interval.

17. SUMMARY

Formal expression of all timing behavior in Chapter 5 of the *PACEMAKER System Specification* has been expressed as BLESS Assertions.

BLESS Assertions can express, declaratively, intricate timing of cardiac pacing, while being clearly understood to express the intent of natural-language requirements. This is crucial to validation; formal specification correctly expresses intent; are doing the right thing.

Ongoing work seeks to devise behaviors (a.k.a. programs) that can be formally verified to conform to this formalization of the *PACEMAKER System Specification*. This provides (hopefully strong) evidence for verification; are doing it right.

Acknowledgement

This work is supported supported by the US National Science Foundation (NSF) (#0932289, #1239543), the NSF US Food and Drug Administration Scholar-in-Residence Program (#1065887, #1238431, #1355778).

18. REFERENCES

[1] David Gries, *The science of programming*, Springer-Verlag, Berlin Heidelberg New York, 1981.

[2] Leslie Lamport, *The temporal logic of actions*, ACM Trans. Program. Lang. Syst. **16** (1994), no. 3, 872–923.

[3] Brian R. Larson, *Behavior Language for Embedded Systems with Software: Language Reference Manual,* 2014, `info.santoslab.org/research/aadl/bless`.

[4] Dominique Méry, Bernhard Schätz, and Alan Wassyng, *The Pacemaker Challenge: Developing Certifiable Medical Devices (Dagstuhl Seminar 14062),* Dagstuhl Reports **4** (2014), no. 2, 17–37.

[5] SAE International, *SAE AS5506B. Architecture Analysis & Design Language (AADL),* 2013.

[6] Boston Scientific, *Pacemaker system specification,* sqrl.mcmaster.ca/pacemaker.htm, 2007.

[7] Chaochen Zhou and Michael Hansen, *Duration calculus: A formal approach to real-time systems,* Springer, Berlin Heidelberg New York, 2004.

UML with Meaning: Executable Modeling in Foundational UML and the Alf Action Language

Ed Seidewitz
Model Driven Solutions
14000 Gulliver's Trail
Bowie, MD 20720 USA
+1.301.455.3681
ed-s@modeldriven.com

1. ABSTRACT

To most in the software community, "modeling" is drawing pictures, something much different than "coding". While programming languages must be specified precisely enough to be executable, this has not necessarily been the case for modeling languages. Indeed, the well-known Unified Modeling Language (UML) has for years had a specification that is far from precise.

However, precise models are quite common in other engineering disciplines, and there has been a minority even in software engineering that have created models that are precise enough to be, themselves, executable. Over the last decade, the UML community has more generally come to realize the benefits of having at least a subset of UML specified with precise execution semantics. While not all models need to be executable, executable models can support early testing and analysis of the design of critical software systems, as well as supporting simulation for communities using UML for modeling beyond just software (such as SysML for systems engineering).

As a result, there has been a great deal of work in recent years toward the standardization of precise, executable semantics for UML models – the "meaning" behind the pictures: Foundational UML (fUML), the Action Language for fUML (Alf) and the recently completed Precise Semantics for UML Composite Structures. These new specifications provide the promise of widespread support for executable modeling across the many UML tools now on the market.

Categories and Subject Descriptors

D.2.2 [**Software Engineering**]: Design Tools and Techniques – *computer-aided software engineering (CASE), object-oriented design methods*, Design – *methodologies*, D.3.3 [**Programming Languages**]: Language Classifications – *design languages*

General Terms

Design, Standardization, Languages

Keywords

Executable modeling, system modeling, UML, action languages

2. INTRODUCTION

For years, "modeling" in the software community has largely seemed to mean simply drawing pictures, either to represent the problem domain or to blueprint a solution, without a precise enough meaning to fully specify the functionality of the system being developed. This is reflected in the specification of the Unified Modeling Language (UML), arguably the most commonly used standard modeling notation for software development, which does not define the semantics of UML models at all precisely.

Though the latest specification (for UML 2.5 [17]) is better than those that came before, this is still not sufficient for many possible real-world applications of modeling, particularly for high-integrity software. For example, modeling may be used to perform correctness and performance analysis on a software system while it is being designed and implemented. This analysis may even go beyond what could be practically validated through testing. But, to create such models, one needs a modeling language with precisely defined semantics that can be supported in standardized analysis, validation and simulation tooling.

On the other hand, there has also been a long standing minority in the software development community that has created models precise enough that they can be executed in their own right. Indeed, commercial executable modeling tools based on the Shlear-Mellor method [21][22], Real-Time Object-Oriented Modeling (ROOM) [20] and Harel statecharts [4] all predated UML. However, such approaches converted over to UML notations (for example, [1] and [7]), and executable UML has been used for significant and critical applications, including fighter aircraft flight software, launch vehicle flight software and telecommunication switches [2][23].

And yet, executable modeling has remained a niche approach dependent on divergent, proprietary tooling. One crucial issue with creating precise, standard UML models has been the imprecision of semantics specification in the UML standard. This issue was finally addressed with the adoption by OMG of the Foundational UML (fUML) specification [15]. This specification provides the first precise operational and axiomatic semantics for a Turing complete, executable subset of UML. The subset encompasses most of the object-oriented and activity/action modeling constructs of UML, which cover not only features commonly found in an object-oriented programming language, but also more advanced modeling features found in UML such as first-class associations and asynchronous signals.

But there has been a second crucial issue with executable UML modeling: the lack of a good surface notation for specifying detailed behavior and computation. UML is a largely graphical modeling language whose legacy is the unification of earlier

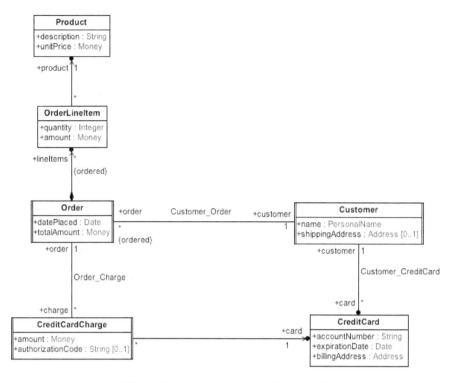

Figure 1 Ordering Example Class Model

graphical modeling languages. This is a great strength of UML for traditional, largely informal "big picture" analysis and design modeling, but it does not work well for representing detailed computations.

The fUML specification does not provide any new concrete surface syntax, tying the precise semantics solely to the existing abstract syntax model of UML. UML does provide a concrete notation for activities and actions that can be used to model, say, the method for an operation, but this requires one to draw a very detailed, graphical activity diagram.

Now, anyone who has ever tried to create an activity diagram down at this level of detail (I have personally done several!) knows that it is a frustrating, time-consuming and error-prone thing to do. The graphical UML activity notation was just not meant to be used at such a level of detail – and, in fact, for most people, trying to do such "graphical programming" is not intuitive or effective.

This issue was addressed with the adoption by OMG of the Action Language for fUML (Alf) [16]. Alf is basically a textual notation for UML behaviors that can be attached to a UML model anyplace that a UML behavior can be. (The "extended" Alf notation actually includes some basic structural modeling constructs, so it is also possible to do entire models textually in Alf.)

Semantically, Alf maps to the fUML subset. In this regard, one can think of fUML as effectively providing the "virtual machine" for the execution of the Alf language. However, this grounding in fUML also provides for seamless semantic integration with larger graphical UML models in which Alf text may be embedded. This avoids the semantic dissonance and non-standard conventions required if one where to instead, say, use a programming language

like Java or C++ as a detailed action language within the context of an overall UML model.

Together, these standards (and more to come) effectively provide a new combined graphical and textual language for precise, executable modeling. In the rest of this paper, I will explore the implications for software and system engineering practice of bringing real meaning to UML, through the presentation of two illustrative examples.

3. EXAMPLE 1: PRODUCT ORDERING

Let's start with a simple example from the domain of ecommerce. In today's world, ecommerce has become a ubiquitous way of doing business, impacting on almost everyone's life in some way. Key to such systems is the maintenance of a large amount of information – on products, customers, orders, etc. Further, an ecommerce system must also efficiently and accurately handle a reasonable volume of asynchronous transactions, both with users on the front end and financial systems on the back end.

For the purposes of our example (which is loosely based on the case study in Appendix B of [19]), let's consider just the functionality of placing and managing orders. The first thing to understand is what information needs to be kept on an order and how this is related to other entities in the problem domain. This can be well represented using a UML class diagram, such as the one shown in Figure 1.

This diagram models an order as having two pieces of attributive information, the date it was placed and its total amount, as well as a set of line items, each of which specifies the quantity of a certain product included in the order. It also shows that an order is placed by a single customer (who may have many orders) and that it may have several credit card charge attempts (each of which is just for this one order).

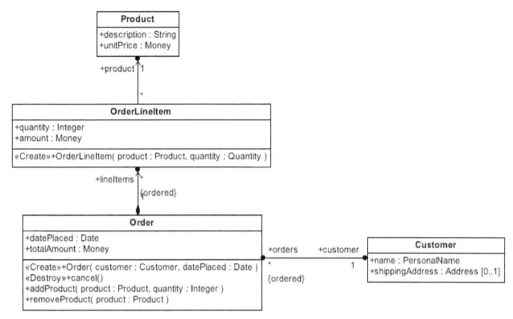

Figure 2 Order Class

Models such as this are particularly useful in discussions with problem domain stakeholders. They are straightforward to understand and a lot of detail can be presented in a well-laid-out, compact diagram. For most people, this is far easier to understand than large blocks of text such as the previous paragraph.

Of course, there is also behavior associated with the classes shown in Figure 1. Some of this can be represented in the typical object-oriented way as operations on the classes, as shown in Figure 2 for the Order class. But, while the names used for the operations on this diagram are suggestive, the model does not actually specify what the operations really *do*.

At this point, we need to decide what this is a model *of*. I introduced the original model in Figure 1 as a way to talk about the problem domain. But, with the introduction of operations, we are seemingly now moving into an object-oriented *solution* domain discussion.

Indeed, a software developer will see a diagram such as Figure 2 as a model of the *software* that needs to be implemented in order to meet the requirements of the problem domain. For example, a Java developer will see this model as representing a Java class called Order that has four fields, one of which needs to be a collection, and four methods, including a constructor. This is also the approach that is often automated by code generation software.

The orthodoxy of object-oriented analysis and design (OOAD) has been to organize programs in a way that reflects a model of basic concepts of the problem domain. In this way, the hope was that the expression of the computational details of the program in terms of these problem domain abstractions would make the program easier to understand, more likely to be correct and with parts that were more likely to be reusable in the future.

The problem was that even specifically object-oriented languages turned out, for the most part, to not be good enough as languages for modeling problem domains in addition to being languages for modeling computations; too much of a typical OO program has to be given over to the details of specifying computation precisely

enough to be executed. As the program grows, the "big picture" of the problem domain model tends to get harder and harder to understand just by looking at the program code.

That is why graphical modeling continues to be useful for visualizing abstractions during the early stages of development, even in today's popular agile approaches. And, when faced with a difficult architectural issue to understand, developers may reverse engineer the code into a model that provides them the picture they need for their discussions. In the end, though, "the truth is in the code", and models are just pictures that may sometimes be useful, but are too difficult to maintain in parallel with the code to any great level of detail. Right?

Indeed, this viewpoint on modeling is still so prevalent that it keeps people from even thinking to ask an important question: Having gone to the trouble of creating diagrams such as Figure 1 and Figure 2, which are humanly understandable from *both* a problem and a solution perspective, why do we have to translate them at all into another language in order to "implement" them? Why can't they *be* the code, and mean to the computer just what they are understood to mean by people looking at them?

The answer is that they *can*. For example, fUML gives precise, operational specifications for what it means to instantiate classes and associations, set values, call operations – indeed for all the constructs used in Figure 1 and Figure 2. And the following is the executable Alf code for a method for the Order class `addProduct` operation:

```
namespace Ordering::Order;
private import Products::Product;

activity addProduct
  (in product : Product, in quantity : Integer){
  lineItem = new LineItem(product, quantity);
  this.lineItems->add(lineItem);
  this.totalAmount =
    this.totalAmount + lineItem.amount;
}
```

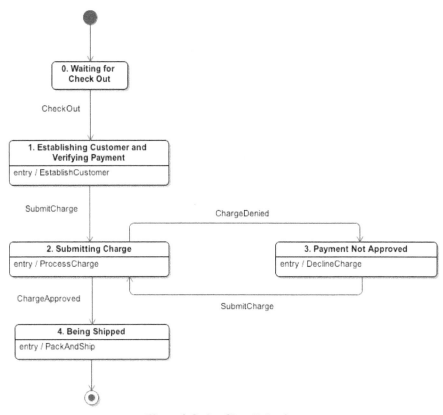

Figure 3 Order Class Behavior

Syntactically, Alf looks at first much like a typical C/C++/Java legacy language. This is the result of a conscious compromise on the part of the team that developed the Alf specification. Since (despite some serious issues discussed below) it is currently not uncommon practice to use Java or C++ as a UML action language, there was a strong desire to have a subset of Alf that would be familiar to such practitioners, to ease their transition to the new action language.

But note the statement "`this.lineItems->add(item);`". Association ends are not really semantically collection objects in UML – rather, they are multi-valued properties with specified multiplicities. This statement simply says to add an item to the set of values on the "`lineItems`" end of the association from Order to LineItem.

The fact that `this.lineItems` would be represented as a collection object in, say, Java, is dissonant with the UML semantics, and any code that relies on this mapping would need to be specifically avoided if Java were to be used as a UML action language. And what kind of collection should it be anyway? A Vector? An ArrayList? A HashSet? And why not map to Java arrays rather than collection objects?

The problem is that the semantic mapping to a programming language requires the introduction of exactly the kinds of implementation decisions that one wants to avoid in executable models. In general, one would like to keep the model independent of the implementation platform (a well-known tenet of the MDA approach [12]), specifying precise system behavior in the model without committing to the non-essential details of a specific target platform. To consider this further, let's take another step with the ordering example.

An order actually has an autonomous, asynchronous lifecycle that extends from when it is placed, through being paid, until it is packed and shipped. Figure 3 models this lifecycle as a simple UML *state machine*. Such a model abstracts the life of an order into a finite number of states, with the order having discrete transitions between these states based on the occurrence of specific events (which are modeled here as the receipt of *signals* that may carry event-specific data).

We can now make the Order class an *active* class, with the state machine as its active behavior. An instance of the class begins in the state "`0. Waiting for Check Out`" and then responds to the reception of various asynchronous signals, transitioning to subsequent states as appropriate. Further, as shown in Figure 3, a state may have an *entry behavior* that executes on entry to that state.

And, of course, these entry behaviors can be represented in Alf. For example, the code for `EstablishCustomer` might be

```
namespace Ordering::Order::Order_Behavior;
private import Utilities::Time::CurrentDate;
private import RealFunctions::'+';

activity EstablishCustomer
  (in checkOut: CheckOut) {
  this.lineItems = checkOut.items;
  Customer_Order.createLink
    (checkOut.customer, this);
  this.datePlaced = CurrentDate();
  this.totalAmount =
    this.lineItems.amount->reduce '+';
  this.SubmitCharge(checkOut.card);
}
```

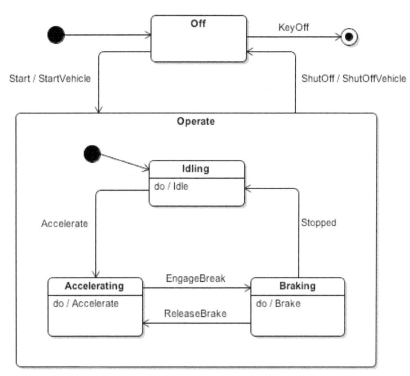

Figure 4 HSUV Operational States

There are a couple more things to note about this Alf code. First, the "Customer_Order.**createLink**" operation is used here to create a *bidirectional* link between the order and a customer, as an instance of the Customer_Order association, without any additional machinery. And the expression "this.lineItems. amount->**reduce** '+'" leverages the inherently concurrent, flow-oriented nature of the underlying fUML activity semantics. It means to get a sequence of the amounts of each of the line items and add them all together.

Once one has specified all the required behavior, a UML model becomes a complete executable program. Executed interpretively, this program can act as a prototype for the desired end system, enhancing the ability to do iterative, rapid development. If the intent is to deploy the end application on a different target platform, then the model could be executed in an emulated target environment, in order to simulate its performance on the target platform. And, finally, given a specification of the target, the model can be compiled into the desired target architecture and deployed for operation on the target platform.

4. EXAMPLE 2: HYBRID SUV

Our second example has to do with systems engineering, rather than pure software development. Systems engineers have long used models and simulation in order to analyze and optimize the designs of systems that usually involved both hardware and software. As the Systems Modeling Language (SysML) profile of UML has become more popular, it has been natural for the systems engineering community to desire similar capabilities for SysML models.

The example we will consider is a simplification of the Hybrid SUV (HSUV) example given in Annex C of the SysML Specification [14]. We can begin with a fairly intuitive state

machine model of the overall operational states of such a vehicle (Figure 4). Note that each of the substates within the Operate composite state has a "do" activity – that is, an ongoing activity that takes place while the system is in the relevant state. Let's consider specifically the Accelerate activity that is active in the Accelerating state.

At this level of the model, it is actually nice to be able to represent the activity using an activity diagram, as shown in Figure 5. In this case we have three subactivities: one that monitors the pushing of the accelerator pedal, one that monitors vehicle conditions and one that takes the output of the other two activities and produces drive power and commands to the vehicle transmission. That is, the activity behavior is basically modeled as three concurrent subprocesses connected by data flow.

Actually, the nodes in Figure 5 are technically not activities themselves, but *actions* that call a separately defined activities (as is indicated by the little "fork" symbol on the nodes). For example, the ProvidePower activity is itself modeled by the activity diagram shown in Figure 6. As is clear in this diagram, central to the behavior of the ProvidePower activity is ProportionPower, which determines how much power is provided by the gas engine versus the electric motors in this hybrid vehicle.

Now, "medium-grained" processes (such as those in Figure 5 and Figure 6) can often be effectively specified using graphical activity diagrams. A benefit of the seamless semantic integration of Alf with graphical UML models is that one can easily move from using graphics at the medium-grained level to using Alf at a finer-grained level, all based on the same underlying fUML semantics. For example, rather than using another level of activity diagramming for ProportionPower, we can more readily specify this computational behavior using Alf:

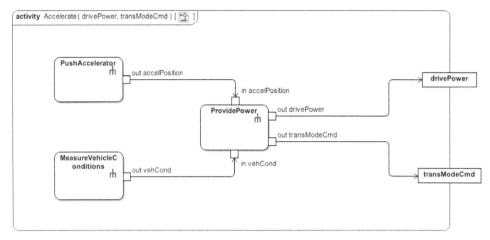

Figure 5 "Accelerate" Activity Diagram

```
namespace HSUV::ActivityModels;
private import HSUV::DataTypes::TransModeCommand;
private import HSUV::Functions::*;
private import RealFunctions::*;

activity ProportionPower (
  in speed : Real,
  in battCond : Real,
  in accelPosition : Real,
  out gThrittle : Real,
  out eThrottle : Real,
  out transModeCmd : TransModeCommand
) {
//@parallel
{
  throttle = (accelPosition * battCond) /
            GetMaxBattLevel();
  eThrottle = Min(throttle, GetMaxEThrottle());
  gThrottle = Min(accelPosition - throttle,
                    GetMaxGThrottle());

  transModeCmd = new TransModeCommand(
    level => speed / GetTransModeConv()
  );
}}
```

Particularly interesting here is the "@parallel" annotation. This indicates that all the statements in the following block are to execute concurrently, not sequentially. That is, the behavior of this Alf-specified activity is just as much that of concurrent processes and data flows as the activities specified using activity diagrams in in Figure 5 and Figure 6.

(Indeed, concurrent execution of nodes is the default semantics in UML activities. The mapping of a sequence of Alf statements *without* the @parallel annotation actually requires the introduction of explicit control flows to force sequential execution. Sequential execution was made the default for an Alf statement sequence simply because it was considered too confusing to have a C-like notation of semicolon terminated statements execute concurrently by default, even though that would have been the more natural mapping to UML activities!)

So, once we have completely specified an executable model for the HSUV, what can we do? Well, the goal is to be able, for example, to run the model as a simulation of the expected performance of the HSUV as designed. The result might be, say, a plot of various performance parameters of interest over simulated

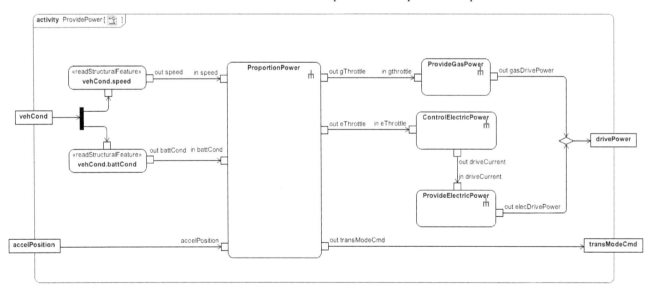

Figure 6 "Provide Power" Activity Diagram

time, as illustrated in Figure 7, in order to determine of the HSUV design meets its performance requirements, in this case the ability of a vehicle of a certain weight and engine power to achieve a required acceleration.

Now, SysML also includes a sophisticated capability to model parametric mathematical models of continuous processes, and tools already exist to simulate SysML models based on integrating differential equations expressed using such parametrics (for example, [5]). Full simulation of a real-world SysML model, however, really requires the integration of continuous simulation of parametrics, behavioral simulation of activity models and discrete-event simulation of state machine models. Achieving this ultimate simulation environment is a very interesting topic of ongoing research on executable SysML modeling.

5. CONCLUSION

The fUML and Alf standards are relatively new and implementations of them have only appeared recently. There are open-source reference implementations available for both fUML [8] and Alf [9]. Being the earlier standard, tooling for fUML is more developed than for Alf, with a number of major UML tools now having features available to execute, animate and debug fUML activities [3][6][11]. And more extensive commercial environments based on fUML and Alf are also under development (see, for example, [10]).

But, as the name "Foundational UML" suggests, the current fUML and Alf standards are really intended as the basis for building out further executable UML specifications. A new

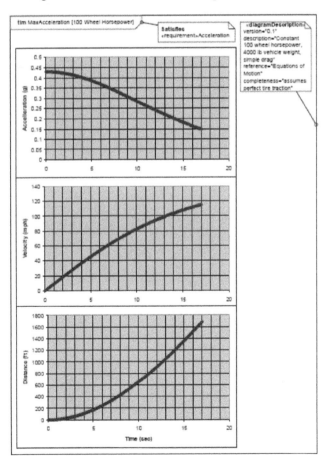

Figure 7 Execution and Analysis Results

standard for the Precise Semantics of UML Composite Structures [18] already extends fUML semantics to include UML component and connection modeling, which is fundamental to both SysML and the MARTE profile for real-time-system modeling [13]. The next area to be addressed is to finally fully standardize the precise execution semantics for UML state machines.

So far, however, most fUML-based execution tooling has been intended to primarily address needs for system simulation and pre-deployment testing. What is still needed is a suite of production-quality model compilers that may be used to provide reliable, high-performance, deployable code, as was available for earlier pre-fUML executable modeling tools. With the availability of such compilers, the executable UML ecosystem will be able to provide truly complete, standards-based, system-development environments, allowing us at last to move up another generation in the level of abstraction in which we are able to program, with greater agility, reliability and integrity.

6. REFERENCES

[1] Abstract Solutions. *MDA with Executable UML.* http://www.kc.com/XUML/

[2] Corcoran, D. 2011. *Model Driven Development and Executable UML at Ericsson.* http://www.omg.org/news/meetings/tc/agendas/va/xUML_pdf/Corcoran.pdf

[3] Eclipse Foundation. *Papyrus/UserGuide/ModelExecution.* https://wiki.eclipse.org/Papyrus/UserGuide/ModelExecution

[4] Harel, D., and Politi, M. 1998. *Modeling Reactive Systems with Statecharts: The Statement Approach.* McGraw-Hill.

[5] InterCAX. *Products.* http://www.intercax.com/products/

[6] Lieber Lieber Software. *Advanced Modeling Using Simulation and Execution (AMUSE).* http://www.lieberlieber.com/model-engineering/amuse/

[7] Mentor Graphics. Bridgepoint. http://www.mentor.com/products/sm/model_development/bridgepoint/

[8] Model Driven Solutions. *fUML Reference Implementation.* http://fuml.modeldriven.org

[9] Model Driven Solutions. *Alf Reference Implementation.* http://alf.modeldriven.org

[10] Mutschall, J. 2014. *ALF: The Standard Programming Language for UML.* Code Generation 2014, Cambridge UK. http://www.slideshare.net/JuergenMutschall/code-generation-2014-alf-the-standard-programming-language-for-uml

[11] No Magic. *Cameo Simulation Toolkit.* http://www.nomagic.com/products/magicdraw-addons/cameo-simulation-toolkit.html

[12] Object Management Group. 2003. MDA Guide Version 1.0.1. OMG Document omg/03-06-01, June 2003. http://www.omg.org/mda/

[13] Object Management Group. 2011. *UML Profile for MARTE: Modeling and Analysis of Real-Time Embedded Systems, Version 1.1.* OMG Document formal/11-06-02. http://www.omg.org/spec/MARTE/1.1/

[14] Object Management Group. 2012. *OMG Systems Modeling Language (OMG SysML™), Version 1.3.* OMG Document formal/12-06-01. http://www.omg.org/spec/SysML/1.3/

[15] Object Management Group. 2013. *Semantics of a Foundational Subset for Executable UML Models (fUML), Version 1.1*. OMG Document formal/13-08-06, August 2013. http://www.omg.org/spec/FUML/1.1/

[16] Object Management Group. 2013. *Action Language for Foundational UML (Alf): Concrete Syntax for a UML Action Language, Version 1.0.1*. OMG Document formal/13-09-01, October 2013. http://www.omg.org/spec/ALF/1.0.1/

[17] Object Management Group. 2013. *OMG Unified Modeling Language (OMG UML™), Version 2.5 Beta 2*. OMG Document formal/13-09-05, September 2013. http://www.omg.org/spec/UML/2.5/Beta2

[18] Object Management Group. 2014. *Precise Semantics of UML Composite Structures, Version 1.0 Beta 1*. OMG Document Number ptc/2014-06-15. http://www.omg.org/spec/PSCS/1.0/Beta1/

[19] Mellor, S. J. and Balcer, M. J. 2002. *Executable UML: A Foundation for Model-Driven Architecture*. Addison-Wesley.

[20] Selic, B., Gullekson, G. and Ward, P. 1994. *Real-Time Object-Oriented Modeling*. Wiley.

[21] Shlaer, S. and Mellor, S. J. 1988. *Object-Oriented Systems Analysis: Modeling the World in Data*. Prentice Hall.

[22] Shlaer, S. and Mellor, S. J. 1991. *Object Lifecycles: Modeling the World in States*. Prentice Hall.

[23] Shubert, G. 2011. *Executable UML Information Day Panelist Presentation. Lockheed-Martin Space Systems Company*. http://www.omg.org/news/meetings/tc/agendas/va/xUML_pdf/Shubert.pdf

Correctness via Compilation to Logic

Thomas Ball
Microsoft Research
tball@microsoft.com

ABSTRACT

Advances in automated theorem provers over the last decade have led to a renaissance in software tools that compile problems of correctness to problems over logic formula.   In this talk, I will review progress in automated theorem provers, such as Z3 from Microsoft Research, and consider a variety of program correctness tools that build upon Z3, such as automated test generators, automated safety/termination checkers, as well as interactive functional verifiers. I'll then describe a number of new projects that make us of the "correctness via compilation to logic" approach, including the design of new programming languages, ensuring the security of data centers, and safely programming gesture recognizers such as Kinect.

Categories and Subject Descriptors

D.2.4 Software/Program Verification

Keywords

program verification; program testing; interactive functional verification; automated theorem proving

Bio

Thomas Ball (Tom) is a Principal Researcher and Research Manager at Microsoft Research. From 1993-1999, he was a member of the technical staff at Bell Laboratories. His 1997 PLDI paper on path profiling with colleagues Ammons and Larus received the PLDI 2007 Most Influential Paper Award. In 1999, Tom moved to Microsoft Research, where he started the SLAM software model checking project with Sriram Rajamani, which led to the creation of the Static Driver Verifier (SDV) tool for finding defects in device driver code. Tom and Sriram received the 2011 CAV Award "for their contributions to software model checking, specifically the development of the SLAM/SDV software model checker that successfully demonstrated computer-aided verification techniques on real programs." Tom is a 2011 ACM Fellow for "contributions to software analysis and defect detection". As a manager at Microsoft, he has grown research areas such as automated theorem proving, program testing/verification, and empirical software engineering.

HILT 2014, October 18–21, 2014, Portland, OR, USA.
ACM 978-1-4503-3217-0/14/10.
http://dx.doi.org/10.1145/2663171.2663189

Specification of Generic APIs,
or: Why Algebraic May Be Better Than Pre/Post

Anya Helene Bagge
Bergen Language Design Laboratory
Department of Informatics
University of Bergen, Norway
http://www.ii.uib.no/~anya/

Magne Haveraaen
Bergen Language Design Laboratory
Department of Informatics
University of Bergen, Norway
http://www.ii.uib.no/~magne/

ABSTRACT

Specification based on Floyd-Hoare logic, using pre and post-conditions, is common in languages aimed at high integrity software. Such pre/postcondition specifications are geared towards verification of code. While this specification technique has proven quite successful in the past 40 years, it has limitations when applied to API specification, particularly specification of generic interfaces.

API-oriented design and genericity is of particular importance in modern large-scale software development. In this situation, algebraic specification techniques have a significant advantage. Unlike pre/post-based specification, which deals with the inputs and outputs of one operation at a time, algebraic specification deals with the relationships between the different operations in an API, which is needed in the specification of generic APIs.

Categories and Subject Descriptors

D.2.4 [**Software Engineering**]: Software/Program Verification; F.3.1 [**Logics and Meanings of Programs**]: Specifying and Verifying and Reasoning about Programs

General Terms

Reliability, Verification, Languages

Keywords

Program specification; API specification; Generic programming; APIs; Axioms

1. INTRODUCTION

Modern interface-oriented and generics-heavy development methods [29, 35] focus on abstract APIs, rather than dealing directly with concrete data structures. In this setting, the implementation of a class will never deal directly with objects of other classes—rather, access is through a well-defined interface that hides the concrete class of each ob-

HILT 2014, October 18–21, 2014, Portland, OR, USA.
Copyright is held by the owner/author(s). Publication rights licensed to ACM.
ACM 978-1-4503-3217-0/14/10 ...$15.00.
http://dx.doi.org/10.1145/2663171.2663183.

ject. One implementation class is exchangeable for another, as long as it complies with the same interface.

Generic libraries for collection classes are prime exponents of this idea. The different collection implementations have specific requirements on the API of the elements. The collection class only accesses the elements through the API. When the API requirements are satisfied, the class provides the service expected of it. Generic programming extends this approach to any algorithm and data structure. The goal is to make the implementation as flexible as possible, stating the minimal requirements needed on the data in order to let the implementation work.

Many languages have mechanisms for syntactic requirements on generic parameters. Examples are interfaces in Java and packages in Ada. This is sufficient to ensure independently that the generic code is type correct and that the instantiation of the generic code will be type correct. In C++ the template mechanism is used for generic programming, but in itself offers no such guarantee, so every instantiation must be fully typechecked. An attempt at remedying this situation was made in the form of *concepts* [17], but the proposal was deemed to complex. Interestingly, the C++ concept proposal included *axioms* to provide semantic constraints as well as the syntactic requirements. Neither the Java nor the Ada mechanisms include any semantic constraints.

Due to the abstract nature of interfaces, semantics are more easily specified by relating the operations of the interface to each other, rather than by trying to specify the inputs and outputs of each operation separately. In particular, specifying the output of an operation may be impossible until we know which concrete data types are involved. Consider the hash and equals methods of Java [15]:

```
public int hashCode();
public boolean equals(Object other);
```

The behavior of hashCode is specified entirely by its relationship to equals: all equal objects must have the same hash value, i.e. a.equals(b) implies that a.hashCode() == b.hashCode() for all a and b. This is an *axiom*, in the algebraic specification sense. In Java, satisfying these properties is necessary in order for collections like HashMap and HashSet to work as specified.

In algebraic specification terminology, a *signature* defines the syntax of an API by listing its types and operations (with argument lists and result types). Together with a set of *axioms* describing the intended semantics, we get a complete API specification. The axioms normally take the form of universally quantified expressions in some logic. The axioms relate the different operations of the API to each other. *Models* (implementations) of a specification can be constructed by associating concrete data structures with the types, and concrete implementation code with the operations, in such a way that the axioms hold (are *satisfied*). A typical abstract data type declaration corresponds to a signature; with axioms we get an API specification; and with implementation class(es) we get one (or more) models.

In contrast, the pre/post specification technique is based on Floyd-Hoare logic, using triples of the form $\{P\}\ C\ \{Q\}$, where the postcondition Q holds after the command C, if the precondition P holds before. This is typically realized in the form of a requires or pre clause for the precondition, and an ensures or post clause for the postcondition, as seen in e.g., Eiffel [27], JML [23] or SPARK [5].

Preconditions are particularly important in specifying *partiality* – the range of valid parameters of a function. In the case of hashCode and equals above, Java enforces an implicit precondition that this != null. For Java's equals, the semantics is normally such that passing null as the argument should give the result false, hence there is no precondition on the argument.

In algebraic specifications, handling of partiality and preconditions has traditionally been inelegant, often leading to significant clutter in the axioms, see [28] for an overview. This may have lead to an impression that algebraic specifications are difficult to use in practical settings. In *guarded algebras* [20], preconditions are stated at the level of the signature (similarly to pre/post specifications), and all axioms are written on the implicit assumption that the preconditions hold. The clutter of guarding against precondition problems thus disappears, while the benefit of specifying the abstract API is retained.

In this paper we do not delve into the theory of the specification technique. Rather we contribute a practical approach to API specifications, where the axioms are written as code using assertions. This allows direct integration with unit testing systems, if the axioms are written using unit testing assertions. Such axioms should also be readily exploitable by language related proof tools, e.g., the machinery used for proving pre/post specifications. The paper shows this technique for writing axioms in Java, C++ and Ada, and relates it to the QuickCheck [8] test framework for Haskell.

The paper is organized as follows. In section 2 we motivate axioms for API specifications, and show several examples related to the Java library. Then we discuss the approach for other languages (C++, Ada, Haskell) in section 3. Section 4 discusses axioms versus pre/post specifications, followed by the issue of purity and side effects (section 5). We will also briefly discuss the background and history of specification techniques (section 6) before we conclude (section 7).

2. API SPECIFICATIONS

Specifications of APIs differ from the specification of individual functions. In APIs there are interaction effects between functions, and the specification focuses on these.

Consider the Java collection classes. These exist in many variations, but the Collection interface defines the basic properties. The method add is in the Java 7 library given the following specification[1].

[1] From http://docs.oracle.com/javase/7/docs/api/
java/util/Collection.html#add(E)

Ensures that this collection contains the specified element (optional operation). Returns true if this collection changed as a result of the call. (Returns false if this collection does not permit duplicates and already contains the specified element.)

Collections that support this operation may place limitations on what elements may be added to this collection. In particular, some collections will refuse to add null elements, and others will impose restrictions on the type of elements that may be added. Collection classes should clearly specify in their documentation any restrictions on what elements may be added.

If a collection refuses to add a particular element for any reason other than that it already contains the element, it *must* throw an exception (rather than returning false). This preserves the invariant that a collection always contains the specified element after this call returns.

This textual description subtly relates the effect of the add method to the result of calling the contains method. Further, there are many conditions which need to raise exceptions. If the collection is immutable, the add method will not be supported and must raise UnsupportedOperationException. For some precondition violations, like adding a null reference to a collection that does not allow this, the NullPointerException should be thrown. For other violations, like adding a duplicate element to a collection which does not allow this, the add method should return normally with a return value of false, not modifying the collection. Thus any method that queries the status of the collection, e.g., the size method, should not observe any difference between the two states of the collection. These properties can be written down as normal Java code[2]. The following procedure captures the specification above.

```
public static <E>
void addEnsuresCollectionContainsElement(
    Collection <E> c, E t) {
  try {
    // Records some data on current status of c.
    int size = c.size ();
    boolean contained = c.contains(t);

    // Attempt to add an element.
    if (c.add(t)) {
      // Element added to the collection .
      assertEquals( size + 1, c. size ());
    } else {
      // Element already present.
      assertTrue(contained );
      assertEquals( size , c. size ());
    }
    // Check that the element is present.
    assertTrue(c.contains(t ));
  } catch (UnsupportedOperationException
    | ClassCastException
```

[2] The Java based axioms used in this paper work with JAxT [19], an axiom based testing tool for Java. JAxT couples axioms and test data to the relevant interfaces and classes, and is integrated with JUnit through using JUnit assertions.

```
22     |  NullPointerException
       |  IllegalArgumentException
24     |  IllegalStateException  e)  {
       // OK: precondition violation indicated.

26     }
}
```

Note the interactions between methods add, contains and size. The specification is as much a description of how these methods interact, as a description of the add method itself. The interaction is somewhat overwhelmed by the code used to handle precondition situations, a problem also in regular Java code that tries to deal with all error situations.

This rather complex interaction between features and preconditions has readily been captured as Java code. We believe many API features can be specified as code, yielding several benefits.

- The axiom reads as normal code, a notation familiar to programmers.

- The axiom is executable as a parameterized unit test, and in fact here we use the JUnit assertion facility to make the claims in the axiom, hence supporting integration with unit testing tools.

- The semantics of the axiom is fully compatible with the semantics of the host language.

The latter implies that any proof tool for API specification needs to understand the programming language syntax and semantics, and *only* needs to understand the programming language's syntax and semantics since no additional specification notation is used.

We can further explore this style of axiom notation by providing specializations for a few of the cases covered above. The next two axioms are mutually exclusive and must be used for appropriate collections; the first for immutable collections where add is not supported, the second requires that the add method is implemented.

```
1  public  static  <E>
   void  add_unsupported(Collection<E> c, E t) {
3    try {
       c.add(t);
5      fail ("add() did not throw.");
     } catch (UnsupportedOperationException e) {
7      // OK: intended behavior.
     } catch (ClassCastException
9      |  NullPointerException
       |  IllegalArgumentException
11     |  IllegalStateException  e)  {
         fail ("add() throws wrong exception.");
13   }
   }

   public  static  <E>
2  void  add_supported( Collection<E> c, E t) {
     try {
4      c.add(t);
       // OK: call succeeded.
6    } catch (UnsupportedOperationException e) {
       fail ("add() is required for this class");
8    } catch (ClassCastException
         |  NullPointerException
10       |  IllegalArgumentException
```

```
       |  IllegalStateException  e)  {
12     // OK: call violated preconditions.
     }
14 }
```

The second axiom above implies that normal values added to the collection have the normal behavior described in the axiom addEnsuresCollectionContainsElement above.

A similar pattern can be used for dealing with collections that disallow, or allow, null references, respectively.

```
   public  static  <E>
2  void  add_null_invalid ( Collection <E> c) {
     try {
4      c.add( null );
       fail ("add() is required to refuse null elements.");
6    } catch (UnsupportedOperationException e) {
       fail ("add() is supposed to be implemented.");
8    } catch (NullPointerException e) {
       // OK
10   } catch (ClassCastException
         |  IllegalArgumentException
12       |  IllegalStateException  e)  {
         fail ("add() should throw NullPointerException.";
14   }
   }

1  public  static  <E>
   void  add_null_valid ( Collection <E> c) {
3    try {
       c.add( null );
5      // OK
     } catch (UnsupportedOperationException
7        |  NullPointerException
         |  ClassCastException
9        |  IllegalArgumentException  e)  {
         fail ("add() is required to accept null elements.");
11   } catch ( IllegalStateException  e) {
       // OK, maybe a buffer overflow
13   }
   }
```

Axioms written as code are generally able to deal with all situations that the programmer must handle in the code.

2.1 Generic Requirement APIs

The purpose of generic programming is to reuse algorithms and data structures by parameterizing them on types and operations, i.e., the *generic requirement API*. The meaning of the parameterized data structures and algorithms very much depend on the semantics of the generic requirement API. For instance, an algorithm for sorting data in an array, requires that the elements have a total order operation available. When implementing a hash map, a hash function compatible with the equality function are the basic requirements, implementing a matrix package requires at least a commutative ring as the element type, and so forth.

Mainstream languages supporting generic programming include Ada, C++ and Java. They all provide means for declaring *syntactic* aspects of generic requirements, possibly bundling generic arguments together in packages, templates or interfaces.

Java is an illustrative example, where the requirements for their collection classes have received extensive documenta-

73

tion in the standard library. Consider the Comparable API from Java[3].

```
interface Comparable<T> {
  int compareTo(T o);
}
```

The Comparable API is one of the standard interfaces offered by Java, and must be implemented in order to use e.g. the sorted collection classes from the Java Library. Classes that implement this interface must provide a total order via the compareTo method. This method has a number of properties. Quoting from the documentation:

> The implementer must ensure sgn(x.compareTo(y)) == -sgn(y.compareTo(x)) for all x and y. (This implies that x.compareTo(y) must throw an exception iff y.compareTo(x) throws an exception.)
>
> The implementer must also ensure that the relation is transitive: (x.compareTo(y)>0 && y.compareTo(z)>0) implies x.compareTo(z)>0.
>
> Finally, the implementer must ensure that x.compareTo(y)==0 implies that sgn(x.compareTo(z)) == sgn(y.compareTo(z)), for all z.
>
> It is strongly recommended, but not strictly required that (x.compareTo(y)==0) == (x.equals(y)).

The compareTo method combines several total comparison relations into one:

- x.compareTo(y) < 0 is $x < y$,
- x.compareTo(y) <= 0 is $x \leq y$,
- x.compareTo(y) == 0 is $x = y$,
- x.compareTo(y) >= 0 is $x \geq y$, and
- x.compareTo(y) > 0 is $x > y$.

The first property from the Java documentation states that < and >, ≤ and ≥ are duals, and also defines *symmetry* for =. The second property is *transitivity* for >, and hence for <. The third gives transitivity and *reflexivity* for =, hence these properties follow for ≤ and ≥. The *antisymmetry* of ≤ and ≥ follow from the first property and antisymmetry for int comparisons. *Connectedness* follows from compareTo being a function (it has to give a verdict for every combinations of arguments). The fourth property encourages a weak form of *congruence*, ensuring that objects that are alike using compareTo also are alike using equals. These semantic requirements can be captured as axioms in Java code.

```
public static <T extends Comparable<T>>
void prop1(T x, T y) {
  try {
    assertEquals(Math.signum(x.compareTo(y)),
        -Math.signum(y.compareTo(x)));
  } catch (RuntimeException e) {
    // OK;
  }
}

public static <T extends Comparable<T>>
```

[3]From http://docs.oracle.com/javase/7/docs/api/java/lang/Comparable.html

```
void prop2(T x, T y, T z) {
  try {
    if (x.compareTo(y) > 0 && y.compareTo(z) > 0) {
      assertTrue(x.compareTo(z) > 0);
    }
  } catch (RuntimeException e) {
    // OK;
  }
}

public static <T extends Comparable<T>>
void prop3(T x, T y, T z) {
  try {
    if (x.compareTo(y) == 0) {
      assertEquals(Math.signum(x.compareTo(z)),
          -Math.signum(y.compareTo(z)));
    }
  } catch (RuntimeException e) {
    // OK;
  }
}

public static <T extends Comparable<T>>
void prop4(T x, T y) {
  try {
    assertEquals(x.compareTo(y) == 0, x.equals(y));
  } catch (RuntimeException e) {
    // OK;
  }
}
```

The specification also makes strong statements on exceptions. The first property states that compareTo is symmetric also for exceptions. Our code-oriented style for writing axioms can deal with this.

```
public static <T extends Comparable<T>>
void strongSymmetry(T x, T y) {
  try {
    x.compareTo(y);
    y.compareTo(x);
    // OK: neither call throws an exception.
  } catch (RuntimeException e) {
    // at least one of the calls throws an exception
    try {
      x.compareTo(y);
      fail("x.compareTo(y) does not throw!");
    } catch (RuntimeException e1) {
      try {
        y.compareTo(x);
        fail("y.compareTo(x) does not throw!");
      } catch (RuntimeException e2) {
        // OK! Both calls fail symmetrically.
      }
    }
  }
}
```

This property is even more specific for comparisons with null, where another part of the specification states that since null.compareTo(x) will cause a NullPointerException, then x.compareTo(null) must also throw NullPointerException.

```
public static <T extends Comparable<T>>
void compareTo_null(T x) {
  try {
```

```
      x.compareTo(null);
5     fail ("Should throw a NullPointerException");
    } catch (NullPointerException e) {
7     // As required
    }
9 }
```

Specifying that throwing of exceptions is symmetric, or when a specific exception is to be thrown, may seem strange from a pre/postcondition viewpoint, where throwing an exception may be thought of as checking a precondition (see section 4). However, considering the generic use cases, knowing that certain exceptions are thrown in specific circumstances makes sense. When writing a sorting algorithm or binary search, the strong symmetry ensures that it does not matter for the user of the compareTo method which element is used for which argument in the call. The method will behave symmetrically with respect to throwing in general. Specifically, if a collection allow null references as elements, its algorithms can possibly be simplified since null pointer exceptions occur consistently whether the null element is used as the left or the right argument of compareTo.

2.2 API Specifications and API Enrichment

Keeping the specification logic limited to program code obviously has limitations. Many properties cannot readily be expressed due to the weakness of code as a specification logic, e.g., lack of quantifiers, no ghost variables, no modal operators etc. Yet there are interesting interplays between specification language power and API complexity: a less powerful specification language can in many cases be compensated by extending the API.

The specification of a sorting algorithm has two components: the fact that the output is sorted, and the fact that the output is a permutation of the input. The sortedness condition is readily specified in a simple logic, but the permutation condition normally requires a more powerful specification logic.

We can stick with the simpler logic by expanding the API. In addition to the sorting method, let the API also contain a function that counts the occurrences of elements in the data structure.

```
1 /** Sorts the data in situ. */
  abstract public void sort ();
3 /** Counts the number of occurrences of t. */
  abstract public int count(T t);
```

Now it becomes possible to write both the sortedness and the permutation condition in a few lines of code.

```
  public static <T extends Comparable<T>>
2 void isSorted (MyArrayList<T> list, int i) {
    if ( list . size () <= i) return ;
4   if (0 == i) return ;
    list . sort ();
6   assertTrue ( list .get( i −1).compareTo(list.get( i )) <= 0);
  }
8
  public <T extends Comparable<T>>
10 void isPermutation(MyArrayList<T> list, T t) {
    int precount = list .count(t);
12  list . sort ();
    int postcount = list .count(t);
14  assertEquals (precount, postcount);
  }
```

The first axiom states that the list is in the correct ordering for an arbitrary selected pair of neighboring indices. The second axiom ensures that for an arbitrary element, sorting the list does not change the number of times the element occurs in the list.

In our experience enlarging the API in order to simplify specifications seems to have several benefits.

- The specification becomes simpler.

- It becomes much easier to test the API as the need for test fixtures and mock objects is reduced.

- Often the richer API turns out to be more reusable than the leaner API.

These effects may be a consequence of the API becoming somewhat more complete and self contained when it is enriched in this way. On the other hand, enlarging the API induces the cost of developing the additional methods.

3. AXIOMS IN OTHER LANGUAGES

3.1 C++ Concepts and the Catsfoot Library

The failed *concepts* proposal for C++11 [17] came with builtin algebraic specification support with axiom definitions as part of the concept interface definitions. The constructs allowed fundamental algebraic concepts to be expressed and integrated with generic libraries [16].

Although the proposal was ultimately rejected, the specification features as well as most of the other features can be provided through libraries such as the Catsfoot C++ template library [2].

The following example illustrates how Catsfoot can be used to specify total orders, for any type T and associated relation Rel. Axioms are placed in specially-structured C++ classes inheriting from the Catsfoot class concept.

```
1 template <typename T, typename Rel>
  struct total_order : public concept {
```

Each concept may be generic, and have a number of requirements. In this case, we require a relation, encoded as a *functor* (class with overloaded function call operator). It should take two arguments, be callable, and return something convertible to bool:

```
  typedef concept_list <
4   is_callable <Rel(T, T)>,
    std :: is_convertible <typename is_callable<Rel(T, T)>
6                   :: result_type , bool>,
  > requirements;
```

Next come the axioms. The operator we are specifying is provided as one of the parameters (this may seem counter-intuitive, but remember that the actual relation is defined by the functor class and not the object itself, which is typically a dummy object obtained through the default constructor):

```
  static void is_antisymmetric (const T& a, const T& b,
10                  const Rel& rel) {
    if ( rel (a,b) && rel(b, a))
12    axiom_assert (a == b);
  }
14 static void is_total (const T& a, const T& b,
                  const Rel& rel) {
16   axiom_assert ( rel (a,b) || rel (b,a));
```

```
18    static void  is_transitive (const T& a, const T& b,
                                   const T& c, const Rel& rel) {
20      if ( rel (a, b) && rel(b, c))
          axiom_assert( rel (a,c));
22    }
```

Finally, the axioms are collected in a list—this allows the tooling to automatically call all axioms with randomized data when testing.

```
   AXIOMS(is_antisymmetric,
24         is_total ,
           is_transitive )
26 };
```

A sample implementation (*model*) of a total order would be the less-than-or-equals operator for integers: total_order< int, op_lt> (this instantiation checks the syntactic requirements). We can state that <= satisfies the total_order concept by specializing the verified type trait (this instantiation records the semantic intent):

```
  template <>
2 struct  verified <total_order<int, op_lt>>
      : public std :: true_type
4 {};
```

A sorting library may then state that it requires a verified total order to provide sorting.

3.2 Expressing Axioms in Ada

The same principle of encoding axioms in the Java and C++ programming languages can be applied to Ada. Below we show a generic specification of the less-than-or-equals operator, with the properties stated as assertions within procedures—one for each property.

The setup is similar to Catsfoot, specifying a type and an operation as parameters:

```
  generic
2   type T is private ;
    with  function  "<="(A, B : T) return Boolean is <>;
```

With Ada's separation of specification and body, the axioms should have descriptive names, so that the behavior is apparent from reading the specification part:

```
4 package Total_Order is
      procedure LessEq_Is_Antisymmetric(A, B : T);
6     procedure LessEq_Is_Total (A, B : T);
      procedure LessEq_Is_Transitive (A, B, C : T);
8 end Total_Order;
```

The package body provides the actual axioms, in the form of assertions:

```
   package body Total_Order is
10   procedure LessEq_Is_Antisymmetric(A, B : T) is begin
       if  A <= B and B <= A then
12       Assert(A = B, "LessEq_Is_Antisymmetric");
       end if ;
14   end;

16   procedure LessEq_Is_Total (A, B : T) is begin
       Assert(A <= B or B <= A, "LessEq_Is_Total");
18   end;

20   procedure LessEq_Is_Transitive (A, B, C : T) is begin
       if  A <= B and B <= C then
```

```
22     Assert(A <= C, "LessEq_Is_Transitive");
       end if ;
24   end;
   end Total_Order;
```

This generic description of how a less-than-or-equals operator should behave can then be reused in other specifications, such as the specification of sorted lists in the following example: First, a straight-forward description of the interface:

```
1 generic
    type Elt is private ;
3   with function "<="(A, B : Elt) return Boolean is <>;
  package Sorted_Lists  is
5   type List is private ;

7   -- insert E into L
    procedure Insert (L : in out List ; E : in Elt );
9   -- get length of L
    function Length(L : in List ) return Natural ;
11  -- get element at index I in L
    function Get(L : in List ; I : in Natural) return Elt ;
13  -- count occurrences of E in L
    function Count(L : in List ; E : in Elt) return Natural ;
```

Next, the semantics. We have split the behavior specification into two parts, Requirements and Axioms, two specially named nested packages.[4] The former is used to specify required semantics for parameters to generic packages, and the latter for specifying the behavior of subprograms provided by the package. For the requirements, we reuse Total_Order:

```
   -- specification of what we require from parameters
16 package Requirements is
     new Total_Order(T => Elt);

18
   -- specification of what we are providing
20 package Axioms is
     -- for any I1, I2,  I1 <= I2 = Get(L,I1) <= Get(L,I2)
22   procedure List_Is_Sorted (L : List ; I1, I2 : Natural);
     -- result of Count increases by one after insert
24   procedure Insert_Increases_Count (L : List ; E : Elt );
     -- result of Length increases by one after insert
26   procedure Insert_Increases_Length (L : List ; E : Elt );
   end Axioms;
28 private
   -- ...
30 end Sorted_Lists ;
```

Code for the axioms is provided in the package body, for example:

```
   -- sample axiom implementation
2  procedure List_Is_Sorted (L : List ; I1, I2 : Natural) is
     N : Natural := Length(L);
4    X1 : Natural := I1 mod N;
     X2 : Natural := I2 mod N;
6  begin
     Assert ((X1 <= X2) = (Get(L, X1) <= Get(L, X2)));
8  end;
```

Parameter behavior and provided behavior can then be tested by instantiating the generic package and calling the axiom procedures with representative data. Tool assistance

---

[4] This format is chosen for technical reasons related to the Ada package system.

may be helpful for this—in Java and C++, axioms can be tested automatically with random data, using reflection or meta-programming (respectively). A verification or testing tool should be able to find the associated algebraic specification by looking into the nested Requirements and Axioms packages.

The package organization shown here would likely not be supported in SPARK, due to limitations in dealing with generics [34]. Since several SPARK features may be helpful (including preconditions and dependencies), finding a SPARK-compatible axiom scheme would be useful.

3.3 Haskell and QuickCheck

QuickCheck [8] is a popular testing library for Haskell based on algebraic specification. Axioms are normal Haskell boolean functions (called *properties*), and QuickCheck can automatically determine appropriate arguments and call the functions with randomly generated data. For example, the less-than-or-equals specification looks like this (note that forward implication is, confusingly, written with a backwards arrow $<=$):

```
propLessEqIsAntisymmetric a b =
    (a <= b && b <= a) <= (a == b)

propLessEqIsTotal a b =
    a <= b || b <= a

propLessEqIsTransitive a b c =
    (a <= b && b <= c) <= (a <= c)
```

We can try the tests on various implementations, for example for integers and characters:

```
> quickCheck (propLessEqIsTotal :: Int−>Int−>Bool)
+++ OK, passed 100 tests.
> quickCheck (propLessEqIsTotal :: Char−>Char−>Bool)
+++ OK, passed 100 tests.
```

In this case, the properties are tied to the *type class* Ord of ordered types, which also contains other ordering operations, min/max operations and equality. A QuickCheck specification library should provide properties for the complete set of operations.

Properties and type classes are fully decoupled in Haskell, unlike how concepts in JAxT and Catsfoot (and our sketched Ada example) combine an interface with a specification. This means that building more complex specification from simpler ones becomes somewhat more difficult. For example, to deal with the sorted list which requires an element type with a less-than-or-equals operator, we would specify Ord as the type of elements (a purely syntactic requirement). Checking conformance with the axioms requires finding each instantiation and running QuickCheck on the appropriate properties.

4. API AND PRE/POST SPECIFICATIONS

Frameworks that rely solely on pre/post specification have problems capturing the properties of *Comparable*.

The JML [23] specification below[5] exposes these differences. It presents the compareTo example used in subsection 2.1 using pre/post specifications. The specification was written for an older, pre-generic version of Java, so needs to

deal with dynamic typing of the second argument. It is also evident that the specification considers being called with null as a precondition violation, rather than being related to throwing a specific exception.

```
Specifications : pure
  public behavior
    requires o != null;
    ensures (* \result is negative
        if this is "less than" o *);
    ensures (* \result is 0 if this is "equal to" o *);
    ensures (* \result is positive
        if this is "greater than" o *);
    signals_only ClassCastException;
    signals (ClassCastException) (* ... *);
  also
  public behavior
    requires o != null &&
        o instanceof Comparable;
    ensures this .definedComparison((Comparable)o,this);
    ensures o == this ==> \result == 0;
    ensures this .sgn(\ result ) ==
        −this.sgn((( Comparable)o).compareTo(this));
    signals (ClassCastException)
        ! this .definedComparison((Comparable)o,this);
int compareTo(non_null Object o);
```

This specification is more monolithic than the algebraic approach. It is monolithic in the sense that all aspects of the description of the method is included, as opposed to in the axiom case where the specification is composed from individual axioms, each dealing with separate aspects of the library specification. Further, we see that the JML specification uses a more powerful logic than the Java only specification of axioms, e.g., the specification language has a built in equality. Yet there are important shortcomings in this specification: the transitivity property (property 2) is missing, so is property 3. Both of these properties relate three variables, one more than provided as arguments to the function call, going beyond what pre/post easily can express.

JML does have features for dealing with this, through universally quantified assertions at the class level, corresponding to axioms in the algebraic sense—which is how the missing properties are expessed in JML.

In Spec# [6], the specification of IComparable[6] deals only with data flow and purity, and does not attempt to specify the full behavior. This seems to be common for Spec# interface specification, and in general Spec# seems focused on specifying purity, object invariants, data flow and exception behavior.

We believe this difference in capturing API properties is archetypal for the two techniques.

- Algebraic specifications are composed of collections of axioms, each relating one or more operations with an unlimited use of free variables.

  They may be incomplete, i.e., important axioms may be missing from the current specification, yet the specification is still useful.

  This encourages modularity and reuse of specification components.

---

[5]From http://www.eecs.ucf.edu/~leavens/
JML-release/specs/java/lang/Comparable.spec

[6]From https://specsharp.codeplex.com/
SourceControl/latest#SpecSharp/Samples/
OutOfBandContracts/Mscorlib/System.IComparable.ssc

- Pre/post specifications are extremal points, the first and the last, of assertions for an algorithm. Assertions play important roles in the verification of algorithms, thus making pre/post natural resources for verification of algorithms.

  In order to meet this goal, pre/post specifications tend to be monolithic and should encompass all relevant properties. They often need quite powerful specification logics to express properties.

These differences are amplified by the different goals: on the one side API specifications with axioms for unit testing, on the other specifications for proving algorithms correct.

However, there are many interesting properties that are less straight-forward to specify algebraically or at the API level. We have already mentioned how preconditions are necessary also in algebraic specification. Tools like JML, Spec#, SPARK and Dafny [24] support a number of such properties, e.g., termination, coarse or fine grained data modification, data dependency between inputs and outputs, data ownership, and algorithm-level assertions.

4.1 API Specifications Subsume Pre/Post Specifications

Using the same specification logic for axioms as for pre/post specifications, we find that axioms subsume pre/post specifications. Assume we have a pre/post specification of the following form in a suitable specification logic.

```
method m(...)
  requires Pre;
  ensures Post;
```

We can write this as an axiom in the following way.

```
axiom PrePost (...) {
  if ( ! Pre ) return;
  call m (...);
  assertTrue( Post );
}
```

The if statement checks for precondition violations in the test data, ensuring that the axiom does not commit the method to any specific behavior in such cases. After calling the method, the post condition is asserted to hold. Picking up the pre and postconditions in idioms like this should be straight-forward. Allowing the axioms to use the same specification power as the pre/post specifications, e.g., local quantifiers and ghost variables, we find that pre/post specifications are a special case of axioms.

Tools that support pre/post specifications often include features beyond just Pre and Post. For instance, Dafny [24] has a decreases clause for attaching termination related information to procedures. Such features are not captured by the translation into axioms sketched above.

5. PURITY AND MUTABILITY

A particular problem that arises when mixing specifications with code, is that of what happens when operations have side effects—i.e., they modify or use global data, access the outside world, or change the objects passed as arguments.

This creates a reasoning problem: *how do you reason about a series of assertions/axioms, if each assertion/axiom may have unknown side effects?*—and a programming problem: *what semantic effect does turning assertion checking on or off have if the assertions can have side effects (and similar for axiom checking)?*

Solutions to this problem include forbidding calls to arbitrary functions from specifications (e.g., as in ESC/Java [11]); introduce a notion of purity, and allow only calls to known pure functions (e.g., as in JML); tell the programmer sternly to avoid using non-pure functions and hope for the best (e.g., as in Eiffel).

In Spec# this problem is dealt with through a notion of *observational purity* [7], where side effects are allowed only as long as they can not be observed by the callers. A static analysis tool is available to determine the property.

For practical use in testing, side-effects are not a huge concern. It mostly affects the way axioms are written. The test framework can take care of ensuring that each axiom is evaluated in a fresh environment, and instantiated with suitable (perhaps aged) objects for its universally quantified variables. Some algebraic-style testing frameworks, such as ASTOOT [9], allows axioms with OO notation, and can also deal with side-effects.

The experimental Magnolia language [4] deals with the side-effect issue by avoiding aliasing (hence no globals) and mapping from procedures (which are allowed to have effects on the arguments) to functions (which are strictly pure). Side effects on the outside world are dealt with through updates on a 'world' object. Each procedure is mapped to a set of functions—one function for each possible output / updated argument of the procedure. Specifications (which are algebraic-style and integrated into the language) are written using functions only, and reasoning happens at the level of pure functions. Implementations, however, may be provided in the form of procedures, and through a process of *mutification* pure function-oriented code is rewritten to use procedures with in-place updates of arguments.

6. HISTORICAL BACKGROUND

Both pre/post specifications [12, 21] and algebraic specifications [26] have a long history in computer science.

Pre/post specifications are a natural extension of assertions used for proving and understanding algorithms. An assertion captures properties of the state of a program, e.g., a loop invariant. The last assertion in a procedure defines its postcondition: what holds when the procedure finishes. Symmetrically, the first assertion in the procedure defines its precondition: what needs to hold in order for the procedure to work properly. Already in the 1970s, languages like Gypsy [1], Euclid [30], CLU [25] and Alphard [33] picked up these ideas. Some, including Euclid and CLU, left the specification syntax and processing to external tools, while Alphard made it directly part of the language. Pre/post specifications were popularized as "design by contract" in Eiffel [27], and have gained popularity in recent languages as Spec# [6], JML [23] and Ada [36] with the SPARK [5] tool set for proving correctness.

CLU and Alphard also pioneered the use of abstract data types. ADTs have an internal implementation, a model, and an external API (in current terminology). Algebraic specifications focus on the interaction between functions, making them natural for specifying APIs [26]. Early work tied algebraic specifications closely to software, e.g., [13] using axioms as test oracles. The research on algebraic specifications soon took on a more mathematical approach, leading to a focus on initial specifications [14, 10]. These are good for building theoretical models, but only have an indirect relationship to software. The LARCH specification language [18] makes this explicit by having a separate algebraic specification language, though not with initial semantics, and explicit programming specific interface languages. Extended ML [31] provided a tight integration between an algebraic specification language and the programming language ML. Although positive experiences were reported [32], there were problems in integrating the semantics of the specifications and of ML.

The Tecton system [22] similarly attempted to leverage algebraic specification; those experiences were later used in the design of C++ concepts [17]—which, if successful, would have provided an industrial-strength language with algebraic specification support. Although axioms played little role in the proposed standard—compilers were for the most part supposed to ignore them, apart from basic syntax and type checking—several initiative attempted to exploit the specifications for optimization [37, 16, 3] and testing [3].

7. CONCLUSIONS

We have discussed the specification of generic APIs and how postconditions fail to deal with this case. Instead, we argue that APIs should be specified through algebraic specification, with axioms that relate the operations of the API to each other. Preconditions still have an important role to play in such specifications, for specifying constraints on arguments—guarded algebras provide a systematic approach to dealing with this.

Though our examples of generic API specifications are primarily related to collection classes, there are similar needs in other domains, e.g., in generic linear algebra codes [16].

An API may be implemented many times. A useful specification should cover all such implementations, and should be useful in determining the correctness of such implementations. This requires a tight integration between the notation and semantics of the specification language and the programming language. Such an integration is readily achieved when axioms are written as tests in the programming language. This provides an immediate approach to using algebraic style axioms for APIs in a high integrity setting.

Proof tools based on pre/post specifications have made huge improvements over that past few decades, so much so that we are approaching the goal of verifying realistic applications. The recent success of such tools gives a vision for developing similar automated proof tools for algebraic style specifications of APIs and the related implementations, possibly on top of existing tools for pre/post specifications.

Tools for proving generic programs seem to be lacking, as up to date tools such as SPARK or Dafny cannot tackle this when requirements on the generic API need to be taken into account. They are however able to prove the correctness of instantiated generic code.

Assertions and invariants in general are useful for reasoning about algorithms and concrete code—regardless of how APIs are specified. The success of assertion-based frameworks such as JML and SPARK are a testament to this.

Acknowledgments

This research is partially financed by the Research Council of Norway, under the DMPL project. Thanks to Eivind Jahren for help in understanding Haskell.

8. REFERENCES

[1] A. L. Ambler, D. I. Good, J. C. Browne, W. F. Burger, R. M. Cohen, C. G. Hoch, and R. E. Wells. Gypsy: A language for specification and implementation of verifiable programs. In *Proceedings of an ACM conference on Language design for reliable software*, pages 1–10, New York, NY, USA, 1977. ACM.

[2] A. H. Bagge, V. David, and M. Haveraaen. Testing with axioms in C++ 2011. *Journal of Object Technology*, 10:10:1–32, 2011.

[3] A. H. Bagge and M. Haveraaen. Axiom-based transformations: Optimisation and testing. In J. J. Vinju and A. Johnstone, editors, *Eighth Workshop on Language Descriptions, Tools and Applications (LDTA 2008)*, volume 238 of *Electronic Notes in Theoretical Computer Science*, pages 17–33, Budapest, Hungary, 2009. Elsevier.

[4] A. H. Bagge and M. Haveraaen. Interfacing concepts: Why declaration style shouldn't matter. In T. Ekman and J. J. Vinju, editors, *Proceedings of the Ninth Workshop on Language Descriptions, Tools and Applications (LDTA '09)*, volume 253 of *Electronic Notes in Theoretical Computer Science*, pages 37–50, York, UK, 2010. Elsevier.

[5] J. Barnes. *SPARK – The Proven Approach to High Integrity Software*. Altran Praxis Ltd, 2012.

[6] M. Barnett, K. R. M. Leino, and W. Schulte. The Spec# programming system: An overview. In G. Barthe, L. Burdy, M. Huisman, J.-L. Lanet, and T. Muntean, editors, *Proceedings of Construction and Analysis of Safe, Secure, and Interoperable Smart Devices (CASSIS 2004)*, volume 3362 of *Lecture Notes in Computer Science*, pages 49–69. Springer-Verlag, 2005.

[7] M. Barnett, D. A. Naumann, W. Schulte, and Q. Sun. 99.44% pure: Useful abstractions in specifications. In *6th Workshop on Formal Techniques for Java-like Programs (FTfJP'2004)*, 2004.

[8] K. Claessen and J. Hughes. QuickCheck: A lightweight tool for random testing of Haskell programs. In *ICFP '00: Proceedings of the fifth ACM SIGPLAN international conference on Functional programming*, pages 268–279, New York, NY, USA, 2000. ACM Press.

[9] R.-K. Doong and P. G. Frankl. The ASTOOT approach to testing object-oriented programs. *ACM Trans. Softw. Eng. Methodol.*, 3(2):101–130, 1994.

[10] H. Ehrig and B. Mahr. *Fundamentals of Algebraic Specification 1: Equations und Initial Semantics*, volume 6 of *EATCS Monographs on Theoretical Computer Science*. Springer, 1985.

[11] C. Flanagan, K. R. M. Leino, M. Lillibridge, G. Nelson, J. B. Saxe, and R. Stata. Extended static checking for java. In *Proceedings of the ACM SIGPLAN 2002 Conference on Programming Language Design and Implementation*, PLDI '02, pages 234–245, New York, NY, USA, 2002. ACM.

[12] R. W. Floyd. Assigning meanings to programs. In *Mathematical Aspects of Computer Science*, volume 19 of *Proceedings of Symposia in Applied Mathematics*, pages 19–32. American Mathematical Society, 1967.

[13] J. D. Gannon, P. R. McMullin, and R. G. Hamlet. Data-abstraction implementation, specification, and testing. *ACM Trans. Program. Lang. Syst.*, 3(3):211–223, 1981.

[14] J. Goguen, J. Thatcher, and E. Wagner. An initial algebra approach to the specification, correctness and implementation of abstract data types. In R. Yeh, editor, *Current Trends in Programming Methodology*, volume 4, pages 80–149. Prentice Hall, 1978.

[15] J. Gosling, B. Joy, G. Steele, and G. Bracha. *Java^TM Language Specification, The (3rd Edition)*. Addison-Wesley Professional, 2005.

[16] P. Gottschling and A. Lumsdaine. Integrating semantics and compilation: Using C++ concepts to develop robust and efficient reusable libraries. In Y. Smaragdakis and J. G. Siek, editors, *GPCE*, pages 67–76. ACM, 2008.

[17] D. Gregor, J. Järvi, J. Siek, B. Stroustrup, G. Dos Reis, and A. Lumsdaine. Concepts: linguistic support for generic programming in C++. In *OOPSLA '06: Proceedings of the 21st annual ACM SIGPLAN conference on Object-oriented programming systems, languages, and applications*, pages 291–310, New York, NY, USA, 2006. ACM.

[18] J. V. Guttag, J. J. Horning, and J. M. Wing. The Larch family of specification languages. *IEEE Softw.*, 2(5):24–36, 1985.

[19] M. Haveraaen and K. T. Kalleberg. JAxT and JDI: the simplicity of JUnit applied to axioms and data invariants. In *OOPSLA Companion '08: Companion to the 23rd ACM SIGPLAN conference on Object-oriented programming systems languages and applications*, pages 731–732, New York, NY, USA, 2008. ACM.

[20] M. Haveraaen and E. G. Wagner. Guarded algebras: Disguising partiality so you won't know whether it's there. In *Recent Trends In Algebraic Development Techniques*, volume 1827 of *Lecture Notes in Computer Science*, pages 3–11. Springer-Verlag, 2000.

[21] C. A. R. Hoare. An axiomatic basis for computer programming. *Commun. ACM*, 12(10):576–580, 1969.

[22] D. Kapur, D. R. Musser, and A. A. Stepanov. Tecton: A language for manipulating generic objects. In J. Staunstrup, editor, *Program Specification, Proceedings of a Workshop*, Lecture Notes in Computer Science, pages 402–414, Aarhus, Denmark, Aug. 1981. Springer-Verlag.

[23] G. T. Leavens, A. L. Baker, and C. Ruby. Preliminary design of JML: A behavioral interface specification language for Java. *SIGSOFT Software Engineering Notes*, 31(3):1–38, 2006.

[24] K. R. M. Leino. Dafny: An automatic program verifier for functional correctness. In E. M. Clarke and A. Voronkov, editors, *Logic for Programming, Artificial Intelligence, and Reasoning - 16th International Conference, LPAR-16, Dakar, Senegal, April 25-May 1, 2010, Revised Selected Papers*, volume 6355 of *Lecture Notes in Computer Science*, pages 348–370. Springer, 2010.

[25] B. Liskov, R. R. Atkinson, T. Bloom, J. E. B. Moss, J. C. Schaffert, R. Scheifler, and A. Snyder. *CLU Reference Manual*, volume 114 of *Lecture Notes in Computer Science*. Springer-Verlag, 1981.

[26] B. Liskov and S. Zilles. Specification techniques for data abstractions. In *Proceedings of the international conference on Reliable software*, pages 72–87, New York, NY, USA, 1975. ACM.

[27] B. Meyer. *Eiffel: The language*. Prentice-Hall, Inc., Upper Saddle River, NJ, USA, 1992.

[28] P. D. Mosses. The use of sorts in algebraic specifications. In M. Bidoit and C. Choppy, editors, *COMPASS/ADT*, volume 655 of *Lecture Notes in Computer Science*, pages 66–92. Springer, 1991.

[29] D. R. Musser and A. A. Stepanov. Generic programming. In P. M. Gianni, editor, *Symbolic and Algebraic Computation, International Symposium ISSAC'88, Rome, Italy, July 4-8, 1988, Proceedings*, volume 358 of *Lecture Notes in Computer Science*, pages 13–25. Springer, 1988.

[30] G. J. Popek, J. J. Horning, B. W. Lampson, J. G. Mitchell, and R. L. London. Notes on the design of Euclid. In *Proceedings of an ACM conference on Language design for reliable software*, pages 11–18, 1977.

[31] D. Sannella and A. Tarlecki. Extended ML: An institution-independent framework for formal program development. In *Proceedings of the Tutorial and Workshop on Category Theory and Computer Programming*, pages 364–389, London, UK, 1986. Springer-Verlag.

[32] D. Sannella and A. Tarlecki. Algebraic methods for specification and formal development of programs. *ACM Comput. Surv.*, page 10, 1999.

[33] M. Shaw, W. A. Wulf, and R. L. London. Abstraction and verification in Alphard: Defining and specifying iteration and generators. *Commun. ACM*, 20(8):553–564, 1977.

[34] SPARK Team. SPARK Generics – A User View. Technical Report S.P0468.42.25, Altran, January 2012. Draft.

[35] A. Stepanov and P. McJones. *Elements of Programming*. Addison-Wesley Professional, 1st edition, 2009.

[36] S. T. Taft, R. A. Duff, R. Brukardt, E. Plödereder, P. Leroy, and E. Schonberg. *Ada 2012 Reference Manual. Language and Standard Libraries - International Standard ISO/IEC 8652/2012 (E)*, volume 8339 of *Lecture Notes in Computer Science*. Springer, 2013.

[37] X. Tang and J. Järvi. Concept-based optimization. In *LCSD '07: Proceedings of the 2007 Symposium on Library-Centric Software Design*, pages 97–108, New York, NY, USA, 2007. ACM.

A Framework for Model Checking UDP Network Programs with Java Pathfinder

William Rathje
University of Puget Sound
1500 N Warner
Tacoma, Washington 98416
brathje@pugetsound.edu

Brad Richards
University of Puget Sound
1500 N Warner
Tacoma, Washington 98416
brichards@pugetsound.edu

ABSTRACT

Complex asynchronous, distributed systems could benefit significantly from model checking, but model checking programs do not natively support verification of distributed software. Several frameworks have been developed recently that apply model checking to networked software, but none of these frameworks support complete modeling of programs that use the User Datagram Protocol (UDP). This paper presents the first framework to model realistic rather than ideal UDP network operations using Java Pathfinder, and describes its use in verifying a distributed UDP-based application.

Categories and Subject Descriptors

D.2.4 [**Software Engineering**]: Software/Program Verification—*Model checking*

Keywords

Model Checking; Java Pathfinder; UDP Networks

1. INTRODUCTION

Model checking is a software verification technique that involves searching every execution path of a program to determine if certain correctness properties always hold. It is particularly useful for safety-critical systems where all possible executions must be systematically verified to ensure that the software will never fail, and it has resultantly been used to successfully verify mission-critical embedded systems like airplane flight software and NASA spacecraft control systems [5].

Model checkers have been developed to verify either an abstracted model of a software program or the software program itself. The latter method is particularly convenient because it avoids the need to develop a separate program model for model checking, and it avoids errors introduced in the process of developing a separate and simplified

model. Model checking systems such as SPIN verify abstracted, formal models of systems (in the case of SPIN, written in the PROMELA language). More recent efforts have developed software models directly from implementation code. The most commonly used system for directly verifying implementation-level code is NASA's Java Pathfinder (JPF) [6]. JPF translates Java code into SPIN's PROMELA code and then verifies the PROMELA model. JPF does not currently provide support for Java's networking packages, including the User Datagram Protocol (UDP) classes `DatagramPacket` and `DatagramSocket`, or the TCP/IP packages `Socket` and `ServerSocket`, although a recent extension is being developed for TCP networks only [11].

Model checking is widely used in verifying asynchronous software systems, where traditional verification techniques such as unit and boundary testing often fail to identify potential error states such as deadlocks and race conditions. Most safety and data-critical systems are networked, and distributed systems spread across a network are asynchronous. The safety-critical and highly asynchronous nature of distributed, networked systems makes model checking tools for networked programs particularly desirable. Unfortunately, networked systems are particularly challenging to model check because:

1. Their execution state space and the number of properties, such as packet loss and corruption, that must be simulated in their models is extremely large relative to non-distributed systems [7].

2. Model checking relies on backtracking when identifying errors, and backtracking involves re-executing program operations. In a networked system, these re-executions can involve transmissions on the network. The state of other clients on the network will have changed by the time the model checker backtracks, which will invalidate the model checking process [2].

Several frameworks have been developed recently that address these issues and apply model checking to networked software. However, none of these frameworks support complete modeling of programs that use the User Datagram Protocol. This paper presents the first framework to model realistic rather than ideal interactions of UDP operations using JPF.

2. RELATED WORK

Recent frameworks for model checking networked programs fall into one of two categories:

1. Process centralization: Frameworks using process centralization convert processes spread across a network into threads, which are then executed within a single process. Network implementations are replaced with simplified stubs, which simulate network operations locally.

2. IO caching: IO caching involves model checking a single process while caching the states of other processes, which can then be restored during backtracking.

2.1 Process Centralization

Process centralization involves converting a multi-process program into a single-process program by wrapping separate processes, like client and server processes, as threads that can be executed in one process. This resolves the backtracking problem because backtracking no longer involves retrieving interactions across a network.

Stoller and Liu [13] outline three transformations for model checking distributed Java programs that circumvent the lack of support in current model checkers for verifying distributed systems. The three transformations are: 1) centralizing distributed processes such that separate processes executed across the network are wrapped as threads and executed in a single multi-threaded process 2) converting methods executed remotely into 'stub' methods that can be executed locally, and 3) developing simulated encryption implementations if the networked system incorporates encryption. Centralizing processes into a single threaded process avoids the backtracking problem described previously, while local 'stub' methods can be simplified to avoid the problem of simulating the complexity of an entire network.

Artho and Garoche have developed a framework [1] for centralizing distributed programs using TCP/IP for model checking software. They list developing extensions for UDP datagrams as future work. Barlas and Bultan have produced a framework, "NetStub," [4] for centralization of both TCP/IP and simplified UDP network software. It replaces the entire `java.net` package with method stubs appropriate for centralized model checking. NetStub is limited to modeling "ideal" networks only, which do not feature packet loss, reordering, or corruption. The authors cite modeling these features of non-ideal networks as future work.

Unfortunately, UDP networks are inherently unreliable. Transmission speed comes at the expense of potential message corruption, loss, and reordering. In order to verify that UDP network code can accommodate all possible use cases, UDP simulation frameworks must simulate this packet loss, reordering, and corruption. Although NetStub was published in 2007 and called for simulation of imperfect networks, to date there has been no progress toward developing frameworks for model checking networks with simulated packet loss, reordering, and corruption. This gap poses significant problems for efforts to model check UDP programs.

2.2 IO Caching

Besides process centralization, caching techniques have been used to model check networking software. These techniques have never been applied to UDP-based network programs. Caching techniques solve the backtracking problem laid out above by caching the state of a distributed system so that it may be retrieved later. As with process centralization, the model checker still verifies only one process, but outside processes are executed and their states are cached.

Artho et al. develop a system for model checking networked systems using IO caching [2, 3]. They implement the system for JPF: Net IO-Cache is available for model checking TCP/IP network programs with JPF. They note that while the framework only works for TCP/IP network programs, they believe the software can be extended for UDP network implementations. To date, there have been no extensions released for UDP network-based programs.

The caching approach benefits from checking distributed code without first simplifying network interactions to an abstract model, which is required for the stub approach. As Artho et al. notes, stubs that oversimplify their model of the original application code can result in erroneous modeling. Stub-based approaches are also generally more difficult to scale than cache-based approaches because they require modeling all interacting processes instead of just one [3].

On the other hand, there are advantages to using process centralization over cache-based approaches. Barlas and Bulton note that modeling a network does not require modeling all of its components, such as router implementations or packet formats, and doing so can lead to state space explosion [4]. An additional limitation of the caching approach is that it can only verify one distributed process, whereas the centralization approach verifies all processes in a distributed system [3]. As a result, caching methods do not provide full coverage of a distributed program.

Moreover, extending a stub-based centralized network framework such that it supports unreliable UDP transmissions (message loss, reordering, and corruption) is fairly straightforward. Because of its superior testing coverage and the ease with which we can extend previous approaches, we use a centralization/stub approach rather than a cache-based approach for model checking realistic UDP network programs.

3. SUPPORTING UNRELIABLE MESSAGE TRANSMISSION

Existing stub-based frameworks only model idealized TCP/IP and UDP network programs. While the TCP/IP protocol ensures reliable message transmission and can be tested effectively with an idealized network model, a UDP-based program must be able to handle unreliable message transmissions. UDP programs cannot be effectively checked without being tested against simulated message loss, reordering, and corruption.

Fortunately, extending stub-based frameworks to implement message loss, reordering, and corruption is relatively straightforward. Stub messages for sending messages must be made nondeterministic such that messages are sent and ordered at random, and all possible transmission cases, both correct and incorrect, are checked. We develop lightweight stubs in JPF that send and order messages at random. These stubs use JPF's `Verify` class, which includes methods for getting every possible random value and then checking one-by-one that each value leads to correct program executions.

4. FRAMEWORK

The framework is composed of two layers. First, there is a process centralization layer that takes user-defined processes to be verified and wraps them as threads. Second, there is a set of stub classes that replace the key classes and methods of `java.net` used for UDP operations.

The process-centralization layer requires some manual implementation so that it can call appropriate user-defined processes in the system under test (SUT). The changes are minimal, and involve inserting appropriate calls to the main methods of processes into the SUT. Unlike the process-centralization layer, the stub classes do not require any manual implementation by the user.

Stub classes are modeled after NetStub's architecture. Replacement stub classes are simply named after classes in the `java.net` package. User-defined code imports these classes instead of those from `java.net`.

4.1 Process Centralization

Process centralization is accomplished using the implementation strategy laid out in [1]. The centralization classes are derived from that paper and are described briefly below.

4.1.1 Centralized Process

CentralizedProcess is a java class modeled directly after that presented in Artho and Garoche [1]. It subclasses `Thread` and adds a process id variable for tracking processes by number.

4.1.2 Process Startup

`ProcessStartup` is the class that centralizes all processes in the distributed system provided by the user to be verified. It provides one main method that calls each individual process's main method within a separate thread. Processes are initialized as threads using the approach presented in Artho and Garoche [1]. Process initialization is straightforward: processes are launched individually using the following code (adapted from code first presented in Figure 1 of Artho and Garoche's paper), which wraps them in threads:

```
Thread t3 = new CentralizedProcess(2)
{
  public void run()
  {
    Sender.main(null);
  }
};
t3.start();
```

Unlike in NetStub, where users must write their own program drivers in order to wrap distributed processes as threads, this mechanism involves simply inserting calls to user-defined application code into the `ProcessStartup` class. Future work includes further automating this process.

Inter-thread communication is enabled via a static queue of type `DatagramPacket` (described below) that holds all packet transmissions. This queue is available for sockets to access concurrently and models the main network channel.

4.2 Stub Classes

We developed stub classes to simulate the operations of several key UDP networking classes in the `java.net` package.

4.2.1 DatagramPacket

`DatagramPacket` provides a replacement stub for the class in `java.net`. It replaces fields and methods with its own. It is primarily used to support `DatagramSocket`.

4.2.2 DatgramSocket

`DatagramSocket` is a stub providing functionality for UDP sockets. It accesses the static queue initialized in `ProcessStartup`, and sends or receives `DatagramPackets`. The `send(DatagramPacket p)` method includes the conditional `Verify.randomBool()` used to determine whether or not to continue the send operation. Discontinuing the send operation simulates packet loss. In a JPF verification run, the method will test all possible combinations of packet loss and transmission. (In this case, there are only two possibilities: the packet is either lost or it is transmitted.)

If `Verify.randomBool()` returns true, the send method will continue execution. If the queue is empty, it will add the `DatagramPacket p` to the queue. If the queue is not empty, it will insert `p` at `Verify.randomBool(queue.size())`. This operation makes JPF place the packet at all available locations in the queue, which simulates packet reordering on an unreliable channel.

The other key method in this class, `send(DatagramPacket p)`, polls the queue and places the contents in packet `p`. It blocks if the queue is empty. This simulates the functionality of the method provided in the `java.net` package.

4.2.3 InetAddress, InetSocketAddress, and Exception Classes

The remaining classes, like `DatagramPacket`, provide replacement stubs for functionality found in `java.net`. Providing these stubs required rewriting networking exception handlers and classes providing support for IP addresses. Most of these simply duplicate the functionality provided in `java.net`.

5. EXPERIMENTS

We apply our UDP model checking framework directly to a large, highly scalable, distributed application: The RF package is a software-based simulation of a wireless transmission system that has been in use for over a decade [9, 10, 8]. It simulates wireless network transmissions on a wired network by broadcasting short sequences of UDP packets in place of the simulated wireless transmissions. In addition to routines for transmitting and receiving simulated wireless broadcasts, the RF package includes status routines for monitoring the state of the simulated radio channel. Collisions between simultaneous user-level transmissions are detected, and the simulated packets involved in the collision are dropped. The system has been used primarily in networking courses, where students develop software implementations of systems like 802.11. It is imperative that RF is free from subtle logic bugs and models collisions correctly so that students using the package can treat it as an accurate simulation of a real broadcast-based system. The need for consistently accurate performance combined with the parallelism used in RF makes model checking an appropriate technique for verifying the software, and the framework developed in this paper makes model checking the UDP functionality in the RF package possible.

Experiments were conducted on a Macbook Pro with 16 GB of memory and four cores running at 2.3 GHz. The computer ran OS X 10.9.3.

5.1 Modifications to RF for Model Checking

RF is a single java class. It provides an interface for transmitting and receiving packets as well as checking whether the UDP transmission channel is in use.

A small number of simplifications to the RF class were required to enable model checking with our framework. RF implements a millisecond timer to detect and report the time of packet collisions. Because JPF attempts to verify all possible combinations of floating point values, retaining the timer results in too many states to check. Most model checking systems, including SPIN, do not provide mechanisms for verifying timing operations because they lead to state space explosion problems. Instead, it is enough to determine that the application software provides an appropriate response in timeout scenarios. In RF, timeout situations occur when the channel is waiting for a final UDP packet, corresponding to a simulated wireless transmission, that is lost and thus never arrives. Removing the timer removes this error check. In an actual execution scenario, a timer would be necessary to catch this class of errors.

The state space becomes similarly unmanageable with RF's existing wireless packet conversion approach. RF simulates a single simulated transmission with a sequence of 10 UDP transmissions – both to intentionally slow the simulated transmission rate and to allow detection of simultaneous wireless transmissions. (Interleaving of UDP packets from multiple hosts implies a collision.) This is too much to check with JPF. Using a sequence of two or three UDP packets for each simulated transmission, however, is enough to check all program properties without encountering the same state space explosion. is a single java class. It provides an interface for transmitting and receiving packets as well as checking whether the UDP transmission channel is in use.

5.2 Sender, Listener, and MAC Layer

We verify RF using three java test classes generated to perform simple network operations. These classes are Sender, Listener, and MACLayer. MACLayer provides an interface for interacting with RF's transmit and receive methods. Sender and Listener share a single instance of the MACLayer class. Sender transmits a byte array of data along the network channel by calling the transmit method in MACLayer and then exits. Listener repeatedly calls the receive method in MACLayer until it received a non-empty packet. It then exits.

5.3 Results

The framework was able to verify up to three threads running simultaneously, corresponding to a system with three simulated wireless hosts, before throwing out of memory errors. In comparison, NetStub's verification of the peer-to-peer system FreePastry with two UDP peers produced out-of-memory errors, requiring the use of a modified approach of saving and replaying states for verifying the UDP application. The figure below shows the execution times and states generated for one, two, and three Sender threads running simultaneously to provide a metric for performance. Performance is comparable to that reported in the NetStub paper on large applications.

We also ran verifications with two Sender threads and one Listener thread. JPF verification runs succeeded (there were no deadlocks or exceptions identified).

Table 1: Verification performance when using our UDP stub framework to verify RF.

Threads	Time	New States	Depth
1	0:01	1779	121
2	0:49	276100	252
3	48:42	5871872	342

6. CONCLUSION

We present the first JPF extension framework offering support for model checking programs with unreliable UDP network operations. We demonstrate that unreliable channel behavior can be simulated using straightforward calls to JPF's Verify routines, and use our new framework to verify the behavior of a large, distributed application making use of UDP communication routines. Future work includes exploiting search optimizations in Java Pathfinder to attempt the verification of more threads, integrating the framework with existing TCP/IP solutions, and expanding the framework to include more elements of the java.net package. We also plan to use the framework to verify more UDP software programs.

7. REFERENCES

[1] C. Artho and P. Garoche. Accurate centralization for applying model checking on networked applications. In *Automated Software Engineering*, pages 177–188. IEEE, 2006.

[2] C. Artho, Leungwattanakit, W., M. Hagiya, and Y. Tanabe. Efficient model checking of networked applications. *Objects, Components, Models and Patterns*, pages 22–40, 2008.

[3] C. Artho, W. Leungwattanakit, M. Hagiya, Y. Tanabe, and M. Yamamoto. Cache-based model checking of networked applications: From linear to branching time. In *Automated Software Engineering*, pages 447–458. IEEE, 2009.

[4] E. Barlas and T. Bultan. Netstub: a framework for verification of distributed java applications. In *Proceedings of the twenty-second IEEE/ACM international conference on Automated software engineering*, pages 24–33. ACM, 2007.

[5] E. Clarke, O. Grumberg, and D. Peled. *Model Checking*. The MIT Press, 1999.

[6] K. Haveland and T. Pressburger. Model checking java programs using java pathfinder. *International Journal on Software Tools for Technology Transfer*, 2(4):366–381, 2000.

[7] M. Musuvathi and D. Engler. Model checking large network protocol implementations. In *Proceedings of the First Symposium on Networked Systems Design and Implementation*, pages 155–168. NSDI, March 2004.

[8] B. Richards. Bugs as features: Teaching network protocols through debugging. In *Proceedings of the thirty-first SIGCSE Technical Symposium on Computer Science Education*, pages 24–33. ACM, March 2000.

[9] B. Richards and B. Stull. Teaching wireless networks with minimal resources. In *Proceedings of the thirty-fifth SIGCSE Technical Symposium on*

Computer Science Education, pages 306–310. ACM, March 2004.

[10] B. Richards and N. Waisbrot. Illustrating networking concepts with wireless handheld devices. In *Proceedings of the Seventh Annual Conference on Innovation and Technology in Computer Science Education*, pages 28–33. ACM, June 2002.

[11] N. Shafiei and P. Mehlitz. Extending jpf to verify distributed systems. *SIGSOFT Softw. Eng. Notes*, 39(1):1–5, February 2014.

[12] N. Shafiei, E. Ruppert, and J. Ostroff. *Model Checking Distributed Java Applications*. Unpublished Thesis Proposal. University of York., 2013.

[13] S. Stoller and Y. Liu. Transformations for model checking distributed java programs. In *Proceedings of the 8th international SPIN workshop on Model checking of software*, pages 192–199. Springer-Verlag, 2001.

Safe Parallel Programming in Ada
with Language Extensions

S. Tucker Taft
AdaCore
USA
taft@adacore.com

Brad Moore
General Dynamics
Canada
brad.moore@
gdcanada.com

Luís Miguel Pinho
CISTER, ISEP
Portugal
lmp@isep.ipp.pt

Stephen Michell
Maurya Software, Inc.
Canada
Stephen.michell@
maurya.on.ca

ABSTRACT

The increased presence of parallel computing platforms brings concerns to the general purpose domain that were previously prevalent only in the specific niche of high-performance computing. As parallel programming technologies become more prevalent in the form of new emerging programming languages and extensions of existing languages, additional safety concerns arise as part of the paradigm shift from sequential to parallel behaviour.

In this paper, we propose various syntax extensions to the Ada language, which provide mechanisms whereby the compiler is given the necessary semantic information to enable the implicit and explicit parallelization of code. The model is based on earlier work, which separates parallelism specification from concurrency implementation, but proposes an updated syntax with additional mechanisms to facilitate the development of safer parallel programs.

Categories and Subject Descriptors

D.3.3 [**Programming Languages**]: Language Constructs and Features – *Concurrent programming structures.*

General Terms

Performance, Standardization, Languages

Keywords

Multi-core; programming language; Ada; safe parallelism

1.   INTRODUCTION

There is a continuing trend of exponential growth of computational elements embedded on a single chip. This has led to significant challenges for software designers and implementers. Prior to 2005, the increase in transistor count corresponded to a similar increase in CPU clock speed, which boosted performance of sequential algorithms. Since then, CPU clock speeds have leveled off largely due to power concerns, and chip manufacturers have instead moved towards multicore technologies as a means of achieving performance increases.

HILT 2014, October 18 – 21, 2014, Portland, Oregon, USA.
Copyright 2014 ACM 978-1-4503-3217-0/14/10...$15.00.
http://dx.doi.org/10.1145/2663171.2663181

This increased parallel execution capability challenges software developers that want to exploit parallelism opportunities that are inherent in algorithms where high performance is critical. To maximize performance, Amdahl's law [1] suggests that it is necessary to minimize the sequential processing in an algorithm, however most mainstream programming languages and development environments lack adequate support for parallelism. In a world of many cores on a single chip executing a single algorithm, the effective use of such capabilities requires a paradigm shift that lets parallel behavior be exposed and captured wherever possible. It is a paradigm that has been for a long time contained within a specialized domain of high-performance computing, but that is now required in all domains of computing systems.

Parallel programming features have a long history. Dijkstra [2], Per Brinch Hansen [3], C.A.R. Hoare [4], and others proposed programming features such as parbegin/parend, cobegin/coend, etc., many years ago. The notion of a light-weight concurrent programming capability remains a key facet of any modern parallel programming capability. In some sense the distinction between "concurrent programming" and "parallel programming" is somewhat arbitrary, but in practice the main difference is that the focus with concurrent programming is to structure a complex program as a set of relatively independent activities to simplify the overall logic, while the primary focus of parallel programming is to divide a compute-intensive problem up to allow it to make better use of parallel hardware. A concurrent restructuring of a sequential program is successful if it simplifies the logic of the program, whereas a parallel restructuring is only successful if it actually speeds up the program on parallel hardware. Concurrent programming has evolved since these early proposals, tending toward explicit task or process constructs, while allowing more explicit control over scheduling of these independent activities. On the other hand, parallel programming has tended to preserve the notion of light-weight, anonymous parallel activities, and to augment the basic cobegin/coend with parallel loops and other data-parallel constructs.

Various parallel programming extensions have been proposed for Ada itself in the past. Mayer and Jahnichen [5] introduce a parallel keyword, which applied to "**for**" loops, allowing a compiler to optimize loop iterations when targeted to a multiprocessor platform. Hind and Schonberg [6] also targeted the optimization of parallel loops, introducing the concept of lightweight (mini) tasks, to reduce the overhead of using tasks for parallelism. Thornley [7] proposed two extension keywords to standard Ada: parallel and single, where parallel was used for declaring that a block or a "**for**" loop would be executed in parallel. Again the emphasis was on keeping the constructs light-weight while introducing parallelism, to ensure that there was a net savings in using the parallel programming features relative to the original sequential program. These efforts occurred in an era when parallel hardware was more the exception than the rule, and these largely academic investigations never reached a stage of widespread consideration for adoption into the language standard.

This paper presents a proposal that combines and extends earlier work into concrete syntax and semantics, allowing parallel programs to be expressed safely and naturally in Ada; this work has been performed in the context of the ongoing evolution of the Ada language standard. This work reuses the notion of a *Parallel OPportunity* (POP) and *Tasklet* from [8,9,10]. POPs are places in an algorithm (code) where work can be spawned to parallel executing *workers* that work in concert to correctly execute the algorithm. Tasklets are the notational (logical) units within a task that are executed in parallel with each other. The goals of this proposal are:

1   To permit existing programs to benefit from parallelism through minimal restructuring of sequential programs into ones that permit more parallel execution;

2   To support the development of complete programs that maximize parallelism;

3   To efficiently guide the compiler in the creation of effective parallelism (without oversubscription) with minimal input from the programmer;

4   To support the parallel reduction of results calculated by parallel computation;

5   To avoid syntax that would make a POP erroneous or produce noticeably different results if executed sequentially vs in parallel.

Earlier approaches [8,9,10] sought to avoid changes to Ada syntax and instead provide parallelism hints to the compiler via aspect and pragma annotations. However, it was recognized that such annotations would alter the semantics currently defined in the standard, and support for such aspects would need to be allowed in places not currently allowed in Ada (for example, aspects are not currently allowed to be specified on loop statements). Since the changes needed involved are more significant than simply defining new aspects, we decided to explore possibilities for new syntax that can be directly tied to the new semantics, leaving the semantics for existing syntax as it was previously for the most part.

Furthermore, an alternative paradigm to implicit parallelization is proposed. Introducing parallel notations can increase the likelihood of data races, which can lead to erroneousness. We address this issue by defining `Global` and `Potentially_Blocking` aspects to enable the compiler to provide better static detection of such problems so that they may be eliminated during development.

This paper is organized as follows. Section 2 presents related work while section 3 presents the fundamental model of a tasklet. Section 4 presents a new parallel block construct, while Section 5 addresses parallelization of loops. Section 6 then proposes ways to provide safety of parallel computation, and to enable safe implicit parallelization by the compiler. Finally, Section 7 presents some conclusions and open issues.

2.   RELATED WORK

Several new programming languages have been developed recently with parallel programming in mind, and a number of existing languages are investigating how best to add support for parallel programming. Some of the "new" languages are in fact special-purpose *extensions* of existing languages, often with an augmented run-time library, while others are *completely* new designs.

Notable examples of the new languages that are defined as extensions of existing languages are Cilk+ [11] (based on C++), OpenMP [12] (with variants based on C, C++, and Fortran), and OpenCL [13] and CUDA [14] (both being languages that are based on C or C++ and used with Graphics Processing Units, GPUs, and other similar accelerators for general purpose parallel computing). All of these languages make no attempt to improve the semantics of the underlying base language to support parallelism, but add new capabilities on top, which are specifically designed to take advantage of parallel hardware of various sorts. Cilk and OpenMP both use a *fork/join*, divide-and-conquer model where light weight threads can be spawned to perform parts of a larger calculation. In Cilk the light-weight threads are scheduled using a *work-stealing* model where heavier-weight *server* threads, roughly one per physical processor, each serve a queue of light-weight threads, stealing from other servers' queues when their own queue is empty. OpenMP provides a number of different scheduling approaches, providing the programmer more low-level control of how the light-weight threads are mapped to the physical processors. In the GPU languages OpenCL and CUDA, the model is more data driven, where a body of code is identified as a *kernel*, which is to be applied to every item in an array or other data aggregate. OpenCL and CUDA are targeted to environments where there is often separate memory for the main processor(s) and the accelerator(s), and so extra control is provided in placing data in particular parts of memory.

In all of these languages, the emphasis is on giving control to the programmer, with more or less of an attempt to provide a level of portability and abstraction, with Cilk providing the highest level model, and CUDA providing the lowest-level model. There is relatively little left to the compiler to decide, as the programmer determines where new threads are spawned, what code is to be run on the accelerator versus the main processor, etc.

These language extensions have to some degree been the inspiration for efforts to extend the C, C++ and Ada language standards themselves. These efforts are still in their early stages, with the C effort being named CPLEX (for C Parallel Language Extensions) [15], and the C++ effort being documented in a "Technical Specification for C++ Extensions for Parallelism" [16]. As with the other language extensions based on C and C++, no particular effort is made to enhance the underlying semantics of the languages to integrate parallelism. The goal is to give programmers an ability to direct how the compiler could insert parallelism. The programmer remains in control, and the compiler has very little leeway to insert parallelism beyond that which is authorized by the programmer, in large part because the compiler rarely has enough information to perform safe automatic parallelization. These extensions rely on the programmer to worry about data races, and provide few constructs beyond thread-local storage [17] to help identify or minimize such races.

A previous effort to extend Ada [8,10] proposed a fine-grain parallel model, based on the notion of tasklets, which are non-schedulable computation units (similar to Cilk [11] or OpenMP [12] *tasks*). However, in contrast to the C and C++ works, the principle behind this model is that the specification of parallelism is an abstraction that is not fully controlled by the programmer. Instead, parallelism is a notion that is under the control of the compiler and the run-time.

There are a handful of new languages that are not merely extensions of existing languages, but are rather completely new designs. Three notable examples of these are *Go* [18] from Google, *Rust* [19] from Mozilla Research, and *ParaSail* [20] from AdaCore. These languages are built around the notion that all computations will be structured as the coordinated execution of multiple light-weight threads, and each provides constructs specifically designed to simplify the safe interaction of these threads. *Go* provides light-weight *goroutines,* with *channels* for safe communication between them. Go does not prevent data races due to unsynchronized access to shared data, but it makes it relatively easy to structure the program using only goroutines and channels, and thereby avoid the need for directly sharing data.

The *Rust* language provides light-weight *tasks,* with a set of library-based mechanisms for them to interact and communicate, including *futures* [21] and channels. Rust goes further to disallow direct use of shared data between tasks, by enforcing unique pointer *ownership* on global data, while providing more conventional garbage-collected pointer semantics for task-local data. Pointer ownership means that only one pointer is pointing at any given piece of global data, and that pointer is accessible only from one task. The value of a pointer may be *moved* or *sent* from one place or one task to another, leaving a null pointer value behind, to ensure that the uniqueness of each such pointer is preserved. By contrast, pointers into task-local memory may be copied to other task-local variables, meaning that multiple pointers to the same local memory are possible. There are explicitly *unsafe* features which allow these pointer rules to be violated, but so long as these features are avoided, Rust ensures there are no data races.

The *ParaSail* language provides a pervasively parallel model, where the compiler creates light-weight *picothreads* (also called *work items)* as it sees fit, as well as under programmer control. There are no pointers and no global variables, meaning that functions may only update variables passed to them via **var** (in-out) parameters. The compiler treats parameter passing using *hand-off* semantics, similar to that pioneered in the Hermes language [22], where when a variable is passed as a **var** parameter to one function, it is no longer available to be passed to any other function until the original function returns. Similarly, if a variable is passed as a read-only parameter to a function, then the variable may not be passed as a **var** parameter to any other function until the first one returns, though it may be passed to other functions as a read-only parameter. This approach ensures that any ParaSail expression may be evaluated in parallel, so that the ParaSail compiler may insert parallelism where it deems it would be worthwhile. In addition to this implicit parallelism, ParaSail allows programmers to explicitly identify places where parallelism can be inserted, and the compiler will verify that there are no data races introduced by performing the specified code sections concurrently. The compiler might still decide not to actually perform the sections in parallel, but it will always verify the programmer's claim that the sections have no data interdependences. ParaSail also allows the definition of explicitly *concurrent* variables; such variables require the use of software or

hardware locks to ensure that concurrent access is properly synchronized. Concurrent variables are allowed to be manipulated concurrently in parallel threads, with no restrictions.

The Ada extensions proposed in this paper, although reusing the tasklet model of [8,10], are closest in spirit to those of Rust and ParaSail, where the compiler has sufficient knowledge to identify all possible data races, and to insert parallelism implicitly where it sees fit. Rather than eliminating global variables and pointers, we have chosen to allow global variable access and pointer dereferences to be specified via the `Global` aspect of a subprogram declaration, to help the compiler determine whether two computations could be safely performed in parallel. Ada's existing synchronization mechanisms based on protected objects, tasks, and atomic objects, provide the equivalent of Rust's library-based synchronization and communication mechanisms, and ParaSail's concurrent objects. Note that support for potentially blocking operations within tasklets is still an open issue (see section 7 below).

Subprograms without any `Global` aspect specified are presumed to update an unspecified number of global variables, and hence cannot be verified to be safe to run in parallel with any subprogram that reads or writes unsynchronized global variables. The overall intent is that introducing explicit parallel constructs into an Ada program will not introduce data races, and that the compiler will also have enough knowledge to introduce parallelism implicitly, when it can identify parallel opportunities that arise in code without explicitly parallel constructs. This is further detailed in section 6.

3. THE TASKLET MODEL

The work in [8] introduced the notion of a *Parallel OPportunity* (POP). This is a code fragment that appears sequential but which can be executed by processing elements in parallel. This could be by-element operations on an array, parallel iterations of a **for** loop over a structure or container, parallel evaluations of subprogram calls, and so on. That work also introduced the notion of a *tasklet* to capture the notion of a single execution trace within a POP, which the programmer can express with special syntax, or the compiler can implicitly create.

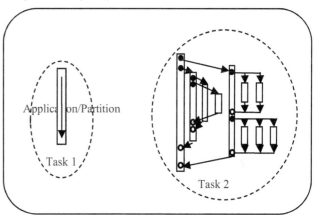

Figure 1. The Tasklet model [10].

As in [10], each Ada task is seen as a graph of execution of multiple control-dependent tasklets (Figure 1), with a fork-join model. Tasklets can be spawned by other tasklets (fork), and need to synchronize with the spawning tasklet (join). In Figure 1, Task 1 denotes the current model of an Ada task where a single thread of control is executing the body of the task; Task 2 denotes the new model, where an Ada task can execute a graph, where rectangles denote tasklets, dark circles fork points, and white circles join points.

An important part of the model is that if the compiler is not able to verify that the parallel computations are independent, then a warning will be issued at compile time (see section 6).

Note that in this model the compiler will identify any code where a potential data race occurs (following the rules for concurrent access to objects as specified in the Language Reference Manual [23, section 9.10]), and point out where objects cannot be guaranteed to be independently addressable. If not determinable at compile-time, the compiler may insert run-time checks to detect data overlap.

Another issue is the underlying run-time. In the proposed model, tasklets are orthogonal to tasks. Regardless of implementation, tasklets are considered to execute in the semantic context of the task where they have been spawned, which means that any operation that identifies a task, such as those in `Task_Identification`, will identify the task in which the tasklet is spawned. This is a major distinction to previous work that left this as an implementation issue. On the other hand, calls by different tasklets of the same task into the same protected object are treated as different calls resulting in distinct protected actions; therefore synchronization between tasklets can be performed using non-blocking protected operations. Note that this is consistent with the current standard which already supports multiple concurrent calls by a single task in the presence of the asynchronous transfer of control capability [23, section 9.7.4].

Our proposed model does not define syntax for the explicit parallelization of individual subprogram calls, since such parallelization can be performed implicitly by the compiler, when it knows that the calls are free of side-effects. This is facilitated by annotations identifying global variable usage on subprogram specifications, a proposal which is detailed in section 6. In sections 4 and 5 we focus on constructs based on explicit specification by the programmer: parallel blocks and loops.

4. PARALLEL BLOCKS

A common parallel language capability is to specify that two or more parts of an algorithm can be executed in parallel with each other. We propose the following syntax for Ada:

```
parallel_block_statement ::=
    parallel
        sequence_of_statements
    and
        sequence_of_statements
    {and
        sequence_of_statements}
    end parallel;
```

Example:

```
declare
    X, Y : Integer;
    Z : Float;
begin
    parallel
        X := Foo(100);
    and
        Z := Sqrt(3.14) / 2.0;
        Y := Bar(Z);
```

```
    end parallel;

    Put_Line ("X + Y=" &
            Integer'Image(X + Y));
end;
```

In this example, the calculation of Z and Y occur sequentially with respect to each other, but in parallel with the calculation of X. Note that the compiler, using the rules specified in Section 6, may complain if the parallel sequences might have conflicting global side-effects. In this particular case, this means that, at a minimum, either `Foo` or both `Sqrt` and `Bar`, need to be annotated with the `Global` aspect. If only one branch of the construct has `Global` aspects, then they must indicate that that branch does not involve any access to non-synchronized globals; alternatively, both branches must be annotated with non-conflicting `Global` aspects.

The parallel block construct is flexible enough to support recursive usage as well, such as:

```
function Fibonacci (N : Natural)
                            return Natural is
    X, Y : Natural;
begin
    if N < 2 then
        return N;
    end if;

    parallel
        X := Fibonacci (N - 2);
    and
        Y := Fibonacci (N - 1);
    end parallel;

    return X + Y;
exception
    when others =>
        Log ("Unexpected Error");
end Fibonacci;
```

4.1 Parallel Block Semantics

A parallel block statement encloses two or more sequences of statements (two or more "parallel sequences") separated by the reserved word "**and**". Each parallel sequence represents a separate tasklet, but all within a single Ada task. Task identity remains that of the enclosing Ada task, and a single set of task attributes is shared between the tasklets.

With respect to the rules for shared variables (see section 9.10 in the Ada reference manual [23]), two actions occurring within two different parallel sequences of the same parallel block are *not* automatically sequential, so execution can be erroneous if one such action assigns to an object, and the other reads or updates the same object or a neighboring object that is not independently addressable from the first object. The appropriate use of atomic, protected, or task objects (which as a group we will call *synchronized* objects) can be used to avoid erroneous execution. In addition, the new `Global` and `Potentially_Blocking` aspects may be specified to enable the static detection of such problems at compile time (see section 6).

Any transfer of control out of one parallel sequence will initiate the aborting of the other parallel sequences not yet completed. Once all other parallel sequences complete normally or abort, the transfer of control takes place. If multiple parallel sequences attempt a transfer of control before completing, one is chosen arbitrarily and the others are aborted.

If an exception is raised by any of the parallel sequences, it is treated similarly to a transfer of control, with the exception being propagated only after all the other sequences complete normally or due to abortion. If multiple parallel sequences raise an exception before completing, one is chosen arbitrarily and the others are aborted.

The parallel block completes when all of the parallel sequences complete, either normally or by being aborted. Note that aborting a tasklet need not be preemptive, but should prevent the initiation of further nested parallel blocks or parallel loops.

We considered allowing the parallel block to be preceded with an optional declare part, and followed with optional exception handlers, but it was observed that it was more likely to be useful to have objects that are shared across multiple parallel sequences to outlive the parallel block, and that having exception handlers after the last parallel sequence could easily be misconstrued as applying only to the last sequence. Therefore we reverted to the simpler syntax proposed above. This simpler syntax is also more congruous with the syntax for select statements.

5. PARALLEL LOOPS

In most compute-intensive applications, a significant proportion of the computation time is spent in loops, either iterating over arrays/container data structures, or systematically searching a large solution space. To benefit from parallel hardware, the computation associated with a loop should be spread across the available processors. One approach, presuming the iterations of the loop have no data dependences between them, is to treat each iteration of the loop as a separate tasklet, and then have the processors work away on the set of tasklets in parallel. However, this introduces overhead from the queuing and de-queuing of work items, and the communication of results from each work item. Furthermore, there often are data dependences between iterations, and creating a separate work item for each iteration can introduce excessive synchronization overhead to deal safely with these interdependences. Therefore, it is common to break large arrays, and/or the loops that iterate over them, into *chunks* (or *slices* or *tiles*), where each chunk is processed sequentially, but multiple chunks can be processed in parallel with one another. Fig. 2 shows how a compiler run-time might decide to break a specific loop into chunks to allow up to four parallel workers to process the loop. Although the chunks are all equal size in this example, the run-time may choose different chunk sizes for each chunk, which would be needed if the number of chunks did not divide evenly into the number of iterations, for example.

```
for I in parallel 1 .. 1000 loop
    Process (I);
end loop;
```

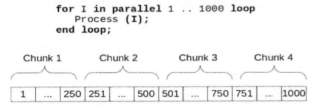

Figure 2. Example of chunking a loop (for 4 parallel workers).

For Ada, we propose giving the programmer some degree of control over the parallelization of **for** loops[1] into appropriately sized chunks, but without requiring that they specify the exact chunk size or the number of chunks. In addition, to deal with data dependences, we would like to provide support for per-thread copies of the relevant data, and a mechanism of reducing these multiple copies down to a final result at the end of the computation.

To indicate that a loop is a candidate for parallelization, the reserved word "**parallel**" may be inserted immediately after the word "**in**" or "**of**" in a "**for**" loop, at the point where the "**reverse**" reserved word is allowed. Such a loop will be broken into chunks, where each chunk is processed sequentially. For data that is to be updated within such a parallelized loop, the notion of a *parallel array* is provided, which corresponds to an array with one element per chunk of a parallel loop. For example, here is a simple use of a parallelized loop, with a parallel array of partial sums (with one element per chunk), which are then summed together (sequentially) to compute an overall sum for the array:

```
declare
    Partial_Sum : array (parallel <>)
                    of Float
                  := (others => 0.0);
    Sum : Float := 0.0;
begin
    for I in parallel Arr'Range loop
        Partial_Sum(<>) := Partial_Sum(<>) +
                        Arr(I);
    end loop;

    for J in Partial_Sum'Range loop
        Sum := Sum + Partial_Sum(J);
    end loop;
    Put_Line ("Sum over Arr = " &
            Float'Image (Sum));
end;
```

In this example, the programmer has merely specified that the Partial_Sum array is to be a parallel array (with each element initialized to 0.0), but has not specified the actual bounds of the array, using "<>" instead of an explicit range such as "1 .. Num_Chunks". In this case, the compiler will automatically select the appropriate bounds for the array, depending on the number of chunks chosen for the parallelized loops in which the parallel array is used.

When a parallel array is used in a parallelized loop, the programmer is not allowed to specify the specific index, but rather uses "<>" to indicate the "current" element of the parallel array, appropriate to the particular chunk being processed. In the above case, we see "Partial_Sum(<>)" indicating we are accumulating the sum into a different element of the Partial_Sum in each distinct chunk of the loop. In this example, if the loop were to be processed in two chunks then the Partial_Sum array would contain two elements, where the first element could contain the sum for the first half of the array, and the second element would then contain the sum for the last half of the array.

---

[1] While loops cannot be easily parallelized, because the control variables are inevitably global to the loop.

The user may explicitly control the number of chunks into which a parallelized loop is divided by specifying the bounds of the parallel array(s) used in the loop. All parallel arrays used within a given loop must necessarily have the same bounds. If parallel arrays with the same bounds are used in two consecutive parallelized loops over the same container or range, then the two loops will be chunked in the same way. Hence, it is possible to pass data across consecutive loops through the elements of a parallel array that is common across the loops. For example, here is a pair of parallelized loops that produce a new array that is the cumulative sum of the elements of an initial array. The parallel arrays Partial_Sum and Adjust are used to carry data from the first parallelized loop to the second parallelized loop:

```
declare
    Partial_Sum: array (parallel <>) of Float
                := (others => 0.0);
    Adjust: array(parallel Partial_Sum'Range)
         of Float
         := (others => 0.0);
    Cumulative_Sum: array (Arr'Range)
                 of Float
                    := (others => 0.0);
begin
    -- Produce cumulative sums within chunks
    for I in parallel Arr'Range loop
      Partial_Sum(<>) := Partial_Sum(<>) +
                        Arr(I);
      Cumulative_Sum(I) := Partial_Sum(<>);
    end loop;

    -- Compute adjustment for each chunk
    for J in Partial_Sum'First..
                    Partial_Sum'Last-1 loop
      Adjust(J+1) := Adjust(J) +
                    Partial_Sum(J);
    end loop;

    -- Adjust elements of each chunk
    for I in parallel Arr'Range loop
      Cumulative_Sum(I):= Cumulative_Sum(I)+
                        Adjust(<>);
    end loop;

    -- Display result
    Put_Line("Arr, Cumulative_Sum");

    for I in Cumulative_Sum'Range loop
      Put_Line(Float'Image(Arr(I)) & ", " &
            Float'Image(Cumulative_Sum(I)));
    end loop;
end;
```

Note that this feature eliminated the need to reference two different elements of the same array (element I and element I − 1) within any of the parallel loop bodies. This reduces expression complexity and eliminates data race issues at chunk boundaries, where the I − 1th element could refer to an element of another chunk.

Note also that chunking is not explicit in parallelized loops, and in the above example, the compiler is free to use as few or as many chunks as it decides is best, though it must use the same number of chunks in the two consecutive parallelized loops because they share parallel arrays with common bounds.

If Arr had been declared as;

```
Arr : array (1 .. 10) of Float
   := (1 => 1.0, 2 => 2.0, 3 => 3.0,
       4 => 4.0, 5 => 5.0, 6 => 6.0,
       7 => 7.0, 8 => 8.0, 9 => 9.0,
       10 => 10.0);
```

and the loops were processed as two chunks of 5 iterations each, then after the first loop the following values would have been stored:

```
Cumulative_Sum:
    (1 => 1.0, 2 => 3.0, 3 => 6.0, 4 => 10.0,
     5 => 15.0, 6 => 6.0, 7 => 13.0,
     8 => 21.0, 9 => 29.0, 10 => 39.0)
Partial_Sum:
    (1 => 15.0, 2 => 39.0)
```

After processing the second and remaining loops, the following values would have been stored:

```
Adjust:
    (1 => 0.0, 2 => 15.0)
Cumulative_Sum:
    (1 => 1.0, 2=> 3.0, 3 => 6.0, 4 => 10.0,
     5 => 15.0, 6 => 21.0, 7 => 34.0,
     8 => 36.0, 9 => 44.0, 10 => 54.0)
```

The programmer could exercise more control over the chunking by explicitly specifying the bounds of Partial_Sum, rather than allowing it to default. For example, if the programmer wanted these parallelized loops to be broken into "N" chunks, then the declarations could have been:

```
declare
    Partial_Sum : array (parallel 1..N)
             of Float
                := (others => 0.0);
    Adjust: array(parallel Partial_Sum'Range)
         of Float := (others => 0.0);
    ...
```

Parallel arrays are similar to normal arrays, except that they are always indexed by Standard.Integer, and they are likely to be allocated more widely spaced than strictly necessary to satisfy the algorithm, to avoid sharing cache lines between adjacent elements. This wide spacing means that two parallel arrays might be interspersed, effectively turning a set of separate parallel arrays with common bounds, into an array of records, with one record per loop chunk, from a storage layout point of view.

Note that the same rules presented for parallel blocks (subsection 4.1) apply to the update of shared variables and the transfer of control to a point outside of the loop, and for this purpose each iteration (or chunk) is treated as equivalent to a separate sequence of a parallel block.

5.1   Automatic Reduction of a Parallel Array

As is illustrated above by the first example, it will be common for the values of a parallel array to be combined at the end of processing, using an appropriate *reduction* operator. In this case, the Partial_Sum parallel array is reduced by "+" into the single Sum value. Because this is a common operation, we are providing a language-defined attribute which will do this reduction, called "Reduced." This can eliminate the need to write the final reduction loop in the first example, and instead we could have written simply:

```
Put_Line ("Sum over Arr = " &
        Float'Image (Partial_Sum'Reduced));
```

The Reduced operator will automatically reduce the specified parallel array using the operator that was used in the assignment statement that computed its value -- in this case the "+" operator appearing in the statement:

```
Partial_Sum(<>) := Partial_Sum(<>) +
                   Arr(I);
```

For large parallel arrays, this reduction can itself be performed in parallel, using a tree of computations. The reduction operator to be used can also be specified explicitly when invoking the Reduced attribute, using a Reducer and optionally an Identity parameter. For example:

```
Put_Line ("Sum over Arr = " &
    Float'Image (Partial_Sum'Reduced(
            Reducer => "+",
            Identity => 0.0)));
```

The parameter names are optional, so this could have been:

```
Put_Line("Sum over Arr = " &
    Float'Image (Partial_Sum'Reduced(
                    "+", 0.0)));
```

Note that an explicit Reducer parameter is *required* when the parallelized loop contains multiple operations on the parallel array. More generally, the parameterized Reduced attribute with an explicit Reducer parameter may be applied to any array, and then the entire parallel reduction operation will be performed. Hence the first example could have been completely replaced with simply:

```
Put_Line ("Sum over Arr = " &
    Float'Image (Arr'Reduced("+", 0.0)));
```

The examples shown here involve simple elementary types, but the Reduced attribute can similarly be applied to complex user-defined types such as record types, private types, and tagged types. The Reducer parameter of the Reduced attribute simply identifies the subprogram to use for the reduction operation.

6. PARALLELISM AND CONCURRENCY SAFETY

One of the strengths of Ada is that it was carefully designed to allow the compiler to detect many problems at compile time, rather than at run time. Programming for parallel execution in particular is an activity that requires care to prevent data races and deadlocks. It is desirable that any new capabilities added to the language to support parallelism also allow the compiler to detect as many such problems as possible, as an aid to the programmer in arriving at a reliable solution without sacrificing performance benefits.

A common source of erroneousness in languages that support concurrency and parallelism are data races, which occur when one thread of execution attempts to read or write a variable while another thread of execution is updating that same variable. Such a variable is *global* in the sense that it is globally accessible from multiple threads of execution. In the current Ada standard, threads of execution are *tasks*. In this proposal, tasklets are another form of execution threads.

Eliminating concurrency and parallelism problems associated with non-protected global variables is an important step towards improving the safety of the language. To that end, we propose the addition of a Global aspect to the language. The main goal in the design of this aspect is to identify which global variables and access-value dereferences a subprogram might read or update.

The inspiration for this aspect comes from the SPARK language [24], which has always had global annotations. Earlier versions of SPARK augmented a subset of Ada with annotations added as specially formatted comments, which were used for static analysis by the proof system. With the addition of aspects to Ada in Ada 2012, SPARK 2014 has changed its annotations to use aspects, including the "Global" annotation.

To encourage convergence with SPARK we are starting from the SPARK Global aspect. However, for Ada, it is necessary to extend this idea to cover a broader spectrum of usage, since Ada is a more expressive programming environment than SPARK.

The Global aspect in SPARK 2014 is applied to subprogram specifications, and is of the following form;

```
with Global =>(Input => ...,
               In_Out => ..., Output => ...)
```

where "..." is either a single name, or a parenthesized list of names, and Input, In_Out, and Output identify the global variables of the program that are accessed by this subprogram, in read-only, read-write, or write-only mode, respectively. If there are no global variables with a particular parameter mode, then that mode is omitted from the specification. If there are only global inputs, and no outputs or in-outs, then this syntax can be further simplified to:

```
with Global => ...
```

where again "..." is a single name, or a parenthesized list of names.

Finally, if there are no global inputs, in-outs, nor outputs, then:

```
with Global => null
```

is used.

We needed to refine the notion of SPARK's Global aspect, because SPARK does not support access types, and because SPARK relies on an elaborate mechanism for handling the abstract "state" of packages. The refinements we are proposing are the following:

1. Allow the name of an access type A (including "access T") to stand-in for the set of objects described by:
   (for all X convertible to A => X.all)

2. Allow the name of a package P to stand-in for the set of objects described by:
   (for all variables X declared in P => X)

3. Allow the word **synchronized** to be used to represent the set of global variables that are tasks, protected objects, or atomic objects.

Note that references to global constants do not appear in Global annotations.

In the absence of a global aspect, the subprogram is presumed to read and write an unspecified set of global variables, including non-synchronized ones.

Another issue for parallel safety is the aliasing of parameters with other parameters and with globals. Ada 2012 has some rules relating to aliasing that apply to the use of functions with out and in-out parameters, which reduce the problem [23, section 6.4.1]. There are also the new attributes `Has_Same_Storage` and `Overlaps_Storage` [23, section 13.3(73.1/3-73.10/3)]. In the absence of preconditions such as:

```
with Pre => not X'Overlaps_Storage(Y)
```

the compiler must presume that two parameters that are passed by reference, or a by-reference parameter and a global, might overlap if their types imply that is possible.

Given a `Global` aspect, and presuming appropriate use of `Overlaps_Storage`, the compiler is able to check for potential data races at compile-time. Our proposal does not specify whether such checks are required in all cases, or only in the presence of some sort of named "restriction."

If one wants to know whether a subprogram has side-effects, it is important to know about *all* data that might be read or written. Access types introduce difficulties in determining such side-effects, since the side-effects might result after a dereference of a series of pointers to reach an object to be updated. Our proposal addresses this by allowing the programmer to specify the name of an access type in a `Global` aspect. This would be essentially equivalent to writing something like;

```
Global => (In_Out => *.all)
```

except we can be more specific about the type of the access values being dereferenced.

For example, consider a visible access type declared as;

```
type Acc is access T;
```

and a subprogram that has a value of type `Acc` in local variable `Local`, which it then uses to read and update an object via `Local.all`. It would not be very useful to write:

```
Global => (In_Out => Local.all)
```

since "`Local`" means nothing to the caller. But it could write:

```
Global => (In_Out => Acc)
```

to indicate that the caller should be aware that a call on this subprogram is updating some object by dereferencing an access value of type `Acc`. Another problematic case involves specifying in a `Global` aspect a variable that is declared inside a package body. Directly naming such a variable would not have meaning to the caller of the subprogram, and would violate encapsulation. Similarly, suppose an access type is declared inside the body or private part of package P. In both these cases, we treat the private updatable objects as a part of the overall state of package P. We then simply indicate that the subprogram is updating some or all of the state of package P:

```
Global => (In_Out => P)
```

Now suppose that the objects being updated are all protected or atomic objects. Then the caller doesn't really need to worry about which objects are being read or updated. It is always safe to call the subprogram concurrently. It has some side effects, so you cannot assume it is a "pure" subprogram. In this case, we could describe the effects as:

```
Global => synchronized
```

if it only reads synchronized objects, or:

```
Global => (In_Out => synchronized)
```

if it might update synchronized objects as well.

One might be concerned that the number of globals in a subprogram higher in the call structure of a larger program might be unmanageable to specify in a `Global` aspect. To address this concern we propose a shorthand for the `Global` aspect:

```
Global => (In_Out => all)
```

where "`all`" represents all global variables. If the number of non-synchronized globals does get large, then it is likely that the subprogram cannot be used in a parallel context anyway, hence using `all` is generally adequate. By default, the global aspect is (`In_Out => all`) for normal subprograms, and `null` for subprograms in a declared-pure package.

Another important piece of knowledge the caller of a subprogram might need to know is whether or not the call is *potentially blocking*. The Ada language defines *potentially blocking* operations to include **select** statements, **accept** statements, **delay** statements, **abort** statements, and task creation or activation, among others. When executing parallel code, potentially blocking operations can cause problems such as deadlocks. Currently there is no standard way in Ada to specify that a subprogram is potentially blocking. If the compiler cannot statically determine that a subprogram call is potentially blocking, the programmer has to rely on run-time checking to detect these sorts of problems. We propose the addition of a boolean `Potentially_Blocking` aspect that can be applied to subprogram specifications to indicate whether they use constructs that are potentially blocking or call other subprograms that have the `Potentially_Blocking` aspect with a value of `True`. Such an aspect enhances the safety of parallel calls, and also generally improves the safety of Ada, since it allows the compiler to statically detect more problems involving calls on potentially blocking subprograms. The default value for the `Potentially_Blocking` aspect is `True`.

We also propose that these defaults can be overridden for a package by allowing these aspects to be specified at package level, with the meaning that they establish a default for all subprograms in the package. For example,

```
package My_Stuff
   with Global => (In_Out => Synchronized),
        Potentially_Blocking => False
is
   procedure Do_Something (X : in out T;
                           Y : in U);

   function Query_Something (A : T)
        return Z;
   ...
end My_Stuff;
```

Indicates that all subprograms in package `My_Stuff` involve access to synchronized globals, and all of these calls are not potentially blocking calls (in particular these cannot include entry calls, delays, select statements, etc. [23, section 9.5.1]). Such an annotation would alleviate the need to repeat the `Global` or

`Potentially_Blocking` aspect on each subprogram, as long as the package-level default is appropriate for that subprogram.

In the absence of such an explicit package-wide default, the default for `Potentially_Blocking` would be `True`, and the default for `Global` would be (`In_Out => all`) in a normal package, and **null** in a declared-pure package.

6.1 Safe Implicit Parallelization

Given the information in the `Global` and `Potentially_Blocking` aspects, the compiler now has enough information to determine whether two constructs can be safely executed in parallel. When the programmer explicitly specifies that two constructs should be executed in parallel, the compiler can use this knowledge to give appropriate warnings wherever data races are possible. However, it can be a burden on the programmer to add explicitly parallel constructs everywhere in a large program where parallel execution is safe. Therefore, this proposal is designed to enable safe *implicit* parallelization of suitably annotated Ada programs.

In general, implicit parallelization can be modeled as the compiler implicitly transforming the algorithm to use explicit parallel constructs. To determine whether data races are possible, the compiler will make conservative assumptions about each subprogram call. It will assume that each (non-synchronized) variable, package, or access collection identified in the subprogram's `Global` aspect, and each by-reference actual parameter in the call, is accessed in its entirety without any synchronization. If there is any overlap between the objects potentially accessed in two constructs, including any nested calls, the constructs will not be candidates for a transformation that would have them potentially running in parallel.

In addition to rules to prevent the introduction of data races, we also currently disallow the implicit introduction of tasklets that invoke potentially blocking operations, because we presume that blocking a tasklet might block the entire task. Therefore the compiler is not permitted to parallelize two constructs where either involves calls on potentially blocking operations.

Note that the compiler could introduce temporary variables to hold the result of parallel evaluations of subexpressions of a single larger expression, to enable a further transformation. For example, given ... `F(X) + G(Y)` ... the compiler could transform this to:

```
declare
    T1, T2 : Float;
begin
    parallel
        T1 := F(X);
    and
        T2 := G(Y);
    end parallel;
    ... T1 + T2 ...
end;
```

where `T1 + T2` is being substituted for what was originally `F(X) + G(Y)`. Other possible transformations would be to change a sequential loop into a parallel loop. In each case, these transformations would only be performed when the compiler can ensure it is not introducing potential data races as a result.

7. CONCLUSIONS AND OPEN ISSUES

This proposal provides an integrated model for safe and natural parallel computation in Ada, adding specific new parallel syntax, that is integrated with the existing syntax of Ada 2012. It provides mechanisms to parallelize blocks and "**for**" loops, as well as syntax to identify potentially shared state.

The following open topics are identified for future work:

- Containers that are to have cursors updated by some tasklet(s) in a parallel computation must be implemented in ways that support such parallel update, with mechanisms to guarantee safe access and update of the cursors by multiple tasklets.

- Ada provides a formal notion of independently addressable components for composite objects, including arrays that satisfy concurrent access requirements (ARM [23] 9.10 and C.6). It is likely that this is sufficient for safe access by tasklets of neighboring components, but more work is required for confirmation. We do not address the requirements to allocate memory for arrays, records, or containers so that access by tasklets on separate cores is optimized to avoid cache contention or similar overheads.

- Whether to support potentially blocking operations within tasklets is yet to be determined (for now we limit tasklets to invoking subprograms where `Potentially_Blocking` is False). Some algorithms might be written using explicit synchronization of tasklets between phases, but explicit blocking synchronization between tasklets puts the algorithm at risk of deadlock with certain mappings of tasklets to underlying computational elements (for example execution of the "parallel" code by a strictly sequential execution may block the task with no way to release it).

- The mapping of tasklets to heterogeneous computational elements that do not match the uniform memory access processor model. Such computation units are becoming more prevalent. Ada's distribution model with partitions and inter-partition communication subsystems may be able to be mapped into a support environment that allows the execution of tasklets across such a system.

- How to use tasklets in a real time domain. Obviously, precise control of the mapping of tasklets to underlying tasks and/or processors is a likely requirement in such a system. Additional syntax and restrictions may be required if parallel computation is to be useable in this environment.

ACKNOWLEDGMENTS
We would like to thank the anonymous reviewers for their valuable comments. This work was partially supported by General Dynamics, Canada; the Portuguese National Funds through FCT (Portuguese Foundation for Science and Technology) and by ERDF (European Regional Development Fund) through COMPETE (Operational Programme 'Thematic Factors of Competitiveness'), within projects FCOMP-01-0124-FEDER-037281 (CISTER) and AVIACC (ref. FCOMP-01-0124-FEDER-020486); the European Union (EU) FP7 program under grant agreement n° 611016 (P-SOCRATES); and by FCT and EU ARTEMIS JU, within project ARTEMIS/0001/2013, JU grant nr. 621429 (EMC2).

BIBLIOGRAPHY

[1] G. M. Amdahl. Validity of the Single-Processor Approach to Achieving Large Scale Computing Capabilities. In AFIPS Conference Proceedings, pages 483–485, 1967.

[2] E. W. Dijkstra. 1965. Cooperating Sequential Processes, Technical Report Ewd-123. Technical Report.

[3] P. B. Hansen. 1973. Concurrent Programming Concepts. ACM Comput. Surv. 5, 4 (December 1973), 223-245.

[4] C. A. R. Hoare (1978). "Communicating sequential processes". Communications of the ACM 21 (8): 666–677.

[5] H. G. Mayer, S. Jahnichen, "The data-parallel Ada run-time system, simulation and empirical results", Proceedings of Seventh International Parallel Processing Symposium, April 1993, Newport, CA, USA, pp. 621 - 627.

[6] M. Hind , E. Schonberg, "Efficient Loop-Level Parallelism in Ada", Proceedings of TriAda 91, October 1991.

[7] J. Thornley, "Integrating parallel dataflow programming with the Ada tasking model". Proceedings of TRI-Ada '94, Charles B. Engle, Jr. (Ed.). ACM, New York, NY, USA.

[8] S. Michell, B. Moore, L. M. Pinho, "Tasklettes – a Fine Grained Parallelism for Ada on Multicores", International Conference on Reliable Software Technologies - Ada-Europe 2013, LNCS 7896, Springer, 2013.

[9] S. Michell, B. Moore, L. M. Pinho, "Real-Time Programming on Accelerator Many-Core Processors", Proceedings of the High-Integrity Language Technologies conference (HILT 2013), November 2013.

[10] L. M. Pinho, B. Moore, S. Michell, "Parallelism in Ada: status and prospects", International Conference on Reliable Software Technologies - Ada-Europe 2014, LNCS 8454, Springer, 2014.

[11] Intel Corporation, Cilk Plus, https://software.intel.com/en-us/intel-cilk-plus

[12] OpenMP Architecture Review Board, "OpenMP Application Program Interface", Ver-sion 4.0, July 2013

[13] OpenCL (Open Computing Language), http://www.khronos.org/opencl

[14] NVIDIA, "NVIDIA CUDA Compute Unified Device Architecture", Version 2.0, 2008

[15] CPLEX, C Parallel Language EXtensions study group, archives at http://www.open-std.org/mailman/listinfo/cplex

[16] Working Draft, Technical Specification for C++ Extensions for Parallelism, available at http://www.open-std.org/jtc1/sc22/wg21/docs/papers/2014/n3960.pdf

[17] D. C. Schmidt, T. H. Harrison, and N. Pryce, "Thread-specific Storage: an Object Behavioral Pattern for Efficiently Accessing per-Thread State," *C++ Gems II*, (Robert Martin, ed.), SIGS, NY, 1999; http://www.dre.vanderbilt.edu/~schmidt/PDF/TSS-pattern.pdf, retrieved 11-Jun-2014

[18] Google Corporation, The Go Programming Language, http://golang.org/

[19] Mozilla Research, The Rust Programming Language, http://www.rust-lang.org

[20] ParaSail – Parallel Specification and Implementation Language, http://parasail-programming-language.blogspot.com

[21] B. Liskov and L. Shrira, *Promises: Linguistic Support for Efficient Asynchronous Procedure Calls in Distributed Systems*. Proceedings of the SIGPLAN '88 Conference on Programming Language Design and Implementation; Atlanta, Georgia, United States, pp. 260–267.

[22] W. Korfhage, A. P. Goldberg, "Hermes Language Experiences," Software—Practice And Experience, Vol. 25(4), 389–402 (April 1995)

[23] ISO IEC 8652:2012. Programming Languages and their Environments – Programming Language Ada. International Standards Organization, Geneva, Switzerland, 2012

[24] J. Barnes. High Integrity Software: The SPARK Approach to Safety and Security. Addison-Wesley Longman Publishing Co., Inc., Boston, MA, USA, 2003.

Spot: A Programming Language
for Verified Flight Software

Robert L. Bocchino Jr.
Jet Propulsion Laboratory
California Institute of
Technology
4800 Oak Grove Drive
Pasadena, CA 91109
bocchino@jpl.nasa.gov

Edward Gamble
Jet Propulsion Laboratory
California Institute of
Technology
4800 Oak Grove Drive
Pasadena, CA 91109
ed_gamble@me.com

Kim P. Gostelow
Jet Propulsion Laboratory
California Institute of
Technology
4800 Oak Grove Drive
Pasadena, CA 91109
kimpgostelow@gmail.com

Raphael R. Some
Jet Propulsion Laboratory
California Institute of
Technology
4800 Oak Grove Drive
Pasadena, CA 91109
Raphael.R.Some@jpl.nasa.gov

ABSTRACT

The C programming language is widely used for programming space flight software and other safety-critical real time systems. C, however, is far from ideal for this purpose: as is well known, it is both low-level and unsafe. This paper describes Spot, a language derived from C for programming space flight systems. Spot aims to maintain compatibility with existing C code while improving the language and supporting verification with the SPIN model checker. The major features of Spot include actor-based concurrency, distributed state with message passing and transactional updates, and annotations for testing and verification. Spot also supports domain-specific annotations for managing spacecraft state, e.g., communicating telemetry information to the ground. We describe the motivation and design rationale for Spot, give an overview of the design, provide examples of Spot's capabilities, and discuss the current status of the implementation.

Categories and Subject Descriptors

D SOFTWARE [**D.3 PROGRAMMING LANGUAGES**]: D.3.2 Language Classifications—*Concurrent, distributed, and parallel languages*; D SOFTWARE [**D.1 PROGRAMMING TECHNIQUES**]: D.1.3 Concurrent Programming; D SOFTWARE [**D.2 SOFTWARE ENGINEERING**]: D.2.4 Software/Program Verification—*Model checking*; D SOFTWARE [**D.2 SOFTWARE ENGINEERING**]: D.2.5 Testing and Debugging

General Terms

Verification; Validation; Safety; Reliability

Keywords

Flight Systems; Avionics; Actors; Message Passing; Domain-specific Annotations

1. INTRODUCTION

Test and verification are the most costly parts of flight software development. Automation, such as model checking, can significantly improve software test coverage over hand-coded tests; but it too can be expensive. To illustrate, time and cost constraints allowed only four of the 150 software modules on board the *Curiosity* rover to be checked by the SPIN model checker [2].[1] The question is: how can we improve the reliability of flight software while reducing the cost?

We have concluded that a significant source of cost lies in the programming languages used to write flight software (primarily C, though C++ is used as well), and in particular two aspects of those languages:

1. Low-level, unsafe programming language constructs.

2. An inability to cleanly express key flight software concepts.

As to the first point, low-level constructs like pointers, semaphores, and callbacks are both powerful and necessary: they are the elementary building blocks from which any algorithm or data structure can be constructed. However, these

---

[1]Model checking is one of a number of formal methods that can help ensure program correctness; it works by exploring all executions of a simplified version of a program, called a model. Other formal methods include abstract interpretation and theorem proving. SPIN is a widely-used model checker.

constructs are also much too primitive for general use; instead they should be hidden wherever possible behind suitable abstractions. Otherwise the code is tedious to write, unsafe and error-prone, hard to reuse, and impossible to analyze.

Unfortunately C — which was originally designed for programming operating systems — often *requires* the use of primitive mechanisms like pointer manipulation, with no satisfactory alternative. C++ has improved capabilities for abstraction-building, but it is very complex; and still it encourages low-level, hard-to-analyze code. The Ada programming language solves many of the expressivity and safety problems of C and C++, but rewriting of C flight code in Ada is simply not practical. Further, Ada's concurrency model is not ideal for flight code.

As to the second point, we claim that flight software can be improved by adding a handful of key concepts to the programming model. In our view the most important concept is an exact accounting of *state*. By state we mean a variable whose value persists across messages or function calls, such as the number of bytes in a telemetry buffer.[2] By exact, we mean the compiler can determine the minimum number of bytes required to represent the state, as well as its location and actual size.

Knowing this information provides several benefits. As a concrete example, the SPIN model checker works by systematically exploring different reachable states of a program. When it reaches a state it has seen before, it stops and backtracks to a different state; there is no use continuing, because any state reachable from that point has already been seen. A basic assumption of SPIN, therefore, is that *every single bit of global state in the program is known and accounted for*. If this assumption is violated, then SPIN cannot work properly; usually it will fail with strange errors or crashes. Moreover, accounting for state in this way is extremely difficult when the language is as unstructured as C. Additional benefits, such as generation of telemetry communication code, are discussed later in this paper.

Finally, we believe the two points are really two sides of a single design philosophy. While it is unrealistic to eliminate all use of low-level constructs in flight code, if programmers have good abstractions for the job at hand, then use of these lower-level techniques will be a last resort, rather than a first choice. The result should be an improvement in the three "R's" of software quality: readability, reliability, and reusability.

2. SPOT

We are developing a *state-aware* programming language called *Spot*, derived from C. On the one hand, Spot disallows unsafe uses of low-level constructs like pointers; on the other, it extends C to provide key abstractions for flight software, particularly in regard to state and real-time processing.

2.1 Design Rationale

At the heart of Spot's design is the very practical consideration that, for better or for worse, we are stuck with the C programming language for flight code at JPL. Therefore,

our main goal is to find a minimal set of extensions and restrictions to C that can provide the expressivity and safety guarantees we seek. In particular the language must do two things:

1. Describe the program state sufficiently that the location and size of all state variables can be communicated to SPIN.

2. Provide a built-in concurrency model, so that a SPIN model can be automatically constructed.

We discussed point 1 in the introduction. As to point 2, modeling a concurrent system is extremely difficult if, as is currently the case in JPL flight code, task creation and message passing are scattered throughout a C program in the form of unstructured library calls.[3] Model construction is much easier (indeed, we believe it can be done mostly automatically) if the language itself provides a structured concurrency model.

We do not aim to design and implement an entirely new language from scratch, for several practical reasons. First, designing a new language (especially a good one!) is extremely difficult; it is much easier to extend an existing language. Second, achieving adoption seems much more realistic for a variant of C than for an entirely new language. Finally, the design and implementation of an entirely new language is beyond our cost budget. We do believe, however, that if Spot is successful, its ideas could form the basis for a new language in the future.

We also believe that any viable solution must maintain linkage compatibility with existing C code, so that wholesale rewriting in Spot is not required from the start. The linkage compatibility must go in both directions, i.e., it must be easy to link both Spot files into C programs and C files into Spot programs. That way, Spot can gradually replace C — for example, on a component-by-component basis — in existing flight code. We believe that strict adherence to C syntax, especially in its more ungainly aspects, is not required, so long as this linkage compatibility exists.[4]

2.2 Features

We now briefly discuss the major features of Spot.

Actor concurrency. Spot follows the *actor model* [1]: a Spot program consists of several *modules* that interact concurrently by sending each other messages. A Spot module is a unit of computation that corresponds to a module in traditional flight code; it is *instantiated* at runtime into one or more *module instances* that encapsulate some state and some related operations on that state.

The code snippet shown in Figure 1 illustrates these concepts. Line 1 defines a module `Counter`, representing a counter variable together with increment and read operations on the variable. Line 2 defines a constructor `create` for creating instances of the module. Line 3 defines the variable `count` and specifies several facts about it: its type is `int`, its initial value is 0, and it is part of the state of the `Counter`

---

[2]Other examples include a control mode or position estimate. We do not mean the state of the bits in a memory word (though that may well be state in some lower-level model of a hardware system).

[3]Our experience has been that constructing a SPIN model for a single JPL flight module takes roughly three man-months, and that most of this time is spent identifying the concurrent tasks and their interactions.

[4]One major design mistake of C++, in our opinion, is that it is both too rigid in its adherence to C syntax and not flexible enough in its linkage idiom. While linking C files to C++ is straightforward, the opposite direction is not.

```
1  module Counter {
2    constructor create () {}
3    state int count = 0
4    priority P qsize 100
5    message void increment (val int i)
6      priority P
7    {
8      next count = count + i;
9    }
10   message int read ()
11     priority P
12   {
13     return count;
14   }
15 }
```

Figure 1: Example Spot code.

module. In Spot, state consists of mutable variables defined inside module definitions, and no other variables. In line 5, for example, variable i is not state, because it is a constant local variable. As in Scala, the keyword **val** denotes a variable that is immutable after initialization (similar to **const** in C), while the keyword **var** denotes a mutable variable. Global mutable variables are not allowed in Spot.

The rest of the code defines the messages that increment and read the state of the counter. Message definitions are given *priorities* that govern the order in which they are handled. Otherwise a message definition looks much like a C function definition. A message may be *sent* by invoking it on a target module inside a **send** statement, as shown in Figure 2. In line 3, the return value of the **read** message is transmitted to the caller via an implicit return message and stored in the variable x. This operation causes the caller to block and wait for the return value; if more concurrency is needed, one may use a non-blocking receive or an explicit callback.

```
1  var int x;
2  val Counter c = Counter.create ();
3  send c.read () receive x;
4  send c.increment ();
```

Figure 2: Blocking receive.

Line 8 of Figure 1 shows how state update occurs in Spot. The keyword **next** specifies that (1) state is being updated; and (2) the update is to the *next state*, that is, the state of the module that will be seen the next time one of its messages is invoked. During the current execution, the message body sees the old value of **count**; updates done via **next** are buffered and applied at the end of message execution.

A message with **void** return type may update remote state, so the Spot runtime does not actually send any such message until the end of the enclosing message. For example, in Figure 2, if lines 3 and 4 were swapped, then the **increment** message would still be sent last. A message with non-**void** return type (e.g., **read** in Figure 1) may not update remote state. These rules ensure that no message updates any state (either locally or remotely) until it is finished executing. They also extend the **next** semantics to remote

memory access: effectively, every remote update acts upon the next state of the updated object, while every remote read sees the current state.

Annotations for correctness and testing. Spot provides a flexible way to write various kinds of program annotations, including the following:

- Standard C-style assertions.

- Design-by-contract-style preconditions and postconditions, i.e., **assumes** clauses stating what is assumed to be true at the start of a function or message and **guarantees** clauses stating what is guaranteed to be true on exit from a function or message, assuming that the **assumes** clauses are satisfied.

- Temporal logic specifications — for example, assertions that a certain value of a state variable must eventually be achieved — for guiding the SPIN model checking.

- Annotations that specify tests: for example, test inputs and expected results for checking the behavior of functions, messages, and modules.

The test input sets can be specified either directly, e.g., as a range of values, or indirectly as one or more conditions. As an example of a conditional input specification, an annotation might say "check all inputs such that the condition b holds," where b is a Boolean function of the inputs.

The syntactic form of a Spot annotation is very simple: it is just the symbol @ followed by an identifier and an optional expression which, if it appears, must be enclosed in parentheses. The expression may be arbitrarily complex and may be (or include) a function call. Very general conditions, assertions, input ranges, and expected test outputs may be expressed with this simple syntax.

As in languages such as Java and Scala, the Spot compiler just provides the syntax of annotations; their meaning (generating executable assertions, for example, or generating tests) is provided by plugin compiler passes or separate analyzers. This approach keeps the annotation language very flexible and lets it be adapted to new purposes.

```
1  message void increment(val int i)
2    priority P
3    @assumes (i > 0)
4    private @guarantees (
5        next count == count + i
6    )
7  {
8    next count = count + i;
9  }
```

Figure 3: Example Spot assertions.

Figure 3 shows a simple of example of contract-style assertions in Spot. Here we have annotated the **increment** message from Figure 1 with assertions stating that (1) the value bound to the message parameter i must be greater than zero and (2) the result of the message is to increase the value of the state variable **count** by i. The second annotation is marked **private** (meaning it is visible only in this translation unit) because it refers to the private state variable `count` of module `Counter`. (All state variables in Spot are implicitly private.) These annotations could generate executable assertions and/or be checked by SPIN.

Other features. Other features of Spot include the following:

- *Improved arrays.* In Spot, arrays store their dimensions, enabling arrays to be safely passed as message arguments. Spot also cleanly separates pointer and array types: for example, array indexing is allowed, but pointer indexing and arithmetic are not.

- *Value types.* Data structures may be created and initialized together, then treated as immutable values. In C, structures require assignments and pointer manipulation.

- *Domain-specific annotations.* Spot supports flight-specific annotations, for example to guide the generation of telemetry information. These are discussed further in Section 3.

Of course genuine arrays and safe references are standard features of most modern languages; but they are also critical to making C suitable as a basis for Spot.

2.3 Benefits

The Spot programming model provides several benefits over writing flight code in plain C. First, by providing higher-level abstractions such as modules, improved arrays, and value types, Spot increases productivity and code quality as explained in Section 1.

Second, Spot's type system ensures that state is always passed by value, never by reference, between modules. This ensures strict partitioning of the memory representing the state of each module. The partitioning enables easy migration of modules from one core to another — for example due to a change in power allocation — even when the cores do not share the same physical memory. By eliminating global variables and separating state from non-state memory, Spot also enables a simple form of memory management: any memory allocated within a message handler can be automatically deallocated after the handler finishes running.

Third, modules update their state *atomically*: no other module may see an inconsistent state (for example, halfway through an update). Thus Spot messages behave like *transactions* in a database or other transaction processing system. As discussed in the next section, this fact enables Spot to generate all telemetry code for the spacecraft, and much of the ground code, automatically. It also simplifies aborting and restarting messages in response to a fault.

Fourth, Spot enables flight code developers who are not expert model checkers to use SPIN, as it solves two of the thorniest issues: what is the state, and what is the model to be checked? Identification of state works as explained above. The model is the program itself, and the Spot compiler produces all the code that SPIN needs to do its work.

Fifth, Spot naturally supports automatic parallelism on multicore architectures. If the programmer follows simple rules (such as using value types instead of pointers and mutable structures), then the compiler will produce code that runs a single module in parallel on multiple cores.

Finally, Spot compiles to C and is fully linkage-compatible with C, as discussed above.

3. DOMAIN-SPECIFIC ANNOTATIONS

As a concrete example of the benefits of Spot, we discuss domain-specific annotations for handling two kinds of spacecraft state: telemetry and parameters. Telemetry is data sent to the ground in real time, so that ground operations personnel can monitor the state of the system and, in the case of a mishap, determine what has gone wrong. Parameters are values that govern spacecraft computations, for example, an alignment correction for a gyro device. Parameters are essentially constants, but sometimes they must be updated from the ground. For example, one might discover after launch that a gyro has moved and requires an alignment adjustment.

```
1   module GnC {
2       @periodic (q, planet)
3       @onchange (planet)
4       state GncVector x
5       ...
6       @param
7       state GncParms z
8       ...
9   }
10
11  type GnCVector = struct {
12      var double[4] q
13      var Planet planet
14      var GncMode mode
15      var int a
16  }
```

Figure 4: Parameter and telemetry annotations.

Figure 4 illustrates how Spot expresses these concepts. Lines 1–9 define part of a module called GnC. (GnC stands for "guidance, navigation, and control.") In the part of the state that is shown, there are two variables: a variable x of type GncVector and a variable z of type GncParms. GncVector and GncParms are both structure types; the definition of the GncVector struct is shown in part in lines 11–16. The annotations appearing in lines 2–6 use the general annotation syntax described in Section 2.2. Here, though, the annotations describe telemetry communications and parameters, instead of providing test inputs or correctness conditions.

The annotations say the following:

- The contents of the structure members q and planet of x should be sent periodically in telemetry communications to the ground.

- The contents of the structure member planet of x should additionally be sent as a telemetry communication to the ground whenever it changes.

- z is a parameter variable.

Notice that the annotations are on the variables, and the variables carry their types. Therefore the compiler has all the information it needs to generate code for transmitting code to and from the spacecraft either in response to ground commands (in the case of parameters) or at specified times or under specified conditions (in the case of telemetry).

In contrast to these simple annotations, the code for telemetry and parameter communication in state-of-the-art flight systems is a mess: it is complex, ad-hoc, and a burden to read, write, and maintain. Typically it consists of handwritten XML specifications. Not only is this needlessly painful, but it forces programmers to maintain essentially the same information (i.e., the types and sizes of the relevant state variables) in two different places. Primarily this is because the state information, while implicit in the C code, is not readily extracted, and so must be specified by hand all over again. By contrast, once the state is known and accounted for, the parameter and telemetry code can be readily generated with a few simple annotations.

We cannot overstate the potential savings from automatic parameter and telemetry code not only in programming time, but also in testing time. Furthermore, ground tools can utilize the information to generate tables needed to display the data on the ground control displays.

4. IMPLEMENTATION STATUS

We have written a specification for Spot consisting of a formal syntax and an informal semantic description. We are implementing a compiler and runtime based on the specification. Our current implementation contains a complete lexer and parser, a mostly-complete Spot-to-C code generator, and enough semantic analysis to support code generation. We plan to implement a full type checker. The current runtime runs on Unix-like systems and uses pthreads as the concurrency mechanism; porting to other systems such as VxWorks should not be difficult.

We have used the compiler and runtime to compile and run a number of small Spot modules. We have also prototyped the verification methodology (annotations plus SPIN code generation) for these modules. We have integrated the annotations into our Spot compiler and are now integrating the SPIN code generation.

Once we have finished the compiler and runtime, we plan to translate several modules from the *Curiosity* flight software into Spot. We will then evaluate the efficacy of the approach. In particular, we plan to investigate two questions:

1. What are the gains in productivity and safety versus plain C?

2. What is the performance cost?

Several flight projects (Mars Science Laboratory, Asteroid Retrieval, and Comet Rendezvous) have expressed interest in Spot, particularly for developing Guidance, Navigation, and Control (GNC) systems.

5. CONCLUSION

We have briefly described Spot, a new programming language based on C for programming flight software systems. Spot offers enhanced programmability over plain C, and it interoperates with legacy C code. By carefully managing program state, Spot also supports semi-automatic verification, automatic memory management, fault tolerance, and multicore parallelism. We believe that Spot is potentially useful not just for flight systems, but for any system in which safety, fault tolerance, or security are essential.

6. ACKNOWLEDGEMENTS

We performed this research at the Jet Propulsion Laboratory (JPL), California Institute of Technology. Our funding came from the Game Changing Development (GCD) program at the Space Technology Mission Directorate, National Aeronautics and Space Administration; and from the Research and Technology Development (R&TD) program at JPL.

7. REFERENCES

[1] G. Agha. *Actors: A Model of Concurrent Computation in Distributed Systems*. MIT Press, 1986.

[2] G. Holzmann. *The SPIN Model Checker: Primer and Reference Manual*. Addison-Wesley Publishing Company, 2003.

The Rust Language

Nicholas Matsakis
Mozilla Research
nmatsakis@mozilla.com

Felix S. Klock II
Mozilla Research
pnkfelix@mozilla.com

1. ABSTRACT

Rust is a new programming language for developing reliable and efficient systems. It is designed to support concurrency and parallelism in building applications and libraries that take full advantage of modern hardware. Rust's static type system is safe[1] and expressive and provides strong guarantees about isolation, concurrency, and memory safety.

Rust also offers a clear performance model, making it easier to predict and reason about program efficiency. One important way it accomplishes this is by allowing fine-grained control over memory representations, with direct support for stack allocation and contiguous record storage. The language balances such controls with the absolute requirement for safety: Rust's type system and runtime guarantee the absence of data races, buffer overflows, stack overflows, and accesses to uninitialized or deallocated memory.

Categories and Subject Descriptors

D.3.0 [**E.2**]: Programming Language Standards

Keywords

Rust, Systems programming, Memory management, Affine type systems

2. MEMORY MANIPULATION IN RUST

Rust is a new programming language targeting systems-level applications. Like C++, Rust is designed to map directly to hardware, giving users control over the running time and memory usage of their programs. This implies, for example, that all Rust types can be allocated on the stack and that Rust never requires the use of a garbage collector or other runtime. Unlike C++, however, Rust also offers strong safety guarantees: pure Rust programs are guaranteed to be free of memory errors (dangling pointers, double frees) as well as data races.

To control aliasing and ensure type soundness, Rust incorporates a notion of *ownership* into its type system. The unique owner of an object can hand that ownership off to new owner; but the owner may also hand off *borrowed references* to (or into) the object. These so-called *borrows* obey lexical scope, ensuring that when the original reference goes out of scope, there will not be any outstanding borrowed references to the object (otherwise known as "dangling pointers"). This also implies that when the owner goes out of scope or is otherwise deallocated, the referenced object can be deallocated at the same time. Rust leverages the latter property by adding support for user-defined destructors, enabling RAII[2] patterns as popularized by C++.

There are two flavors of borrows: mutable and immutable. Mutable references have a uniqueness property: There can be at most one active mutable borrow of a given piece of state (the owner itself is not allowed to mutate the object for the duration of the mutable borrow, nor are any of the inactive mutable borrows). Immutable references, on the other hand, can be freely copied, and their referents can be the source for new immutable borrows (subject to the restriction that all borrows still respect the lexical scope of the object's owner).

Rust functions can manipulate objects that are owned by local variables arbitrarily far up the control stack. Such functions need to support operations like `*ptr1 = *ptr2;` (writing the dereferenced value of `ptr2` into the memory referenced by `ptr1`), but must also respect the rules: such assignment statements must be prohibited from injecting dangling pointers.

A function that manipulates borrowed references needs to constrain its input parameters to ensure that executing the function body will not break the rules. Rust has an optional explicit syntax for describing the *lifetime* bounds associated with a reference. Lifetime bounds mix together with *lifetime-polymorphism* (analogous to *type-polymorphism*) to provide functions the expressive power needed to manipulate memory references, without breaking type safety.

---

[1] Type soundness has not yet been formally proven for Rust, but type soundness is an explicit design goal for the language.

---

[2] RAII: "Resource Acquisition Is Initialization"

Panel Summary: Finding Safety in Numbers
New Languages for Safe Multicore Programming and Modeling

Robert Bocchino
Jet Propulsion
Laboratory

Niko Matsakis
Mozilla Research

Tucker Taft
AdaCore

Brian Larson
Kansas State
University

Ed Seidewitz
Model Driven
Solutions

ABSTRACT

This panel brings together designers of both traditional programming languages, and designers of behavioral specification languages for modeling systems, in each case with a concern for the challenges of multicore programming. Furthermore, several of these efforts have attempted to provide data-race-free programming models, so that multicore programmers need not be faced with the added burden of trying to debug race conditions on top of the existing challenges of building reliable systems.

Categories and Subject Descriptors

D.3.2 [**Programming Languages**]: Language Classifications – *concurrent, distributed, and parallel languages.*

General Terms

Reliability, Human Factors, Languages

Keywords

Safe Parallel Programming; Spot; Rust; ParaSail; AADL Bless; UML alf

PANEL SUMMARY

It has been almost a decade since single processor performance began to level off, and chip makers began to move seriously toward multicore architectures, in large part to address a growing concern with power consumption at higher clock rates. To address this irreversible move toward parallel, multicore architectures, there has been a burst of new programming language design activities over the past decade, with new concurrent and/or parallel programming features being added to existing languages, and completely new languages being designed with a significant focus on supporting multicore programming.

This panel brings together designers of both traditional programming languages, and designers of behavioral specification languages for modeling systems, in each case with a concern for the challenges of multicore programming. Furthermore, several of these efforts have attempted to provide data-race-free programming models, so that multicore programmers need not be faced with the added burden of trying to debug race conditions on top of the existing challenges of building reliable systems.

Robert Bocchino of the *Jet Propulsion Laboratory* will discuss the design of the *Spot* language, which adopts the *actor* model for safe parallel programming as part of an overall focus on building reliable aerospace systems. Niko Matsakis of *Mozilla Research* will discuss the *Rust* language, which restricts access to global data through the use of *owning* pointers, thereby avoiding concurrent access from multiple tasks. Tucker Taft of *AdaCore* will discuss the *ParaSail* family of languages, which eliminate pointers, global data, and parameter aliasing while adding expandable pointer-free data structures as part of an inherently safe parallel programming model. Brian Larson of *Kansas State University* will discuss the *BLESS* language which provides behavioral specification to the *AADL* architecture definition language. And finally, Ed Seidewitz of *Model Driven Solutions* will discuss *Alf*, the *action language for Foundational UML*.

HILT 2014, October 18-21, 2014, Portland, Oregon, USA.
ACM 978-1-4503-3217-0/14/10.
http://dx.doi.org/10.1145/2663171.2663190.

Author Index